PAWNS
in the
GAME

IRISH HUNGER STRIKES 1912–1981

BARRY FLYNN

The Collins Press

First published in 2011 by
The Collins Press
West Link Park
Doughcloyne
Wilton
Cork

British Library Cataloguing in Publication Data

Flynn, Barry
Pawns in the game: Irish hunger strikes, 1912–1981.
1. Hunger strikes—Ireland—History—20th century.
2. Ireland—Politics and government—20th century.
3. Ireland—History—20th century. 4. Irish question.
I. Title
303.6'1'09415'0904-dc22

ISBN-13: 9781848891166

Typesetting by The Collins Press
Typeset in Bembo 10.5 pt
Printed in Great Britain by CPI Cox & Wyman

Cover photographs
(left) courtesy Presseye.com; *(right)* courtesy Shutterstock

Contents

Acknowledgements   vii

Introduction   ix

1 A game of cat and mouse   1

2 Thomas Ashe: death by force-feeding   18

3 Terence MacSwiney: a means to a bitter end   39

4 Hatred, pain and hunger: 1922 and 1923   60

5 De Valera: poacher turns gamekeeper   85

6 Seán McCaughey: If you had a dog . . .   102

7 Short-term gain, long-term pain   126

8 Take me home to Mayo   142

9 Frank Stagg: death and humiliation   162

10 Beating the terrorists?   174

11 1981: It's gonna happen   202

12. Diplomacy and duplicity   224

13. Intervention and disintegration   243

Appendix I: 'For Micheal Gaughan and Frank Stagg'   262

Bibliography   267

Index   269

For Katrina, Meabh and Deirbhile

Acknowledgements

I would like to thank the following individuals for their assistance: Raymond McCartney, Danny Morrison, Pat Sheehan, Gerry Kelly, Liam McBrinn, the staff of the Linen Hall Library in Belfast and Belfast Central Library. I would also mention those individuals who asked to remain anonymous.

Regarding the sources for this book, there has been an abundance of interviews, articles, research and journals published in recent times on the subject of republican hunger strikes. A majority of those, especially in respect of 1981, are interviews or recollections that use the tool of hindsight. Therefore, a number of the quotations and references contained within the book are subsequent to the events and the dates attributed should, hopefully, not be a cause for confusion.

Introduction

In October 1920 the name of Terence MacSwiney entered into the annals of republican folklore when he died in Brixton Prison. What is not widely recalled is that two other prisoners, Michael Fitzgerald and Joseph Murphy, died on hunger strike in Cork Prison at the same time as MacSwiney. As Terence MacSwiney's fast progressed, the world's media followed and reported every twist and turn of events. For Fitzgerald and Murphy, their agony was played out in private, far away from the public eye and their deaths and sacrifice have been, for the most part, forgotten. Seán McCaughey is another hunger striker whose suffering is largely forgotten. He died in May 1946 after a hunger and thirst strike; out of sight and out of mind of the Irish government and public. Yet again, who can even dare to imagine the conditions under which Seán McCaughey lived for four years as he was denied basic human rights in a protest for political status? If it had not been for Seán MacBride, who gained an admission at McCaughey's inquest that the prisoner had effectively been treated like a dog, the suffering of Seán McCaughey would have gone unremarked for future generations to contemplate. Sadly, history has a habit of being selective in its recall. The names of Ashe, MacSwiney and Sands are world renowned but, perhaps, it is time that the names of all those Irishmen who died on hunger strike were recorded in one book.

The history of hunger strikes in Ireland is one of struggle

and indifference. When the island was partitioned the Civil War that broke out in the twenty-six counties showed that Irishmen could act in a most inhuman way against former comrades. In the midst of the murder, executions and incarcerations, three men were allowed to die when those in power displayed total indifference to their plight. Within the carnival of hatred that had gripped Ireland, it is not surprising that the names of Joseph Whitty, Denis Barry and Andrew O'Sullivan have been lost to collective folk memory. Seventeen years later further deaths of hunger strikers would also vanish into the historical ether. As the Second World War began the IRA was to receive no mercy from Éamon de Valera and his Minister for Justice, Gerald Boland, who seemed determined to destroy what was left of the organisation. In 1940 Jack McNeela and Tony Darcy would lose their lives on hunger strike; with media censorship in full flow throughout the twenty-six counties, both men's deaths went widely unreported. The hierarchy of death in Irish history has been cruel to both men.

In the 1970s hunger striking again entered the political equation but it was not until the fast of 1981 that the protest reached its zenith. It is perhaps timely that the publication of this book coincides with the thirtieth anniversary of the 1981 hunger strike. The events that year, both inside and outside the Maze Prison, helped to shape the political reality that is the island of Ireland today. Indeed as I write this introduction, the results of the 2011 Irish election are still being digested, particularly the remarkable showing of Sinn Féin. The rise of Sinn Féin as a renewed electoral force can be traced back to the victory of Bobby Sands in Fermanagh and South Tyrone in April 1981. That fact is not disputed, but placing it within the broader picture of republican hunger striking is something that is slightly more onerous.

I hope that this book has in some small way put the record straight and placed each of the hunger strikers within the context of their times and their struggle.

Barry Flynn
March 2011

Chapter 1

A Game of Cat and Mouse

'If the prisoners in Mountjoy are determined to commit suicide by starving, they must be allowed to do so.'

George Bernard Shaw, *Evening Post*, 26 October 1912

The death of Michael Devine from Derry on hunger strike in the Maze Prison outside Belfast on 21 August 1981, strange as it might seem, may be linked to a simple act of vandalism seventy-two years earlier. Devine was the last of ten republican hunger strikers to die in a protest for political status during 1981, but it was an example set by a Scottish semi-aristocrat in Holloway Prison that arguably set in motion the sad and bitter history of republican hunger striking. On 22 June 1909 a female artist from Ayrshire in Scotland by the name of Marion Wallace-Dunlop visited St Stephen's Hall in the Houses of Parliament at Westminster with the intention of lobbying her local MP on the subject of a Bill of Rights, due to be read in the Commons on 29 June. Accompanied by Victor Duval, an avid supporter of the concept of women's suffrage, Wallace-Dunlop produced a rubber stamp and an ink pad in the marble hall and pressed a simple message onto wall, which read: 'June 29. Bill of Rights: It is the right of all subjects to petition the

1

King. All commitments and prosecutions for such petitioning are illegal.' It was a simple act of publicity on behalf of the suffragettes that would have far-reaching consequences. Whilst she was trying to leave the palace, the Sergeant-at-Arms spotted the misdemeanour, apprehended Wallace-Dunlop and brought her to the office of the Commissioner of Works, where she was admonished but released.

Two days later the determined Scot returned in disguise to the scene of her original transgression to repeat the act, close to the statue of the Earl of Chatham. This time the authorities were not prepared to show leniency and the miscreant was arrested and brought before Mr Curtis Bennett, the magistrate at Bow Street Police Court, where she was charged with 'wilfully damaging the stonework of St Stephen's Hall, House of Commons, by stamping it with an indelible ink, doing damage to the value of ten shillings.' Surprisingly, given the limited cost of the damage, the prosecution was very keen to impress upon the magistrate the 'seriousness' of the charge. They advised Mr Bennett that this had been the second such 'outrage' committed by the defendant and pointed out that, after cleaning, some of the imprint would still be visible on the marble wall. The following day Wallace-Dunlop was deemed guilty of 'wilful damage' but when she declined the opportunity to pay the fine she was sent to Holloway Prison for a month. She immediately applied to the Home Secretary, Herbert Gladstone, for treatment as a 'first division' prisoner, namely to be granted special status since she had been incarcerated for a political offence. She added, pointedly, that she would fast until this concession had been granted.

Marion Wallace-Dunlop thus became the first modern hunger striker and risked her life for recognition as a political prisoner. It was a principled stand and the gauntlet had been thrown down to a somewhat bewildered government. Its choice, however, was crystal clear: either permit Wallace-Dunlop to fast and die, thus becoming a martyr to the suffragette cause, or grant her special status. It was a game of risk that the government could not win. Faced with this newfangled and innovative form of protest, the government procrastinated for three days until it decided to free Wallace-Dunlop. It was a climb-down that exposed the authorities as vulnerable when threatened by the prospect of a hunger strike. The euphoria caused within the women's movement by Wallace-Dunlop's triumph would inspire further protesters to copy her tactics, with similar success. The political and legal dilemma that hunger striking posed to the government was simple: permitting a prisoner under its care to starve to death would cause extreme embarrassment, create willing victims and leave the authorities open to a charge of criminal manslaughter. It was a conundrum that the government needed to address post-haste. Accordingly, other options, including deportation and the 'sectioning' of fasting suffragettes under the Mental Health Act, were considered as alternatives. However, when these options were ruled out, the authorities felt that they could no longer stand idly by. The solution was simple, yet also brutal, degrading, undignified and cruel. The government decided to address the issue of hunger striking by borrowing a method from lunatic asylums known as 'artificial' feeding (better known as force-feeding).

The first clash of wills between the government and the suffragettes in which force-feeding was applied came at Winston Green Prison in Birmingham in the autumn of 1909. The event that led to this was the suffragettes' disruption of a visit to the city by Prime Minister Herbert Asquith, who spoke at Bingley Hall on 17 September. Six women, led by Mary Leigh and Charlotte Marsh, were arrested during the incident and subjected to force-feeding. Soon horrifying stories were leaked from the prison concerning the degrading treatment that the women were enduring. Brute force was used, as a number of wardens restrained the prisoner and bound her to a feeding chair. Most frequently the prisoner's jaws were clamped open with a wooden block to enable the insertion of a rubber tube into the stomach, although the tube was sometimes pushed through the nose instead. When the prison doctor was satisfied that the tube was inserted correctly, a mixture of warm milk and raw eggs was poured into the victim's stomach until she was considered 'fed'. It was, to the prison authorities, a 'medical procedure' that would save the life of the prisoner. For the victim it was an act that bore similarities to institutionalised rape.

In the House of Commons on 28 September the former Labour leader and personal friend of Emmeline Pankhurst (a leader of the Suffragettes, along with her sister Christabel), Keir Hardie, raised the plight of the six women and labeled the practice as a 'horrible outrage, beastly outrage'. The public was shocked that the women had been subjected to a violent process that the authorities referred to as an 'operation'. Upon her release from Winston Prison, Mary Leigh provided an insight into what she and her colleagues had had to endure:

> Held by the four wardresses the two-foot long tube was forced up my nostril by the doctor. The sensation of the tube's progress up my nose and down my throat was very painful. The drums of my ears seemed to be at bursting point and there was a terrible pain in my throat and chest. They pushed nearly two feet of the tube into me. Then I was forced to lie down on the bed by the four wardresses and held there. The doctor then stood on a chair holding the funnel end of the tube above my head. He then started to pour a liquid mixture of milk and egg into the funnel. After a few moments, the doctor decided that the liquid wasn't going down fast enough so he pinched my nostril with the tube in it and squeezed my throat, causing me even more pain. When they had finished, the doctor checked my heart and they all left.

> *Votes for Women*, 1 October 1909

The act of force-feeding was truly appalling and took the government's 'duty of care' to the extreme. In 1910 the American suffragette Lady Constance Lytton wrote candidly of her experiences in Wilton Jail in Liverpool, saying that being force-fed was 'a living nightmare of pain, horror and revolting degradation'

(*The New York Times*, 30 January 1910). Whilst the decision to use force-feeding lay, in theory, with the Board of Governors of each prison, it was the government which stood indicted. For the prison authorities, and the government, the 'operation' was a 'caring' attempt to prevent a prisoner committing 'suicide by starvation' and it was therefore a necessary evil to be endured. To the public, it was perhaps a different matter.

Despite the public outcry the practice continued unabated, but the very public battle of hearts and minds had been won by the suffragette movement. The Asquith government, under Home Secretary Reginald McKenna, was aware of the limitations of the procedure and acted in April 1913 by introducing the Prisoners (Temporary Discharge for Ill Health) Act or, more famously, the 'Cat and Mouse' Act. In essence the practice of force-feeding suffragettes was to cease and, whilst they would be permitted to fast in prison, they would be released on licence when their lives were deemed to be in danger. It was a pragmatic solution, of sorts, that provided both sides with an opt-out clause. Most tellingly, it was a move that won back the moral high ground for the Liberal government. The horrific stories of force-feeding prisoners ceased with the temporary release of hunger strikers. The public battle was defused somewhat by the Act and, six months after its introduction, the Tory-leaning *Daily Mail* saw fit to report that 'militant suffragettism is dead in England. It was killed by the one-time much derided Cat and Mouse bill' (7 June 1913). The key to the success of the Act, according to the *Daily Mail*, was the fact that the element of 'martyrdom' had been taken out of the equation and the article continued:

> There is now no martyrdom in force-feeding. If they [the suffragettes] refuse food they are allowed to go hungry until they are medically certified to be unfit for prison life. Release, convalescence and re-arrest on the recovery of health is the process, leaving no room for public demonstrations by the prisoner. It is a trial wherefrom the law emerges triumphant.

Whether the 'Cat and Mouse' Act was a strategic success is a cause of much debate. The suffragette movement, though, had its campaign curtailed significantly and nine months after its introduction the number of women embarking on the tactic of hunger striking had fallen by three-quarters. It seemed that by defusing the dramatic and often propagandist element of hunger striking, the government had played a tactical masterstroke.

Soon the tactics adopted to publicise the suffragette cause would become ever more extreme. The events of Derby Day in 1913 brought the issue back into the public domain in the most emphatic fashion. As the horses in the Derby passed Tattenham Corner, Emily Davison made her way on to the track and collided with King George V's horse, Anmer. Davison, who had previously been released from prison under the 'Cat and Mouse' Act, would never regain consciousness and became the first true martyr to the suffragette cause. A friend of Davison and fellow campaigner Emily McGowen, said, 'Miss Davison had always held the view that a woman's life would have to be sacrificed before the women of this country get justice' (*The Daily Telegraph*, 11 June 1913).

The death of Emily Davison was a horrific spectacle – and one that arguably backfired on the suffragette movement. Although the 'Cat and Mouse' Act had denied the suffragettes a martyr through the drama of a hunger strike, the death of Davison provided a ready-made and newly minted idol. Outside of the women's rights movement the perception of Davison was different. In the days after her death Davison was described as a 'lunatic', a 'zealot' and a 'fanatic'. The general public could not have been enamoured of her by her previous record of militancy: she had once been arrested for attacking a Baptist minister in Aberdeen in the mistaken belief that he was Lloyd George. Her funeral procession through London was a *cause-célèbre*, with thousands marching behind her coffin and militant banners prominent. One banner, using the famous words of the American revolutionary Patrick Henry, said, 'Give me Liberty or give me Death', while another stated (perhaps ironically), 'He who loses his Life shall find it.' It was evident that the mood among the suffragettes was one of honouring a martyr to its cause.

The fact remained, however, that had Davison died on hunger strike rather than in a violent accident, public perception of her death would probably have been more sympathetic. In truth, suffragette militancy was not popular among the masses and the death of Davison stirred revulsion, not compassion. Christabel Pankhurst incurred the wrath of the establishment when she said that Davison had 'died for women'. She compounded this sentiment by adding that Herbert Jones, the King's jockey who had been badly injured in the incident, had been 'injured for women'. The poet Alfred Noyes, who had previously been sympathetic to the suffragette movement, described the militants as the 'wild women of the Pankhurst contingent'. *The New York Times* was forthright in its condemnation of Pankhurst's tactics when it said, 'there is not a constructive idea in the heads of these malcontents. They seek only to destroy and have chiefly destroyed their own cause.' Chancellor of the Exchequer, Lloyd George, whose house had previously been torched by suffragettes, summed up the feelings of the government when he said of Pankhurst, 'Hasn't she the sense to see that the very worst way of campaigning for the vote is to try and intimidate a man into giving them what he would gladly give otherwise?' (Priestley, *The Edwardians*, p. 215).

The suffragette movement waned in importance as the Great War approached, yet their violent actions continued regardless. When war was eventually declared in August 1914, Emmeline Pankhurst showed her patriotic streak and advised suffragettes to desist from their campaign and support 'in every way' the government and the war effort. The declaration was pragmatic indeed, as soon the remaining prisoners were released from prison and fell in with the war effort.

On 19 June 1917 the Representation of the People Bill (Women's Suffrage clause) was passed in the House of Commons by a landslide majority of 385 votes to 55. With hindsight it is clear that the 'Cat and Mouse' Act effectively curtailed the ability of the suffragette movement to use the weapon of hunger strike effectively. In reality it was inevitable that the votes for which they fought would be granted in due course. The tactic of hunger striking amid militancy forced the government to act against the movement in what was a very public battle. However, the use of the Act was seen as compassionate measure in the face of protest, particularly when it was protest organised by women. How the government would react to a hunger strike from an individual who was not English, female or upper-class had still to be determined.

★

Despite the more pressing issue of Home Rule, Ireland would not be exempt from suffragist agitation, or indeed hunger-striking. In July 1912 the Theatre Royal in Dublin was to be the venue for a keynote speech on the future of Ireland by Herbert Asquith. It was the first time that a serving Prime Minister had visited the island since the introduction of the Act of Union in 1801, and thousands lined the streets to witness his procession through Dublin. However, on the evening prior to his address, four Irish suffragettes, led by Gladys Evans, attempted to set fire to the Theatre Royal by pouring oil over the carpets and curtains, as well as placing gunpowder in a projector. Their plan failed and Evans was sentenced to five years imprisonment, immediately embarking on a hunger strike.

However, the drama of the attempted burning of the Theatre Royal was to be eclipsed the following evening when another suffragette, the aforementioned Mary Leigh, threw a hatchet into a carriage containing Asquith, Irish Parliamentary Party leader, John Redmond (whose party after December 1910 held the balance of power in the House of Commons), and the lord mayor of Dublin, Lorcan Sherlock. This reckless act occurred as the carriage made its way through the streets of Dublin and Redmond was slightly injured. In court Leigh was to claim that she had intended only to harm Asquith, but nonetheless she was given three months' hard labour for her moment of madness. The meeting at the Theatre Royal went ahead regardless and Asquith was given a standing ovation when he assured the assembled audience that Home Rule for Ireland would be granted. Outside, the Dublin crowds took umbrage at a group of suffragettes and police officers had to intervene when a group attempted to throw some women into the River Liffey.

The drama then moved to Mountjoy Prison where Leigh joined Evans on hunger strike. The practice of force-feeding was utilised by the prison authorities who eventually relented 44 days later and released Leigh after she had collapsed. The *Daily Mail* was to comment, most colourfully, on Leigh that 'her collapse was due to deliberate starvation, she having acquired the knack of ejecting food as soon as it was administered by means of a tube' (20 September 1912). The hunger strike and subsequent force-feeding of Mary Evans lasted until 3 October, when she was released to convalesce.

The debate on the morality of hunger striking as a political weapon waged on as the battle of wills between the government and the suffragettes continued. In late September George Bernard Shaw added his own strong opinion to the mix when, referring to the hunger strikers in Mountjoy Prison, he wrote: 'My conclusion, therefore, is that if the prisoners in Mountjoy are determined to commit suicide by starving, they must be allowed to do so, and that the government could not be held responsible for their deaths if it could convince the public that the prisoners had plenty of food within their reach.'

Not surprisingly, Bernard Shaw's sentiments on letting the suffragettes die were not universally popular. Indeed, Christabel Pankhurst dismissed his views by adding that such opinions were 'the most convincing vindication of militancy'. However, the practice of hunger striking continued. In all, between 1912 and August 1914 when the Great War broke out, a total of thirty-five women were sentenced in Ireland for incidents associated with women's suffrage. Of these, twelve went on hunger strike, but only two, Evans and Leigh, were ever force-fed. In February

1913 four suffragettes, Margaret Cousins, Margaret Connery, Barbara Hoskins and Mabel Purser were sentenced to one month's hard labour for their part in an incident at the Custom House in Dublin when several windows had been broken in a disturbance. On their arrival at Tullamore Prison, County Offaly, they demanded political status and when this was refused they began a hunger strike. After six days the prison authorities yielded to their demands for political prisoner status.

With the onset of the Dublin Lockout on 26 August 1913 the issue of hunger striking would again make an appearance on the Irish political scene. Spearheaded by Jim Larkin and James Connolly, the Irish Transport and General Workers' Union began a titanic struggle against the employers who were led by the media baron, capitalist entrepreneur and conservative nationalist William Martin Murphy. It was a bitter battle that saw much hardship on the streets of Dublin as employees were locked out of their places of work, whilst cheap labour was sourced from Britain. On Saturday 31 August Jim Larkin addressed a meeting of striking workers in Beresford Place, Dublin, at which he burned publicly a proclamation prohibiting the holding of union meetings. It was at this meeting also that James Connolly made a speech in support of the strikes that saw him arrested and placed before the courts. Connolly refused to guarantee his own good behaviour and he was sent to Mountjoy Prison for a period of three months.

Connolly began a hunger strike on 7 September and when he began refusing liquids serious concerns began to circulate regarding his health. Connolly, though, was upbeat during his plight and wrote to his wife Lillie 'do not fret', while adding 'many more than I, perhaps thousands, will have to go to prison before our freedom is won' (Yeates, *Lockout – Dublin 1913*, p. 149). During his stay in Mountjoy Connolly was treated well and received visitors, letters and newspapers for the first three days of his fast. With the condition of Connolly worsening, the Lord Lieutenant for Ireland, Lord Aberdeen, received a union deputation led by William O'Brien demanding Connolly's release. Given that the

'Cat and Mouse' Act was in operation, it was perhaps logical that Connolly and his supporters felt that Connolly's release would be granted at the earliest opportunity. It was a conviction based on the potential for serious disorder in the streets should he die and the understanding that his life, as in the case of the suffragettes, would not be allowed to become a bargaining chip. On Saturday 13 September Connolly was granted his freedom courtesy of a signed declaration, which arrived at the prison via Lord Aberdeen's official car. On his release, Connolly recuperated at the home of Constance Markievicz at Surrey Place in Rathmines.

The first death of the twentieth century in Ireland that could be attributed in part to hunger striking was that of Dún Laoghaire's James Byrne, who died on 1 November 1913, having been released from prison after a hunger and thirst strike. Born in 1875, Byrne was the secretary of the Bray and Kingstown Trades Council and had been arrested on the alleged charge of intimidating a tram worker during the Dublin Lockout. Remanded to Mountjoy Prison, Byrne immediately commenced a hunger strike in a protest at not being granted bail. After three days, in an attempt to force his release, Byrne began to refuse water and, when his condition deteriorated significantly, he was released to await trial whilst recuperating. It was, however, only then that it was discovered that Byrne had contracted pneumonia in Mountjoy and he succumbed in Monkstown Hospital on 1 November. His funeral was attended by over 4,000 and it fell to James Connolly to deliver a bitter graveside oration to the assembled crowd. He told them that their comrade had been murdered as surely as any martyr in the long list of those who had suffered for the sacred cause of liberty. He added that Byrne had been 'thrown into a cold, damp, mouldy cell', but while in prison, so contemptuous had he been of those who put him there that he had refused food and drink; if their murdered comrade could send his fellow strikers a message, it would be to 'get on with the fight for the sacred cause of liberty', even if it brought them 'hunger, misery, eviction and even death itself', as it had done Byrne (cited in Yeates, *Lockout – Dublin 1913*, p. 374).

Byrne, with hindsight, is the forgotten martyr of Irish hunger striking. Whilst his death was due to pneumonia, it was the fact that his fast had weakened his body sufficiently that caused his untimely passing. His grave in Deansgrange Cemetery lay unmarked for many years until it was identified and on 1 November 2003, 90 years after his death, a memorial was erected to him on behalf of a number of Irish trade unions.

One strange case that displayed the ability of the prison authorities to indulge in clever mind games was reported in January 1914. Frank Moss was an organiser for the Irish Transport and General Workers' Union who had been arrested and sentenced for disturbances connected with a strike in Swords, County Dublin. Following the example of James Connolly, he immediately started fasting in an attempt to win his freedom under the 'Cat and Mouse' Act. As his condition deteriorated he was removed from Mountjoy Prison to hospital and placed in an isolation cell. The cell contained the bare minimum of furniture, however, on the bedside table were placed two bottles of Guinness Double Extra stout, as well as a tumbler, some biscuits and a corkscrew. Moss was left alone and when the warder returned later he found the two bottles of stout empty and, accordingly, the fast had been broken. Temptation, it seems, had had the better of Frank Moss.

The question of 'Votes for Women', whilst stealing the political limelight, was secondary in importance to the Home Rule debate. As unionism geared itself for open rebellion, the Irish Question again came to prominence and the island braced itself for civil war. History, however, intervened and the progress of the Home Rule Bill was delayed as the Great War commenced. Thousands of nationalists and unionists immediately joined up in support of the British and their bravery amidst the carnage was seen as vital to the war effort. However, 'England's difficulty is Ireland's opportunity' is an old adage from Daniel O'Connell and the war afforded the more radical opponents of English rule an opportunity to mount their own rebellion.

Winston Churchill wrote famously that 'as the mists of battle cleared, there arose from them the dreary spires of Fermanagh and Tyrone' – meaning, of course, that as Great War ended, the problems of Ireland again came to the fore in British politics. He was correct and Irish republicanism was to be re-born during the aftermath of the Easter Rising in 1916. In reality it was not the rising itself that hardened Irish nationalist opinion against Britain; it was the management – or rather mismanagement – of the issues of prisons and prisoners by Britain that fomented further discontent. By 1917 the notion that Home Rule would solve the Irish Question was off the agenda. In essence, the parliamentary path to Home Rule was eclipsed by the ideal of physical force nationalism.

Despite being caught cold, there was to be no game of 'cat and mouse' played by the British hierarchy with the leaders of the Easter Rising. Whilst the actions of the rebels in 1916 were criticised by a majority of the Irish population, the tide turned in favour of the rebels when they were subjected to what William Gladstone once referred to as 'wild justice of revenge'. The Catholic Primate of All Ireland, Cardinal Michael Logue, who was vehemently opposed to the Easter Rising, described it as 'this foolish and pernicious insurrection'. However, in strangely prophetic words, the Cardinal suggested that in the aftermath of the rising, the 'public authorities will muddle this, as sure as the sun shines.' He was to be proved correct.

In essence, Ireland was put under martial law as the British sought to exert control and the reprisals began in earnest. Despite the fact that the rebels had fought in accordance with the accepted rules of warfare, it fell to General John Maxwell to determine how the insurgents would be dealt with when he arrived in Dublin on 28 April. Essentially, Maxwell assumed the role of supreme military governor, a grandiose title that rivalled that of a military dictator, and he determined that the rising was an act of treason in a time of war. He was given carte blanche to deal with the situation, but his actions created a chasm between the two countries that would never be bridged. Maxwell oversaw the wholesale arrest of 3,400 men and women, many of whom were merely suspects, of which 1,700 were deported to Britain where they were held in internment camps. The greatest mistake, however, was in the private court-martialling of 183 men, 90 of whom received the death sentence for their alleged part in the rising with Maxwell overseeing all the 'trials'.

The policy that Maxwell imposed on Ireland showed how much Britain feared an insurrection at its back door. Granted, there was panic among the establishment that Germany could use the chaos in Ireland as a means to attack or infiltrate Britain, thus the reassertion of order on the island was essential at the time. However, there was a malicious overtone to the reaction that sowed the seeds of future conflict. The Irish Parliamentary Party MP John Dillon, who warned Britain that its policy would see the rebellion 'drowned in a sea of blood', was instrumental in having a vast majority of the death sentences commuted, but the leaders of the rising would not escape Maxwell's wrath. Amid the ongoing carnage of the Great War, Britain exacted retribution on fifteen of the leaders of the rising. On 3 May Padraig Pearse, Thomas MacDonagh and Thomas Clarke were executed by firing squad and the following day Edward Daly, M Joseph Plunkett, Michael O'Hanrahan and Padraig Pearse's brother William were all shot dead. The retribution continued and on 5 May John MacBride was put to death, while Constance Markievicz was given a reprieve and sentenced to life imprisonment. The deaths followed of Con Colbert and Sean Heuston, while de Valera's sentence was commuted. Éamonn Ceannt and Michael Mallin were shot by firing squad in Kilmainham Prison on 8 May. The following day Tomás Ceannt (no relation to Éamonn) was executed in Cork Military Detention Centre for his part in the death of Head Constable William Rowe in Cork during Easter week, but his brother William was acquitted.

The 'wild justice of revenge' continued unabated with the deaths of James Connolly and Seán MacDiarmada on 12 May, but, by this stage, the actions of the military under Maxwell had turned Irish public opinion irrevocably against Britain. The iron fist had been used with avenging force on the rising and the situation had changed utterly. In what was akin to a diplomatic version of the slamming of the stable door after the horse had bolted, the military issued a statement justifying their actions to largely deaf Irish ears:

> In view of the gravity of the rebellion and the connection to German intrigue and propaganda, and in view of the great loss of life and destruction of property resulting therefrom, the General Officer Commander-in-Chief has found it imperative to inflict the most severe sentence on the known organisers of this despicable uprising . . . It is hoped that these examples will be sufficient to act as a deterrent to intriguers and bring home to them that the murder of his Majesty's subjects or other acts calculated to imperil the safety of the realm will not be tolerated.

> Kiberd, *1916 Rebellion Handbook*, p. 60

With Ireland under martial law, the administration at Dublin Castle was further weakened by the resignation of Lord Wimbourne, the Lord Lieutenant of Ireland, who had been criticised in some quarters for perceived inaction before and during the rising. On 12 May Prime Minister Herbert Asquith travelled to Dublin to seek clarification on the situation that had developed since the rising. Before he departed for Ireland, Asquith, in words that must have caused revulsion across the Irish Sea, paid tribute to Maxwell and his handling of the executions and said that 'we have the greatest confidence in General Maxwell's discretion to conduct delicate and difficult jurisdiction.' However, in the midst of the Great War the arrival of Asquith in Dublin was unprecedented and an indication of the disquiet that had been felt at Maxwell's handling of the executions.

Meanwhile the recriminations continued, with the editor of *The Irish World*, Robert E. Ford, labelling the execution of Padraig Pearse 'a piece of base bestiality that will no doubt cause reprisals by the people of Ireland'. The *Manchester Guardian* went further and called the actions of Maxwell et al an 'atrocity', while Timothy Healy, the MP for Cork, claimed in the House of Commons that 'we [the Irish people] are not going to stand here and see our people shot. We are not Prussia.' *The New York Times* stated that the executions were a 'proceeding of absolute stupidity', while the *Daily Chronicle* pointed out astutely that, on top of the executions, Maxwell had made the 'even more serious mistake of wholesale arrests in the southern provinces'. The situation created by Maxwell needed to be addressed and pressure grew on Britain to make a gesture towards the political prisoners incarcerated in British jails or prison camps. Far from quelling the rebellious nature of Irish republicanism, the reprisals had only reinvigorated those held in the prisons in their determination to finish the 'business' that began at Easter 1916.

In December 1916 David Lloyd George replaced Herbert Asquith as British Prime Minister. This change coincided with a new sense of optimism regarding a political settlement in Ireland. For the British the issue of the Irish prisoners in England and Wales presented an opportunity to display some goodwill that would help ease the antagonism of the nationalist population of Ireland. By Christmas Henry Duke, Chief Secretary for Ireland, was to advise the House of Commons that there existed on the island a 'steady improvement' and that he would be sympathetic to the early release of internees from a number of camps, most notably Frongoch in North Wales. These sentiments were expressed within the wider context of finding a political solution to the Irish Question when the Great War had ended. Accordingly, as a leap of political faith, Lloyd George made an enormous gesture by authorising the release of large numbers of internees and the closure of the Frongoch Camp.

With hindsight this act can be seen as a catalyst to further insurrection in Ireland. The notion that the revolutionary zeal of republicanism had been extinguished by incarceration and execution was an error. In the case of the Frongoch Camp, it would become known as *Ollscoil na Réabhlóide*, or the University of Revolution, such was the ability of internees to use their time to educate themselves in anticipation of re-entering the republican struggle after their release. Prominent among the

1,800 ex-internees of Frongoch were Éamon de Valera, Terence MacSwiney, Michael Collins and Arthur Griffith. Lloyd George was fully aware of the reputation of Frongoch as a centre for revolutionary thinking but the outcry over the terrible conditions in the camp may well have influenced his decision in 1916. However, history would dictate that the most fertile fields for the growth of republicanism throughout Ireland would be found in the fateful denouement of prison disputes.

Chapter 2

Thomas Ashe: Death by Force-feeding

'If I die, I die in a good cause.'

Thomas Ashe, 1917

History has an uncanny habit of repeating itself, especially in Ireland. With hindsight 1917 and 1981 appear similar, since both years witnessed radical republican breakthroughs in electoral terms. Similarly, the political changes in both years coincided with a period of prison disputes that would see men die whilst on hunger strike, protesting against their designated status as common criminals. However, in reality this coincidence was perhaps pure chance, although the deaths of sitting members of the House of Commons, which would enable the emergence of republicanism through the ballot box, certainly provided an alternative dynamic to armed insurrection.

Thomas Ashe died on 25 September 1917. He was the victim of circumstance. Whilst Ashe did die while on hunger strike, his cause of death was heart failure with complications brought about by fluid in his lungs. The bottom line was that he died from the effects of force-feeding. In fact, the authorities were to shoulder the blame for Ashe's death, since a prolonged inquest was turned into a damning indictment of British Government

and the Catholic establishment in Dublin Castle. And the tide of public opinion turned even further against Britain in the wake of the public fallout following the death of Ashe.

Somewhere in the higher echelons, a decision was made to address a hunger strike by forty republican prisoners in September 1917 with the use of brutality and force-feeding. It backfired and Thomas Ashe died – his death a direct result of the combination of incompetence and ignorance that marked the authorities' pig-headed determination to face down republican prisoners. What was evident, however, was that Irish society had changed utterly and those who sought to deny that fact were forced to face it with the death of Ashe.

Coinciding with the 1916 Christmas releases of the republican internees and prisoners by Prime Minister Lloyd George, the death was announced of the nationalist MP for North Roscommon, James Joseph O'Kelly. The resulting by-election presented a prime opportunity for republicanism to test the depth of feeling in nationalist Ireland in the aftermath of the Easter Rising. By the use of what was to be referred to as the 'Reading Policy' – so named because it was devised by republican prisoners in Reading Prison – the cause of republicanism would soon eclipse all the other nationalist parties. This strategy was simple in its logic, with Sinn Féin (or a candidate representing the party by proxy) partaking in elections to gain a mandate for its revolutionary stance. The bottom line was that the Irish Parliamentary Party (IPP), under John Redmond, was seen as lacking in dynamism and had brought its moderate political position as far as it could go. By testing public opinion through elections, militant republicanism sought democratic legitimacy to add to its revolutionary potential, thus undermining the accepted limitations of the nationalist Home Rule strategy.

Accordingly, the by-election for North Roscommon was set for 6 February 1917 and George Noble Plunkett was chosen to represent a wide and loose coalition of parties opposed to conscription and, more pointedly, to the Irish Parliamentary Party. Whilst not being considered the most prominent candidate,

Plunkett, who had been made a Papal Count in 1877, was an art historian and director of the National Museum from 1907 until 1916. He was a scholarly character, a former follower of Parnell who had made a slow transformation to radical republicanism. His credentials were impeccable, given that he had three sons who fought during Easter week, with his son Joseph Mary (the most well-known of the trio) executed as one of the signatories of the proclamation. In May 1916 Count Plunkett was sent to Oxford Prison, at which point he had already been ostracised by 'respectable' Dublin society for his sympathetic and active support of the rebels. Plunkett's campaign was fought with gusto with, and aided by, Michael Collins and the other released internees from Frongoch Internment Camp in Wales.

The canvassing and polling was carried out in treacherous conditions and became known as the 'election of the snows'. In the end Plunkett, 'the man for Ireland', was victorious, out-polling the Nationalist T. J. Devine by 3,022 votes to 1,708. The Irish Parliamentary Party was rocked by the result but Devine's manager chose to blame the bad weather for the poor turnout of the nationalist farming vote. However, he added that Devine 'was a local man who was not personally popular', which was far from a glowing endorsement of his own candidate. In his victory speech Plunkett was forthright on his political position: 'My place henceforth will be beside you in your own country for it is in Ireland, with the people of Ireland, that the battle for Irish liberty will be fought. I recognize no Parliament in existence as having a right over the people of Ireland, just as I deny the right of England to one inch of the soil of Ireland' (*An Phoblacht*, 3 March 2005)

The second by-election that saw Sinn Féin's rise to prominence occurred in South Longford where Joe McGuinness, who was serving three years in Lewes Prison for his part in the Rising, was elected on a republican ticket on 10 May. The election was fought on the simple logic of 'Put him in to get him out. Joe McGuinness, the man in jail for Ireland.' By standing a serving prisoner as a candidate, republicans were taking an enormous risk since a defeat could have been a fatal blow. However, in a closely fought contest, McGuinness was victorious over the Nationalist Patrick McKenna by 37 votes. The result was to signal mass celebrations in many parts of Ireland and in Mullingar, County Westmeath, a coffin was paraded through the streets bearing the words: 'The Irish Party died in Longford, 10th May, 1917. RIP.' A meeting was held at the Market House, and one of the speakers declared that John Redmond's day was done in Ireland. *The Daily Telegraph* in London commented that 'there is talk of a petition against McGuinness but the situation is in any case grave', while *The Irish Times'* correspondent said of the result that 'Partition is dead, agreement is the alternative to coercion.'

On his release from Pentonville Prison in London, Éamon de Valera was told that he was to be the republican candidate for a by-election in the constituency of East Clare. The by-election was scheduled for 10 July and was caused by the violent death in Flanders of John Redmond's brother, William, who had been a major in the Royal Irish Rifles. Republicans sensed that the mood had changed in Ireland and that the revolutionary alternative offered to the electorate had mass appeal. The choice of de Valera was an ace in the pack, given his prominence and reputation as a hard-liner. His opponent was to be Patrick Lynch, a prominent King's Counsel, who it was felt might benefit from a sympathy vote after the death of William Redmond. It was a fierce contest with personal attacks galore, particularly the following assault, which was published in a republican leaflet: 'Are you giving Patrick Lynch the vote? He's fat with English pay / For he sat at home in comfort, when de Valera was away.'

The result, when it was announced, was a sensation, with de Valera a victorious 3,000 votes ahead of the Nationalist Lynch. There were wild scenes of celebration in Ennis as the old order had been routed by a party that was confident and emboldened by its emphatic mandate. The *Daily Chronicle* (12 July 1917) commented on de Valera's victory, saying, 'it is a hare-brained gesture of inconsequential destructiveness which makes Englishmen almost despair at Ireland's political future.' In essence, the personal tragedy of his brother's death was to be compounded for Redmond by the political demise of his party and Home Rule. Suffering as he was from ill health, he would never recover from the double body blow as the truth dawned that no seat beyond Dublin or Ulster was immune to the growth of Sinn Féin.

With support for the new republican policy now unstoppable, the concept of Home Rule lay in tatters. Inevitably, the British Government attempted to shore up support for the waning Nationalist Party, but it was too little, too late. In May 1917 the British Prime Minister David Lloyd George wrote to John Redmond, the leader of the Irish Parliamentary Party, in response to his suggestion that an Irish Constitutional Convention be set up. With the Great War at its height, any initiative that could assist Lloyd George in pacifying Ireland in the interim was welcomed and the premier was enthused at the prospect: 'Would it not be too much to hope that Irishmen of all creeds and parties might meet in convention which will secure a just balance of all opposing interests which will finally compose the unhappy discords which so long have distracted Ireland and impeded harmonious development?' (Letter from Lloyd George to John Redmond (16 May 1917), given in an appendix to *The Report of the Proceedings of the Irish Convention*, presented to the House of Commons, 18 April 1918).

For John Redmond the Irish Convention was a last proverbial throw of the political dice. Home Rule as a solution to Ireland's quarrel was waning in significance and the political situation had moved on significantly since 1916. The growth of Sinn Féin, together with the rise of John Dillon within the IPP, had reduced the importance of Redmond within political circles. In fact, the notion of setting up the Convention was to be Redmond's swansong, given that his health continued to deteriorate and he would die in May 1918 of heart failure.

When the news of the initiative broke, Sinn Féin leader Arthur Griffith made the release of the republican prisoners a precondition to his party's participation in the Convention. In late May a hunger strike commenced at Lewes Prison, which led to concessions to republicans – however, optimism was the order of the day in London and soon it was rumoured that a general amnesty would be granted to the remaining republican prisoners as an act of goodwill. Accordingly, in the House of Commons on 15 June, the then Chancellor of the Exchequer, Andrew Bonar Law, announced that the government was satisfied that public security would not be compromised and that the remaining republican prisoners would be freed. Acknowledging that the handling of the prison disputes had been something that had caused much consternation, Bonar Law added that 'the government has decided therefore to remove the one cause by which serious misunderstanding had been inspired'. In essence, it can be argued that the government, in light of the perceived improvement in the situation in Ireland, was prepared to take a massive leap of faith. Within the establishment there was a body of opinion that felt that keeping the prisoners incarcerated was counter-productive. The disaster of the revengeful tactics of Maxwell in the wake of the Rising still stirred anti-English feeling in Ireland. *The New York Times* commented astutely when the news of the releases became public: 'England may well have released a boomerang.'

The Convention, which consisted of fifty-nine members, met for the first time at Trinity College Dublin on 25 July 1917. Chaired by County Meath-born unionist Horace Plunkett, a first cousin of Count George Plunkett, it would meet periodically until March 1918 throughout Ireland, but it was a mere talking shop that failed to appreciate the new political reality. Sinn Féin, despite the release of the prisoners, boycotted the Convention in protest at its terms of reference, which foresaw a solution to the Irish Question only within the British Empire. Also, given the new political reality, the party was still only offered 5 seats out of a membership of 101, with every member having to be 'approved' by Lloyd George. In the background, however, the political battle between Home Rule Nationalism and Sinn Féin had moved in favour of the republicans, and the Convention was seen as somewhat dead in the water. Sinn Féin was a party in the ascendancy and chose to ignore the Convention as irrelevant. Accordingly, by the summer of 1917 a political vacuum existed throughout Ireland. Into that vacuum would burst a new, if sadly familiar, drama: once more prison disputes, tragic death and political martyrdom would further sap Britain's will to stay in Ireland.

★

On 25 September 1917 Thomas Ashe claimed a place for himself in the annals of Irish history when he died in the Mater Hospital, Dublin, while on hunger strike. His death caused shock waves across the island and the bitter recriminations that followed only deepened further the chasm between republicanism and the authorities in Dublin Castle. The inquest into Tom Ashe's death became a prolonged and bitter exposition of the prison regime in Ireland, and the determination of the authorities to face down a hunger strike by stubborn force. His death would ultimately reinvigorate anti-British feeling and prove that hearts and minds could be won by passive struggle against an enemy that was deemed cold and indifferent.

Thomas Ashe was 32-years-old when he died. He was born in Kinard near Dingle, in County Kerry, and was the seventh child of Gregory and Ellen Ashe. In 1905 Ashe enrolled at the De La Salle Training College in Waterford where he undertook a teacher-training course and immersed himself in Irish language and culture, becoming a member of the Gaelic League. On graduating, he was appointed as the principal of Corduff National School in Lusk, County Dublin, where he became involved with the Irish Volunteers. Ashe was also deeply involved in sporting activities in the north County Dublin area and was instrumental in forming the Black Ravens Pipe Band.

By Easter 1916 Ashe had become the Commandant of the 5th Battalion of the Irish Volunteers based in Fingal. During the Rising his battalion made strategic raids across north Dublin, capturing arms and destroying communications equipment and cutting the railway line between Dublin and Dundalk. The most notable incident, however, came at the Battle of Ashbourne, which was considered to have been one of the few successes of the Easter Rising. Under the command of Ashe an attack was mounted on the Royal Irish Constabulary (RIC) barracks in Ashbourne, County Meath, where, despite being heavily outnumbered, the battalion were able to force the police to withdraw and the barracks were taken. After the Rising Ashe was captured and sentenced to death. This was commuted to penal servitude for life and he served time in both Dartmoor and Lewes prisons. Ashe was to benefit from the general amnesty declared in June 1917 and returned to west Kerry to a hero's welcome. His time in prison had only served to reignite his revolutionary zeal and he was soon immersed in revolutionary politics.

Ashe had succeeded Padraig Pearse as President of the Irish Republican Brotherhood (IRB) and his position was to bring him under close scrutiny from the British authorities. On 25 July Ashe made what was described as a 'seditious speech' at Ballinalea in County Longford. He was soon arrested in Dublin and was, under the Defence of the Realm Act, court-martialled on 4 September in Dublin Castle.

At the court martial Constable Thomas Bowers stated that he had witnessed the meeting in Ballinalea and that Ashe had told the crowd to form literary and military societies, to train, arm, and equip themselves. Ashe was permitted to cross-examine Bowers about his verbatim recollection of events, to which he responded that he had taken a mental note of the speech and afterwards had written it out. It was evident that Ashe was fighting a losing battle and he was sentenced to a year's imprisonment with hard labour and transferred to Mountjoy Prison. There Ashe was advised that he would be treated as an ordinary prisoner with no special status. He and the other republican prisoners initiated a policy of non-cooperation with the authorities and this soon escalated into a hunger strike. Outside the prison walls pressure was mounted to secure the release of the strikers and soon the authorities moved Ashe and some others for treatment to the Mater Hospital. On 25 September Thomas Ashe died. The full story of what had occurred in the week leading to his death would never be revealed. His inquest gave a tantalising flavour, however, of what had taken place, and at its close the authorities stood undeniably accused of brutality and responsibility for the death, thanks to the skill of the Ashe family barrister, Timothy Healy.

The funeral was organised by the IRB and was, perhaps, the greatest show of republican strength seen in Ireland since the Easter Rising. Scenes in the city on the return of Ashe's body to Dublin City Hall were described as 'without parallel' (*The Daily Telegraph*, 29 September 1917), outstripping the emotion that possessed the city on the burial of O'Donovan Rossa or Parnell in 1891. There was one long, seemingly unending procession passing through the City Hall to view the remains. Given the massive show of emotion, the authorities in Dublin Castle ordered the military to keep their distance and clashes were avoided in the streets. At Amien Street a crowd of suffragettes marched on the home of Doctor Lowe who had been implicated in the force-feeding of Ashe and were only dispersed when a crowd of constables arrived.

The funeral cortège was observed by well in excess of 150,000 people as it made its way from the City Hall to Glasnevin Cemetery. In the hours preceding the event shops were closed and blinds were drawn as vast crowds converged along the route in expectation of a truly historic spectacle. By midday the doors of the City Hall were closed and only the family of Ashe and a select few mourners were allowed to stay with the body. At 1:30 p.m. the coffin emerged into Dame Street from the City Hall flanked by hundreds of Volunteers representing all corners of the country. From County Kerry over 120 Volunteers had travelled for the burial, while 100 priests were in attendance. On cue, the crowds fell into silence as Father Kennedy from Dingle recited the rosary in Irish and the coffin, which was draped in an Irish tricolour, was placed in the hearse by six comrades of Ashe who had served time with him in Lewes Prison.

It was an occasion of exceptional unity and order. The hearse was followed by scores of carriages representing the various civic and public bodies within Dublin. As the procession passed Mountjoy Prison, two of Ashe's fellow prisoners were spotted by a window while St James's Band played 'The Soldiers' Song'. In Sackville (O'Connell) Street the scenes were unparalleled as tens of thousands filled every vantage point in the road, still in ruin after the events of Easter 1916. By the time the cortège reached the cemetery, it was almost four o'clock. The sound of the 'Death March' accompanied the coffin as it was borne to the grave. As the Latin chants of the priests filled the air, the body of Thomas Ashe was laid to rest. After a volley of shots was fired in the air, Michael Collins gave the oration at the graveside, which was brief in the extreme. What he did say was pointed: 'Nothing remains to be said. That volley is the only speech that it is proper to make above the grave of a dead Fenian.'

The inquest into the death of Thomas Ashe opened on 28 September and caused a political sensation when the true circumstances of his death became apparent (widely reported in the press, most of the quotes in the following account are from *The Irish Times* and *The Irish News*). It was a prolonged and bitter clash of intellects between Timothy Healy KC, who represented the Ashe family and whose sympathy for the Sinn Féin cause was evident, and Henry Hanna KC, the Belfast-born unionist barrister representing the Crown. The gallery at the Mater Hospital on the opening day became a veritable *Who's Who* of prominent republicans, including Éamon de Valera and Count Plunkett. Immediately the fraught tone for the inquest was set when Healy protested at the composition of the 'remarkable' jury, pointing out that at least half of the sixteen jurors summoned to the inquest were, to his knowledge, 'Tories' and that a fair hearing could not be achieved. The coroner, Dr Louis A. Byrne, advised Healy that the 'usual procedures had been followed'. Soon Healy was again on the offensive and rose to accuse the government of insensitivity as John Ashe, the brother of Thomas, confirmed to the court that he had identified the body. 'The government should prove its own handiwork,' stated Healy, obviously playing to an applauding gallery, 'instead of getting this unfortunate brother of the deceased to act in this way.'

Healy warmed to his task and called as a witness the Lord Mayor of Dublin, Laurence O'Neill. As Lord Mayor, O'Neill was an ex-officio Visiting Justice of Mountjoy Prison and explained that he had felt it his duty to attend the prison on hearing that a 'disturbance' had developed in the week of Ashe's death. Ashe, whom O'Neill described as lying in the corner of a cell without bed, bedding, boots or furniture, told the Lord Mayor that he had been seized by four warders who had manhandled him and taken his boots off, leaving him in the cell. Ashe was evidently weak, but said that he had no complaints to make against the prison officials and insisted that the reason they were fasting was due to their treatment as criminals. O'Neill urged Ashe to eat for the sake of his health and undertook to raise the situation with Max Green and the Chief Secretary for Ireland, Henry Duke.

Max Sullivan Green was the Chairman of the Irish Prisons Board and had been described in the House of Commons in 1916 as the 'chief gaoler for Ireland' by the Nationalist MP Laurence Ginnell. This criticism arose as stories circulated about the harsh treatment of Irish prisoners in the aftermath of the Easter Rising and Green's name became synonymous with this ill-treatment. Green was also married to Johanna Redmond, daughter of John Redmond, founder of the Irish Parliamentary Party, and had enjoyed a smooth rise through the ranks of government at Dublin Castle. In essence, he was one of those who would be dubbed 'Castle Catholics', a derogatory label that inferred such individuals had prospered under British rule and had no vested interest in seeing the political situation change. In 1922 he was shot and killed while trying to stop a robbery in Dublin by elements linked to republicanism. In the latter part of September 1917 the fate of Thomas Ashe and the other fasting prisoners would ultimately lie in his hands.

The Lord Mayor told the jury that at the meeting with

Duke and Green, Duke had seemed sympathetic, but had explained that the matter was out of his hands. The Lord Mayor had specifically raised the case of James MacDonagh, the brother of the executed 1916 rebel Thomas, and reported that Green had been less sympathetic and had informed the Lord Mayor that 'these men were handed over to me as criminals' and that he had had 'no alternative but to treat them as such'. In response, O'Neill had warned both men of the gravity of the situation and that they would shoulder the blame should anything tragic happen. On 24 September O'Neill, together with another Visiting Justice, Sir John Irwin, again visited the prison and recounted that they had found Ashe in his cell standing staring at its window. Ashe explained that he had been forced to break four panes in order to get some air and he spoke of the 'revolting experience' that he was being put through by force-feeding. The Lord Mayor then said that Ashe had told him that 'they branded him a criminal' and 'if he died, he knew it was in a just cause'. At that moment, to the consternation of the coroner, the gallery erupted again with applause; it was pure theatre. Within an hour of the visit Ashe had been transferred from his cell to the prison hospital. Sir John Irwin explained to the court that he had found the prisoner to be in good spirits when he visited him with the Lord Mayor and that Ashe had objected to being treated in the same manner as a 'pickpocket'. O'Neill had explained that there was little that he could do as Ashe was serving a sentence imposed by a military court.

The following day the inquest was moved to the City Morgue for medical evidence. Professor MacWeeney described Ashe as a muscular and well-developed man, adding that he could be considered 'fat'. He also stated that, on examination, he had found evidence of a former bout of tuberculosis and added that Ashe had a 'slight affection of the lung' and that his arm had evidence of punctures due to hypodermic needles. Pointedly, he stated that the deceased did not die of hunger, given that there were traces of food in his stomach. On further examination he admitted that death had been in part due to 'passive congestion of both lungs', which had most likely brought about heart failure. Further medical evidence by Dr McKenna, house surgeon at the Mater Hospital, revealed that Ashe, on the evening of his admission to the hospital, had complained of difficulty in breathing and that part of his heart was in a 'weak condition'. Ashe had added that he had collapsed earlier that day after a bout of coughing brought about by force-feeding.

Healy then examined Lieutenant-Colonel Sir Thomas Myles, who had presided at the *post mortem* on Ashe. Myles, a prominent surgeon and Home Ruler, had stated that the cause of death in Ashe's case had been heart failure, given that his heart, when examined, had been described as 'dilated and flabby'. He added that oedema (fluid) in the lung could well have been a contributory factor. This assertion was questioned by Healy, to which Myles, who admitted that he had only ever witnessed force-feeding in lunatic asylums, added that the fact that the prisoner had been refusing food for two days would have contributed to cardiac failure. The crux of Healy's questions was whether it had been advisable to remove Ashe from Mountjoy Prison to the Mater Hospital for treatment, since he was in a 'state of collapse' and his removal could therefore endanger his life. Myles agreed that moving Ashe could have been construed as dangerous in his condition; he also admitted that force-feeding might have posed a serious threat to the patient's health.

The next witness was Sir Arthur Chance, the eminent surgeon based at the Mater Hospital, whom Healy described facetiously as a 'medical giant'. Chance explained the process of force-feeding and stated that the 'operation' was acutely dangerous – moreover that the danger increased if there was resistance on behalf of the prisoner and inexperience among the administering staff. He suggested that the greatest threat to a life during the procedure would come about by a prisoner choking due to a vomiting fit. Healy then went for the jugular and asked Chance if there was, perhaps, a possibility that malpractice could have been involved in the death of Thomas Ashe. Again there was uproar in the court, but Chance retorted, rather illogically, that he could not answer because Healy's question was 'political' rather than 'medical'. The *coup de grâce* lay with Healy as he continued relentlessly, 'You see, Sir Arthur, I don't object to you throwing the shield of your great authority over the prison authorities', to which the cry of 'unchivalrous' was shouted by Hanna. Unperturbed, Healy carried on, 'If I said anything that was offensive, even to the most sensitive, I would withdraw it. I only wished that the same chivalry had been shown to the late Mr Ashe.'

Healy was using his undoubted skill to dramatise the proceedings. However, the fact remained that he had produced no concrete evidence that Ashe had been the victim of malpractice, and had only aroused well-founded suspicion. At the time of Ashe's death forty prisoners had been undergoing the 'operation' of force-feeding and there was clear suspicion that the truth surrounding Ashe's death was being withheld. The fact remained that Ashe had died whilst under the care of the prison authorities in Mountjoy Prison, and that those authorities (when directed by their superiors) had adopted a policy aimed at breaking the resistance of the republican prisoners. Healy knew that he was going to require first-hand accounts of events within the prison and indicated that he intended to seek authority in the High Court to call four fellow prisoners of Ashe before the inquest.

It was, therefore, a case of damage limitation by the time that Henry Hanna KC stood up to present the case for the Crown. The main thrust of his argument was that Ashe and his comrades had been dealt with in accordance with the law and were entitled to the, albeit limited, rights as afforded by the Defence of the Realm Act. Hanna provided a chronology of Ashe's time in prison and the way in which 'he and his fellows' had disregarded prison rules by refusing to sew mailbags and had 'talked at exercise and set the whole place at a defiance'. The ultra-conservative nature of Hanna's persona soon became apparent as he criticised Healy for describing the republican prisoners as 'soldiers and heroes' and, in reference to the ongoing

Great War, said: 'But heroes sleep out in the open at the present moment and obey orders. These men have disobeyed the law and cannot expect prison to be a "palace of delights".' Sympathy from the Crown was in short supply.

Dr Dowdall, a medical officer at the prison, explained that Ashe had first been force-fed on Sunday 23 September and that he had offered no resistance. Dr Lowe, who had assisted Dr Dowdall in the procedure at Mountjoy, explained that Ashe had not resisted the attempts to feed him on the Tuesday either. He reported that Ashe had told him that he 'felt weak' and he had noted that Ashe's lips were somewhat blue as he was fed a pint of milk and two raw eggs through a tube inserted down his throat. Two days later, on 25 September, Ashe approached Dr Dowdall and told him that he felt weak and the decision was taken to move the prisoner to the Mater Hospital. In essence, the removal of Ashe and other prisoners to the hospital could be seen as tactical, given that the possibility existed that they could be freed on humanitarian grounds under the provisions of the 'Cat and Mouse' Act. Dowdall explained to the court that he had assured Ashe, whom he noted to have at that time an irregular heartbeat, that he would secure his release since, in the medic's view, Ashe was seriously ill. Ashe went to the Mater Hospital on Tuesday 25 September under the impression that he would be freed. He was, in fact, hours away from his own death.

By now news of Ashe's inquest was being reported in the press under the heading 'The Mountjoy Tragedy', giving the impression that Ashe's death had been an accident. The inquest was still arousing passions as it entered its third week and the Deputy Governor of Mountjoy, Mr Clerk Boland, was called to testify. Boland had been in charge of the prison while Ashe was incarcerated because the then Governor, Charles Monro, was on leave. Boland explained that on two occasions Ashe had been brought before him and charged with idleness and that on 20 September he was called to C Division in the prison when republican prisoners, including Ashe, began to wreck their cells. Boland explained that he had ordered the cell to be stripped of furniture. In response to a query regarding a report that Boland had submitted to Max Green and the Prison Board in respect of the conditions in Mountjoy, Healy was advised that this was 'confidential' and could not be produced in the court. In Healy's eyes Boland was involved in a cover-up and he interjected, perhaps inadvisably, that 'the case was to establish how Mr Ashe had been killed by Mr Hanna's friends'. This was a serious and outlandish accusation and he did not help his case by insulting Hanna and accusing the government, indirectly, of murder.

The squabble between the two barristers continued unabated. Hanna protested at Healy's use of the word 'murder' when referring to Ashe's death, and to the way in which Healy was playing to the public gallery when he used such emotive terms. In response, Healy, suggesting that the government had not played fair in choosing the jury, said, 'you may pack a jury, but you cannot pack a gallery.'

The proof that there had been a high-level cover-up over the death of Thomas Ashe now lay, in Healy's view, in the document that Boland had forwarded to the Irish Prisons Board setting out his view of the situation. Accordingly, Healy brought the matter to the High Court where the Secretary of the Prisons Board, Mr Douglas, produced a minute of the Board signed by Max Green. The minute was emphatic that the information sought was not to be produced as 'it was prejudicial and injurious to the public service of His Majesty', nor was Douglas to attend the inquest or give evidence. In essence, the document held the key to solving the mystery and in the hands of Healy it threatened to undermine, perhaps destroy, the government's case. The failure of the authorities to permit it to be produced as evidence only added to the claims of conspiracy and cover-up. Healy did, however, enjoy a pyrrhic victory in the High Court when it was it was agreed that Austin Stack, Joe MacDonagh, Finian Lynch and Philip McMahon, all of whom had been force-fed along with Ashe, were to be permitted by the Lord Chief Justice, James Campbell, to give evidence.

It was apparent that unless Healy could produce

unequivocal evidence of a conspiracy to murder, then he was fighting a limited battle. His view that the new Catholic class of authorities in Dublin Castle had covered up Ashe's death was popular with Ireland's public, but it would not shake the 'powers that be'. On 16 October Healy made an attack on those who he felt were standing in the way of the truth in the case. His then political leanings towards Sinn Féin were evident because his ire was reserved for the new Catholic and pseudo-nation-alist establishment who had, in his view, assumed semi-power under the British Crown. In essence, Healy was attacking Max Green and those on the Irish Prisons Board who had vetoed the production of Boland's document in evidence. Given that he was unable to produce the vital document, Healy deviated somewhat from the matter at hand and indulged in political point-scoring. Referring to the ironic fact that the British had pardoned Ashe from his death sentence, the new Irish establishment came in for severe criticism. He began:

> It has been pretended on one side that Ashe was a suicide, and in another quarter that he was a victim of the old guard in Dublin Castle – the victim of Toryism and Unionism. Nothing of the kind. He was the victim of the new gang who have usurped the spectre and the throne of the stern, unbending Tories. He was a victim of those who owe their position to the pollution of political power.

Healy, in perhaps a desperate measure, then stated that Thomas Ashe had died at the order of Max Green who had transmitted this message to Deputy Governor Boland. 'The Prisons Board', Healy stated, 'made up their minds that the pluck of the prisoners could not win' and that their will was to be broken. Again, Healy's rhetoric was theatrical, but, without evidence to back them up, his comments could only be construed as conjecture.

The addition of the four fellow prisoners of Ashe into the proceedings did not add much to the notion that Ashe had been the victim of malpractice. Austin Stack, who had told the hunger strikers that they must see the fast through to the 'bitter end', described the process of force-feeding and suggested that it was something that was carried out with more 'force than skill'. Finian Lynch described how he had told Ashe to 'stick at it, Tom Boy' as he was led from his cell to the hospital. In addition, Warder McManus described how Ashe had kept his humour, asking where the 'executioner' was as he was being shackled before being force-fed. In essence, the evidence of the prisoners and the warders would not explain what had happened to Thomas Ashe to bring about his death.

On 18 October the foreman of the jury handed the coroner a note to the effect that the jury was unanimous in the view that it could not discharge its duty properly until the documents withheld by the Prisons Board were produced. Should this not be feasible, the jury requested that the Chief Secretary for Ireland, Mr Henry Duke, who ultimately held responsibility for prison matters, appear before the inquest. It was a bold move that caused a further adjournment of the proceedings. On 29 October the inquest was reconvened and told that the documents withheld by the Prisons Board would not be produced. A letter was then read on behalf of Mr Duke outlining his reasons for not acceding to the jury's request that he attend. The Chief Secretary stated that he had 'no personal knowledge' of the individual case and that no documents were under his control that could add to the case. From the very top of the establishment, it was clear that the authorities were intent on playing a 'straight bat' in the matter of the death of Thomas Ashe. The jury retired to consider their position and returned to hear the remaining evidence.

The inquest ended on 1 November. By this stage Timothy Healy, perhaps in dismay, was absent and the Ashe family was represented by Mr Dixon. The Coroner summed up the evidence for the jury and told them that, whilst it would be easy to agree with the view that Ashe had died of heart failure, he 'could not satisfy himself' as to why the authorities insisted on using a mechanical pump to feed the prisoners. Throughout the inquest, the Crown had referred to the practice of force-feeding as 'mechanical feeding' since the food was administered to the stomach by means of a pump. In reality though, the use of this pump meant that control of the process was not totally in the hands of the doctors on duty. The Coroner's comment suggested that there could have been an accident. The jury retired to consider their verdict and returned fifty minutes later. Their findings were damning and it seemed that Timothy Healy's performance had won the day:

> 'We find that the deceased, Thomas Ashe, died of heart failure and congestion of the lungs on 25th September, 1917; that his death was caused by the punishment of taking away from the cell bed, bedding and boots, and allowing him to be on the cold floor for 50 hours, and then subjecting him to forcible feeding in his weak condition after hunger striking for five or six days. We censure the Castle Authorities for not acting more promptly, especially when the grave condition of the deceased and other prisoners was brought to their notice. That the hunger strike was adopted against the inhuman punishment inflicted and a refusal to their demand to be treated as political prisoners. We find that the taking away of the deceased's bed, bedding and boots was an unfeeling and barbarous act and we censure the Deputy Governor for violating the Prison Rules and inflicting a punishment which he had no power to do, but we infer he was acting under instructions from the Prisons Board at the Castle, which refused to give evidence and documents asked for.

It was victory, if bitter-sweet, for the Ashe family. The Dublin authorities had been embarrassed emphatically. However, by the time that the inquest returned its verdict, force-feeding had been stopped within Irish prisons because the folly of the practice had caused a backlash against the British. After the death of Thomas Ashe the authorities had continued to force-feed prisoners for a further four days. In all, thirty-seven fasting prisoners in Mountjoy and other prisons across Ireland were subjected to the practice, which stopped abruptly on the day before the burial of Thomas

Ashe. All were released within six weeks under the temporary discharge provisions of the 'Cat and Mouse' Act. In essence, the authorities had been shocked by the public reaction to the death of Thomas Ashe and the option of 'mechanical feeding' was quietly dropped as a method for dealing with hunger strikers.

The 'lie' that force-feeding was an instrument of last resort in order to keep a 'prisoner alive' and from committing 'suicide' had been laid bare. The Ashe case was an acute embarrassment and world opinion had read with disdain the verdict of the inquest. As the inquest came to prominence, significant concessions were soon granted to the republican prisoners. In the House of Commons on 17 November Alfie Byrne, the Irish Parliamentary Party MP for Dublin Harbour, asked the Chief Secretary, Henry Duke, what action he intended to take over 'bringing criminal indictments against those who have been held responsible by the jury for this event.' The Chief Secretary advised the House that he was looking into the matter and planned to 'inform myself fully as to the parts of the subject which are not within my personal knowledge'. The matter was never raised again.

Thomas Ashe wrote the following poem while incarcerated in Lewes Prison in 1917. It is a poignant and personal example of Ashe's committment to the republican cause that would end tragically on 25 September 1917:

'Let me Carry your Cross for Ireland, Lord'

Let me carry your Cross for Ireland, Lord
The hour of her trial draws near,
And the pangs and the pains of the sacrifice
May be borne by comrades dear.
But, Lord, take me from the offering throng,
There are many far less prepared,
Though anxious and all as they are to die
That Ireland may be spared.
Let me carry your Cross for Ireland, Lord
My cares in this world are few.
And few are the tears will for me fall

When I go on my way to You.
Spare. Oh! Spare to their loved ones dear
The brother and son and sire.
That the cause we love may never die
In the land of our Heart's desire!
Let me carry your Cross for Ireland, Lord!
Let me suffer the pain and shame
I bow my head to their rage and hate,
And I take on myself the blame.
Let them do with my body whate'er they will,
My spirit I offer to You.
That the faithful few who heard her call
May be spared to Roisin Dubh.
Let me carry your Cross for Ireland, Lord!
For Ireland weak with tears,
For the aged man of the clouded brow,
And the child of tender years;
For the empty homes of her golden plains;
For the hopes of her future, Too!
Let me carry your Cross for Ireland, Lord!
for the cause of Roisin Dubh.

Thomas Ashe, 1917

Chapter 3

Terence MacSwiney: A Means to a Bitter End

'We are urged to action by a beautiful ideal.'
Terence MacSwiney, *Principles of Freedom*, 1913

The year 1920 was quite possibly the most distressing and bloodthirsty in the history of Ireland. In particular, the city of Cork and the south-western counties suffered greatly as the Irish War of Independence manifested its fullest horrors throughout the island. Atrocity followed atrocity as the Irish Republican Army and the Crown Forces rewrote the rules of guerrilla warfare in the midst of a vengeful and spiteful madness. It was a year of bitterness and bloodshed during which Cork City was to witness the death of not one, but two of its elected Lord Mayors: Tomás MacCurtain through brutal assassination and Terence MacSwiney through an agonising and prolonged hunger strike. On both occasions the deaths and funerals of the civic leaders produced a profound sense of shock and a carnival of reaction on the streets of republican Cork and beyond, epitomising the absolute terror that reigned throughout the period.

The turn of events that led to the death of Terence MacSwiney in Brixton Prison in October 1920 can be traced directly to the murder of Lord Mayor Tomás MacCurtain on the morning of Saturday 20 March that year. As the frenzy of assassinations and attacks against the RIC intensified, the quest for revenge from within that force manifested itself brutally at the mayor's home in Blackrock. Late on Friday 19 March the IRA murdered Constable Joseph Murtagh as he returned home from attending the funeral of a murdered police colleague. Consequently, in the early hours of the following morning, rogue elements of the RIC, led by District Inspector Oswald Ross Swanzy, took matters into their own hands and went to the home of MacCurtain, where they murdered him.

As well as being the Lord Mayor of Cork and leader of the Cork No. 1 Brigade of the IRA, MacCurtain was the first republican to hold civic office on Cork Council and his election to the post six weeks previously had made him a prominent target for reprisal. After the Murtagh killing MacCurtain's house was ransacked while his distraught wife Mary ran for help. Despite the fact that Ireland was in a state of absolute anarchy at this time, this particular malevolent act sent grim shockwaves and repulsion across the country and MacCurtain's funeral became a massive show of republican strength. In murdering MacCurtain, elements of the British establishment were showing their willingness to engage in a so-called 'dirty' war. This point was epitomised when the then Lord Lieutenant of Ireland, Lord French, who had four months previously narrowly survived an IRA assassination attempt himself, told the press that the murder of the Lord Mayor had been due to a 'split' within Sinn Féin. At the coroner's inquest into MacCurtain's death the jury judged it 'wilful murder', with the chief perpetrator named symbolically as Prime Minister Lloyd George and (more crucially, as would soon be apparent) certain members of the RIC. The death of Tomás MacCurtain at the hands of the police marked a watershed in the War of Independence. Five days later on 25 March the first members of the Auxiliary Force, better known as the Black and Tans, arrived in Dublin and the seeds of further conflict had been sown.

The IRA took swift vengeance against those whom it deemed culpable in the death of MacCurtain and any index previously used to measure violence became redundant. On 24 April the republicans shot and killed two members of the RIC, Sergeant Cornelius Crean and Constable Patrick McGoldrick, as they were returning to the barracks in Bandon, County Cork. It had been 'noted' that both men had previously been stationed in King Street Barracks in Cork City, where the IRA claimed that the murderers of Tomás MacCurtain had originated. The old adage that vengeance is a 'dish best served cold' is perhaps best illustrated by the most audacious act of reprisal associated with the death of MacCurtain. On Sunday 22 August 1920 the IRA exacted cruel revenge on the RIC District Inspector Oswald Swanzy, implicated by the jury at the inquest into the murder of MacCurtain.

Swanzy had been quietly relocated to Belfast after the MacCurtain assassination and, acting on a tip-off from RIC Sergeant Matthew McCarthy (who had proved to be a valuable mole for Michael Collins within the force), the 1st Cork Battalion of the IRA dispatched Sean Culhane to the north to link up with local IRA members in the city. On that Sunday morning they set off for Lisburn, ten miles outside Belfast, and Culhane, together with Belfast IRA man Roger McCorley, assassinated the officer as he emerged from church just after 1 p.m. Afterwards a backlash of sectarian violence was unleashed on the Catholic population of Lisburn and hundreds were driven from the town.

Two days before the assassination of Swanzy, MacCurtain's successor as Lord Mayor of Cork, Terence MacSwiney, had been sentenced to two years' imprisonment in Brixton Prison. He would never return to the city alive, as fate would have it. His election to office had taken place immediately after MacCurtain's death and, at a special meeting held on 30 March, MacSwiney gave a speech that outlined his political philosophy and (in common with Padraig Pearse before him) the concept of blood sacrifice that was central to his outlook. It is evident that Pearse's fight and ultimate death in 1916 had influenced the Cork man and the notion of dying for the cause of Ireland was by this time an accepted reality for him. He spoke of the 'cleansing power' of the shedding of Irish and English blood as a necessary evil that had to be endured, essential to the winning of Irish freedom. In addition MacSwiney affirmed that 'they who can suffer most' would be victorious in the struggle – this adage became a standard rationale for those partaking in future hunger strikes. He stated:

> This contest of ours is not on our side a rivalry of vengeance, but one of endurance – it is not they who can inflict most but they who can suffer most will conquer . . . It is not we who take innocent blood but we offer it, sustained by the example of our immortal dead and that divine example which inspires us all for the redemption of our country.

An Phoblacht, 27 September 2001

Born in Cork City to an Irish father and an English mother in 1889, Terence MacSwiney was educated in the Christian Brothers' North Monastery and left there in 1895 to work for the wholesalers Messrs Dwyer and Co. Ltd. However, his appetite for learning was insatiable and he returned to the Royal University of Ireland where he completed a Batchelor of Arts degree in Accounting and was soon employed as a teacher of Commercial Studies by Cork County Council. MacSwiney took a keen interest in the Gaelic culture and was influenced greatly by the new school of Irish drama and literature. In 1913 MacSwiney founded the Cork Branch of Sinn Féin, having laid out his republican political aspirations in his book *Principles of Freedom*. In essence, MacSwiney was skilled as an effective organiser as well as being an astute republican, talents which saw him elevated within revolutionary circles. History records that the Easter Rising in 1916 by-passed Cork because com-munications advising that the rebellion was to commence failed to reach the republican leadership in the city. MacSwiney was by that stage the organiser of the Irish Volunteers but was reluctant when news of the Rising broke to permit his volunteers to 'come out', given that the element of surprise had been lost and the initiative lay with the British. It was a decision he would regret, since the Dublin uprising was floundering and a second offensive in Cork might have impacted the British powerfully.

Thereafter, from Easter 1916 until his death, Terence MacSwiney's life was characterised by imprisonment, struggle and defiance. Soon after the Rising he was arrested under the Defence of the Realm Act and incarcerated in Reading and Wakefield jails until his release in December 1916. In October 1917 he was arrested again and sentenced to nine months' imprisonment for wearing an Irish Volunteers' uniform. Within a month MacSwiney and a number of other prisoners had embarked upon a three-day hunger strike in protest at their incarceration and were afforded their release – a positive outcome that he would never forget.

In June 1917 MacSwiney married Muriel Murphy, the daughter of wealthy Cork man Nicholas Murphy, a director in the Cork Distilleries Company. In March 1918 he was again imprisoned and spent time in Belfast, Dundalk and Lincoln jails. During this time he published a volume of poetry called *Battle Cries* and was elected unopposed to the first Dáil Éireann to represent the constituency of mid Cork. In addition to his public persona as a political leader, Terence MacSwiney was the leader of the IRA's 1st Cork Brigade. This grouping had been at the forefront of the vicious campaign of resistance to British rule since the War of Independence had begun in 1919.

Despite MacSwiney's elevation to high civic office in late March he continued to play a prominent role in the ongoing struggle for Irish independence. On 12 August 1920 he and four other prominent Cork IRA leaders (including Cork sec-ond-in-command Liam Lynch) were captured at Cork City Hall in possession of 'seditious material' that included an RIC cipher key, which could be used to intercept and translate coded police messages. From the moment of his arrest until his death, the Lord Mayor fasted. Four days later MacSwiney stood trial before a military court, which he refused to recognise, and was sentenced to deportation to Brixton Prison. From the dock MacSwiney remained defiant as he outlined his intention to fast to the death in order to win his freedom: 'I will put a limit to any term of imprisonment you may impose as a result of the action I will take. I have taken no food since Thursday and therefore will be free within a month' (O'Hegarty, *A Short Memoir of Terence MacSwiney*, p. 90).

In essence, MacSwiney had laid out his intention to die rather than serve a sentence imposed by an authority he did not believe had jurisdiction in Ireland. It was a game with high stakes and his speech – especially the assurance that he would 'be free within a month' – was based not on bravado, but on absolute conviction that the British Government would not countenance the death by hunger strike of someone as prominent as the Lord Mayor of Cork.

It was a belief that was based on British capitulation in the face of the mass hunger strike in April that year at Mountjoy Prison, and the way in which the authorities had baulked when faced with a similar protest by republican prisoners in Wormwood Scrubs in London. However, his speech from the dock was a challenge to which the British showed absolute indifference. On 25 October 1920, the news broke of the death of the Terence MacSwiney; he had died on the seventy-fourth day of his strike in London's Brixton Prison, true to his word and his cause. The man labelled by the British media as the 'brains of the Republican Army' in Ireland had been unconscious for almost a week and his passing was expected. Terence MacSwiney's prediction of freedom was a miscalculation; the authorities were prepared to let a second Cork Lord Mayor die in 1920 and, within the context of the ongoing war, the British felt that the martyrdom of MacSwiney was easily addressed.

To place MacSwiney's speech from the dock in its proper context, it is essential to understand that the concept of hunger striking as a form protest had again become widespread in the course of 1920. More crucially, MacSwiney had failed to take into account the enactment, on 9 August 1920, of the Restoration of Order Act, which suspended all coroners' courts and replaced them with 'military courts of enquiry'. In addition, the powers of military courts martial were extended to cover the whole population and these courts were empowered to use the death penalty – by firing squad – and internment without trial. It can be seen that the government's policy had hardened severely just at the point when MacSwiney commenced his fast. In essence the British Government, led by Lloyd George, had criminalised Irish republicanism and withdrawn the political status that had been won in the aftermath of the death of Thomas Ashe. The British position had changed and changed utterly and MacSwiney was to test the resolve of the government to the absolute extreme.

The extent of the sheer lawlessness that prevailed in early 1920, as well as the draconian measures that the British government implemented in a vain attempt to reassert its waning power, led to the rejuvenation of the prisons as a second front for the republican struggle. In truth, British rule in large parts of Ireland was on its knees. The government's key tool in the maintenance of law and order was the RIC; however, in April 1919 the Sinn Féin-dominated first Dáil adopted a policy of ostracising the force as a preliminary step towards the campaign of widespread guerrilla warfare and RIC officer assassination that was to follow. Within months the RIC had been forced to abandon over 500 of its barracks and drill halls in outlying areas, because scores of attacks, murders and widespread intimidations had cost the force greatly – deaths and resignations began to cripple it from within. In many parts of the country law and order virtually ceased to exist, with courts failing to sit and communications and general administration coming to a halt.

Backed into a corner, the British response was both forthright and counter-productive. As well as introducing the Auxiliary Force (the loathed Black and Tans) into the mix, the Westminster government implemented a policy of holding republican prisoners in English jails to diminish any influence or threat that they might have on the campaign in Ireland. But in moving the republican prisoners to England, the government, in effect, opened up a second front from where a battle of hearts and minds could be fought through the means of prison protest – and hunger-striking in particular. Moreover, events in Mountjoy Prison in early April and an apparent capitulation by the British government in the face of those events would have far-reaching consequences for hunger strikers later in 1920. On 5 April the Dublin-based prisoners, led by Frank Gallagher and Thomas Hunter, began a mass hunger strike and within ten days over seventy prisoners had been released unconditionally. It seemed that hunger striking, as a political weapon, was a means to an end for republicanism.

The Mountjoy protest began as an act of solidarity by republican internees seeking to have political status granted to Irish prisoners who had been incarcerated under the draconian British Defence of the Realm Act. The fast commenced on Easter Monday and occurred in the aftermath of Ireland's most violent weekend since the Rising itself, during which over 200 RIC barracks had come under attack. Within days over ninety men had joined the strike and a policy of confrontation had been adopted by the prisoners, with chaos ensuing as the regime struggled to exert control. The situation within the prison prompted the threat of a general strike in Dublin if the demand for political status was not met. By 12 April the situation was at breaking point when the Attorney-General for Ireland, Mr Denis Henry, reported in the House of Commons that he had received a telegram that day which stated: 'Mountjoy Prison under strike. The Prisons Board report that the condition of all the prisoners on hunger strike in Mountjoy Prison this morning was weak and some were nearing the danger zone.'

Inside the prison Frank Gallagher had kept a diary since the fast had begun. On 12 April he read in the papers that Lord French had stated there would be no concessions to the prisoners. Gallagher summed up the situation facing the prisoners and the likely outcome if one of the fasters died. However, his writing also was fatalistic and predicted that a tragedy or death either inside or outside the prison was needed to bring the situation to a head.

> They [the British Establishment in Ireland] will eat, drink and be merry in their mansions and Viceregal Lodges . . . we shall lie awake, starve and be mad in this evil-smelling hell hole . . . But it is we who shall win . . . There will be trouble outside . . . a great horror must be upon the people . . . Their helplessness makes it worse . . . Their imagination is on fire and they see in through these walls a gruesomeness that will come eventually, but is not here yet. If it lasts much longer a tragedy must occur outside as well as inside . . . outside there will be a terror in it and dignity, there will be the anger of God in it . . . yes, and of the devil.
>
> Gallagher, *Days of Fear*, p. 42

It fell to the Irish Nationalist MP for Liverpool, T. P. O'Connor, to plead the prisoners' cause and also remind the British government of the effect the death of a prisoner would have on so-called moderate nationalist opinion. Referring to the impact that the death of Thomas Ashe had had across Ireland, O'Connor pointed to the absence of Sinn Féin MPs within the Commons, saying that Ashe's death was the reason why 'we [nationalists] have only seven representatives here today instead of seventy-seven'. As the pressure grew, Dublin Corporation adjourned for a week, while the Archbishop of Dublin, William Walsh, added further to the mix when he stated: 'If the prisoners die we shall be faced with the near prospect of an appalling calamity' (Press Association, 14 April 1920). When news was received of the resignation of the chief medical officer at the prison, Dr Cooke, Dublin Castle responded by offering what was termed 'ameliorative' treatment, in other words an improvement in conditions for those held under the Defence of the Realm Act. This was not enough as the prisoners believed that they had taken the moral high ground, and calls for the release of the hunger strikers, led by the chief officer of the prison board, gave them renewed optimism that the authorities were at breaking point.

Public opinion was tipping towards a surge of support for prisoners, and a strike by Dublin railway workers only added to the sense of crisis. The atmosphere in the city was brought to fever pitch as distressful scenes were witnessed outside the prison when families and supporters of the prisoners awaited news while hundreds remained on their knees to recite the rosary in Irish. In the midst of the turmoil it was reported that the Catholic populace of Dublin was hotly debating the issues of the hunger strike – whether or not it was an immoral act and, most tellingly, whether a priest could give absolution to the dying hunger strikers. Regardless, the morality of the situation had given way to a groundswell of popular support that was almost unstoppable and the situation held the explosive potential last seen during Easter Week 1916.

Within two days it seemed that the authorities in Dublin Castle had capitulated and again a fudged solution, of sorts, ended the protest. The key to the climb down by the government came with the appointment, in place of Ian MacPherson, of Sir Hamar Greenwood as Chief Secretary for Ireland on 2 April. As the *Irish Independent* reported, Greenwood had expressed the view that 'the hunger-strike should be got out of the way' before he took up the reins at Dublin Castle (*Irish Independent*, 3 April 1920). The authorities in Mountjoy Prison, on advice from the British government, relented and transferred the strikers en masse to hospitals for convalescence as a precursor to immediate release. The government, in effect, had blinked first and, faced with the prospect of a second uprising in four years on the streets of Dublin, it had admitted defeat: it was game, set and match to the hunger strikers. In his diary, *Days of Fear*, Frank Gallagher recorded the total victory despite the attempts of the government to save face. He also recorded the humiliation that the Governor had suffered at the capitulation:

> The Governor looked like a very old parrot; just as sad looking and as frail looking . . . The helpful warders brought me opposite him and he started reading from a slip of paper, his staccato voice sounding very low and

mechanical . . . Guessed this had something to do with the parole we would not give, so I turned to the doctor, feeling a pang that I should be discourteous to so tired and well-meaning a Governor . . . Told the doctor that I felt very fit and was going home to be nursed . . . He nodded and smiled as I turned back to the Governor, who had ceased reading. 'You know I am not coming back,' I said. I said 'good-bye.' 'Good-bye and good luck,' he said.

The precedent, according to the government, for a mass release of the hunger strikers came in the treatment that had been afforded to the veteran nationalist William O'Brien, who had been on hunger strike in Wormwood Scrubs and had, in March 1920, been removed from prison to a nursing home to enable his recovery. There was wild excitement when certain men were released without parole, but the vast crowds were instantly quiet when ambulances appeared carrying men to hospitals. Sir Nevil Macready is also credited with responsibility for the dramatic reversal of the government's policy. It is believed that he told Lord French he must have a 'clear field' as General Officer Commanding-in-Chief of the British troops in Ireland.

In Wormwood Scrubs Irish republican prisoners undertook a number of fasts between February and April 1920 to try to establish their right to be treated as political prisoners, the right to a jury trial, and, most emphatically, the unconditional release of internees. The first fast was mildly successful, since it ended within two days when the authorities addressed the prisoners' demands for better food and the transfer of several inmates to Brixton Prison, where they joined their former prison leader, Joseph McGrath, who was being held in isolation away from the other Irish prisoners. In fact, the reason for this success was the British government's lack of appetite for a prolonged conflict; when prisoner Willie Ryan became seriously ill after two days, the Permanent Secretary to the Home Department, Sir Edward Troup, wrote to the Cabinet to advise them of Ryan's condition and that 'his death will be made an excuse for attempted murder of ministers of this country'. Accordingly, the concessions were made and the strike was called off. The general perception of the strike was that it was a double bluff. In the House of Commons on 13 April the MP for Edinburgh West, John Jameson, felt compelled to advise his fellow parliamentarians that conditions in the prisons were commendable:

> As recently as last Saturday I was told by an officer that these Sinn Féin prisoners were regarded by their escort with the greatest envy, that they occupied their time in playing 'The Wearing of the Green' upon Irish pipes, and that their bill of fare and the other amenities of their life were very far removed from those of the ordinary inhabitants of the prison.

The prisoners were convinced that the authorities would not countenance the death of an inmate, while the authorities believed that the prisoners were only half-hearted in their intention to fast to the death. Accordingly, the end of the fast was a pragmatic but short-lived solution.

Spurred on somewhat by the success of the Mountjoy protest in April 1920, the republican inmates of Wormwood Scrubs commenced another strike on 25 April. The aim on this occasion was to win their absolute freedom and within three days over ninety inmates had joined in the protest. The London hunger strike was as public an affair as the Mountjoy strike had been, with thousands of London-based Irishmen and women holding a daily vigil at the prison. Each night, however, there were violent anti-Irish protests staged that saw hand-to-hand fighting in the streets surrounding the Scrubs as tension flared to anger. In Glasgow and Liverpool dock unions with strong Irish memberships threatened to strike in solidarity with the prisoners. Within days twelve inmates had been granted freedom because their health had deteriorated sufficiently to warrant release. It seemed that the will of the government was being sapped again in the face of concerted protest.

The Sinn Féin hunger strikers released from Wormwood Scrubs were sent to a large hospital and, according to the

Associated Press, they 'became indignant because of temporary shortage of food at the mid-day meal, and quitted the hospital after reducing the nurses to tears at their unreasonableness. They have not yet returned. The authorities of the hospital say they have no power to compel the prisoners to stay if they are dissatisfied'.

Meanwhile, in Belfast's Crumlin Road Prison on 26 April a communication was sent to the Governor on behalf of 145 republican inmates demanding their unconditional release 'as they were uncharged and untried'. This request was naturally refused and a mass hunger strike commenced immediately. The capitulation of the British government in the face of the Mountjoy protest had exposed the government's weakness and the prisoners at Crumlin Road had also taken note. Within a week the authorities had agreed to release thirty-four of the inmates, again on the grounds that their health had given grave cause for concern.

★

In London the drama over the hunger strike of Terence MacSwiney began in earnest. With a very public battle to win support for her husband's cause on her hands, the Lady Mayoress, Muriel MacSwiney, was not found wanting in courage. She took to her task as her husband's spokesperson with gusto, remaining his constant companion as his condition worsened. In retaliation the British government and media vilified MacSwiney and dismissed his plea for freedom. In a crude form of pincer movement, eleven republican prisoners in Cork Prison commenced a hunger strike to coincide with that of MacSwiney's. On 26 August the British Cabinet affirmed its position regarding MacSwiney's fast, stating that 'the release of the Lord Mayor would have disastrous results in Ireland and would probably lead to a mutiny of both military and police in the South of Ireland'. Evidently the very existence of British rule in Ireland was considered to be at stake.

MacSwiney was housed in the same cell in which Roger Casement had stayed before being transferred to the Tower of

London, and, from an early stage, his condition became a cause for concern as reports of his ill health emanated from Brixton Prison. On 7 September Prime Minister Lloyd George stated that if assurances were given that the murder of police officers would cease in Ireland, then he was 'convinced' that MacSwiney and all the other hunger strikers would be released. Unsurprisingly, the following day it was reported that MacSwiney had described Lloyd George's statement as 'unrealistic' because it failed to acknowledge the part played by the Crown Forces in the murderous campaigns. Regarding the statement of the British premier, Arthur Griffith was scathing in his criticism and issued a repost stating that 'you English are, as Tolstoy said, the most barbarous of all peoples pretending civilisation'.

Daily, the newspapers carried reports of MacSwiney's dwindling condition. The ongoing negotiations and the intransigence of both sides were relayed to a volatile Irish public that braced itself as the moment of truth drew near. In Cork Prison the situation became grave also, as the hunger strikers' health (especially that of Limerick men Sean Hennessey and Thomas Donovan) became a cause for concern. The correspondent of *The New York Times* reported on the mood in Cork on 8 September, saying that when a group of men were asked what the reaction would be subsequent to the death of an inmate 'they winked and looked at each other. Then finally one tossed away his cigarette, scrambled down from a fence and remarked, "Well, if you want to know it will be a case of 'Up boys and at 'em.'"'

The reality was that in the protracted game of poker in which the life of Terence MacSwiney was at stake, none of the protagonists were bluffing on their ability to hold firm. On 13 September a letter was forwarded to the American Ambassador to London from Mary MacSwiney and the brothers and sisters of the Lord Mayor, appealing for help. The sentiments of the letter were heart-felt and placed the case of the Lord Mayor within the context of the death of Tomás MacCurtain:

> Lord Mayor MacCurtain was murdered for the same

reason for which Lord Mayor MacSwiney is now being murdered – because he was fighting for self-determination for his country. If the present tragedy is now allowed to proceed, we are confronted with the unparalleled crime of two Lord Mayors of the same city being murdered within six months of each other by a supposedly civilised government.

Letter reproduced in *The Times*, 13 September 1920

Within days MacSwiney issued his own statement to the world's press in the form of an appeal to all Irishmen, both on his own behalf and that of the strikers in Cork Prison. It was a statement that, perhaps, demonstrated MacSwiney's dawning belief that the situation was indeed terminal and that the British had resolved that he would die. It was also evident that, in the absence of a solution, justice and retribution for England would be forthcoming from on high:

> If this cold blooded murder is passed through, it will leave a stain on the name of England which has no parallel (even in her history) and which nothing will ever efface. We feel singularly privileged at being made instruments of God for invoking such expressions of support for Irish independence . . . I believe that God is watching over our country and by his divine decree her resurrection is at hand. I believe that this is her last battle for liberty and that God will crown it with complete victory.

Associated Press, 20 September 1920

The use of religious imagery and the invocation of the name of God in MacSwiney's hunger strike were commonplace among supporters of the Lord Mayor. The notion of the supreme value of self-sacrifice can be found in the New Testament in St John's Gospel (15:13), where it is stated, 'Greater love has no one than this: to lay down one's life for one's friends.' The belief that God was on the side of MacSwiney was a powerful message and one that took on a special meaning in Ireland. However, the biggest obstacle that was faced by the MacSwiney supporters was that hunger striking was defined as an act of suicide, and, as such, was not only against the teachings of the Catholic Church but also a mortal sin. The hunger strikers' plight was considered by Pope Benedict in early October; however, the Pope opted not to speak on the matter and referred it to the Congregation of the Holy Office where it would be debated by the Cardinals of the Church. This, of course, would take many years.

At the same time as the Pope was procrastinating on the issue of hunger striking, MacSwiney's sister Mary sent a letter to the Catholic Archbishop of Westminster, Cardinal Francis Bourne, in which she appealed for his intervention, writing, 'Those of us who have been watching him through all these weary days have come to the inevitable conclusion that he has been supernaturally sustained in his struggles.' Meanwhile, Archbishop Daniel Mannix, the Irish-born leader of Catholicism in Australia, said of MacSwiney: 'I find him to be a veritable miracle.' Supporters frequently implied that MacSwiney's ability to sustain his hunger strike had been subject to divine intervention.

While the debating and the diplomacy and the stand-off continued throughout October, the situation in both Brixton and Cork Prisons became acute and the expectations grew daily that a death was imminent. Just after 10.00 p.m. on the evening of Sunday 17 October news broke that Michael Fitzgerald, the Battalion Commandant, 1st Battalion, Cork No.2 Brigade, had died in Cork Prison on the sixty-eighth day of his fast. Fitzgerald had been the secretary of the local branch of the Irish Transport and General Workers' Union. He joined the Irish Volunteers in Fermoy and had previously been captured after he successfully took control of Araglen police barrack on April 1919. Ammunition was found in the house in which he lived and he was sentenced to two months' imprisonment. He was released at the end of August, but was involved in the holding up of a party of British Army troops at the Wesleyan church in Fermoy. The troops were disarmed although one of them was killed.

He was one of eleven hunger strikers within the jail and had commenced his fast a day earlier than MacSwiney. Newspapers reported his death in all its gruesome detail, yet Lloyd George saw fit to release a statement justifying the incarceration of Fitzgerald, even though he had never been before a jury. He said: 'Michael Fitzgerald was in custody for a charge of having murdered Private Jones at Fermoy on September 7, 1919 . . . At Cork Assizes last July a true bill was found against him. Owing to the non-attendance of jurors, however, it was impossible to take him before the court constituted under the Restoration of Ireland Act' (*The New York Times*, 18 October 1920).

Despite the suspicions of the authorities that Fitzgerald was responsible for the murder of Private Jones, he had never been proved guilty and died an untried man. The doctor on duty in the prison hospital, Dr Pearson, expressed amazement that Fitzgerald had lasted so long, describing his determination as akin to a 'nun's devotion'. As the news of his death broke, there was immediate rioting on the streets of Cork and beyond, while in Dublin three soldiers were killed in an attack on a hall near Rutland Street. The Black and Tans were sent to the cities to quell the disturbances, but order, of a sort, was naturally restored the following day when the body of Fitzgerald was released from the jail. The procession through Cork was a massive show of strength and solidarity with the plight of Fitzgerald, MacSwiney and the other hunger strikers. Terence MacSwiney delivered his own personal message from his cell on the death of Fitzgerald and said, 'No tears, but joy for our comrade who was ready to meet his God and die for his country.' Michael Fitzgerald was buried in Kilcrumper Cemetery in Fermoy on 19 October; the previous week, in a ceremony taking place in his own cell, he had been married to a Miss Condon from the village.

Almost inevitably, early in the morning of 25 October, Terence MacSwiney died on the seventy-fourth day of his hunger strike. The end was witnessed by his priest, Father Dominic, Seán MacSwiney, the Home Office doctor, Dr Peppard, together with two nurses on duty. As the moment arrived, MacSwiney was reported to be motionless in his bed, eyes staring although he was unconscious. Father Dominic and Seán said a rosary in Irish, while the doctor administered strychnine in a vain and final attempt to stimulate his heart. MacSwiney died as the final prayers were being said. His last reported words to Father Dominic were, 'I want you to bear witness that I die as a soldier of the Irish Republic' (Bennett, *The Black and Tans*, p. 108).

The authorities at Brixton had begun to force-feed MacSwiney, but he was too close to death for his body to recover. The news of his death was received 'calmly and with profound sorrow' in Cork. The flags of municipal buildings flew at half-mast, while shops left their shutters partially down and 'places of amusement' were closed. Despite the fact that the authorities had issued an order banning any military formation in London, a large number of Volunteers from the city left for England to provide a guard of honour for the Lord Mayor's journey home. By 9.40 that morning a telegram penned by Father Dominic was posted outside the City Hall in Cork. It read: 'The Lord Mayor of Cork completed his sacrifice for Ireland at 5.40 this morning. Sean (his brother) and myself present . . . May his noble spirit be with us always to guide and guard.' It fell to the Deputy Lord Mayor of Cork, Donal O'Callaghan to speak on behalf of the Corporation and in paying tribute to his predecessor he reaffirmed that the fight for Irish independence would go on. He added, 'The only message that I, on behalf of the Republicans of Cork, give today over the corpse of the late Lord Mayor, is that Cork has definitely yielded its allegiance to the Republic.'

Late on the evening of 25 October another prisoner, Joseph Murphy, died in Cork Prison on the seventy-sixth day of his fast. In what the *Irish Independent* described as 'a pathetic death-bed scene' the seventeen-year-old died in the presence of his extended family after what the paper said was a 'prolonged agony'. The article continued that the prisoner's death occurred while prayers were recited by the prison's chaplain,

Father Fitzgerald, and, accordingly, 'another soul left its earthly tenement to join the spirits of those who died that their country may be free.' Educated at the Togher National School in the parish of St Finnbarr's West, Murphy, who had been born in the United States but had been living in Cork's Pouladuff Road, had been associated with the Irish-Ireland movement in the city and was arrested in July 1920 on suspicion of being in possession of explosives. However, he was not convicted when he was put before a military tribunal under General Willis in September and was returned to Cork Prison. Given Murphy's American citizenship, the Secretary of State in Washington, Bainbridge Colby, requested a full report from the American Consul in Cobh on the prisoner but he was to die before any move could be made to secure his freedom. Coming so soon after the death of Terence MacSwiney, the death of Joe Murphy was overshadowed by the events at Brixton Prison. He was buried at St Finnbarr's Cemetery in the republican plot on Wednesday 27 October amid scenes that were described as 'remarkable manifestations of sorrow'. The cortège was led by Volunteers carrying wreaths and, fittingly, an American flag. As the funeral approached the cemetery a military officer using a megaphone warned the mourners that 'not more than 100 people would be allowed to follow the coffin' to the graveside. Joseph Murphy's mother, who was comforted by the recently widowed Muriel MacSwiney, wept loudly as her son's body was placed in the ground and later that evening a volley of shots was fired over the hunger striker's grave. On St Patrick's Day 1960 a plaque was unveiled in honour of Joseph Murphy at his former family home on the Pouladuff Road.

The funeral of Terence MacSwiney was one of the biggest ever witnessed in Ireland. His body lay in state in Southwark Cathedral in London before removal, on 29 October, by train to Holyhead for transporting to Dublin. However, the government was not prepared to let the body of Terence MacSwiney become a focus for mass hysteria as it travelled through Ireland and at Holyhead Sean MacSwiney was handed a letter signed by

Hamar Greenwood, Chief Secretary for Ireland:

> I am advised that the landing and funeral of the Lord
> Mayor in Dublin may lead to a demonstration of a political
> nature. I regret, therefore, that I cannot allow the disem-
> barkation of his remains at any other port except Cork.
> In order to save you every inconvenience, I have directed
> that a suitable steamer carry the remains from Holyhead
> to Cork. This steamer will carry you and twenty of your
> friends, if you so desire.
>
> Hansard, HC (series 5) vol. 134, cols 347–50 (3 Nov.
> 1920)

The attempt to take the body caused scuffles to break out at the
dock. Onlookers jeered as seventy Black and Tans moved in. In
the mêlée Deputy Lord Mayor Donal O'Callaghan shouted in
protest, 'You and your government are body snatchers, you are
going to seize a dead body but we will refuse to accompany
you in this nefarious act' (Associated Press, 29 October 1920).
Mary MacSwiney's fingers were prised away from the coffin
and three police cars, which had accompanied the train and the
body from London, halted and placed the coffin on a steamer
called *The Rathmore*. The family refused to accompany the body
and kept to their plan to travel to Dún Laoghaire. The news of
the 'body snatching' reached Ireland and eventually the body of
Terence MacSwiney reached Cobh Harbour, where the Bishop
of Cloyne refused to oversee its unloading. In solidarity with
the family, the railway workers also refused to unload the body
and eventually a tugboat was commissioned to take the body to
rest next to Cork Custom House, where thousands awaited the
arrival of the family, before it was moved to the City Hall.

Throughout the night thousands of mourners filed past the
coffin of the Lord Mayor. The following morning, 31 October,
the coffin was taken in procession to St Mary's Cathedral where
Archbishop John Harty of Cashel presided over the requiem
Mass. Throughout Ireland demonstrations were held in most
cities and towns as the funeral took place. The funeral procession

was led by 180 priests for the whole of the two-mile route to the republican plot at St Finnbarr's Cemetery. Tens of thousands followed in silence as lorry loads of Black and Tans kept a discreet distance. A revolver was produced at the graveside and a volley of shots fired as a last salute. Arthur Griffith gave the oration at the grave and said that 'Joan of Arc would find a martyr in the Lord Mayor and a worthy comrade in Heaven.' On the day following the funeral of Terence MacSwiney another martyr, eighteen-year-old Kevin Barry, was hanged at Mountjoy Prison. Within a month a wave of violence had engulfed Ireland as the War of Independence renewed itself with ferocious gusto. Undoubtedly, the final phase of the bloody battle for Irish independence was inspired in part by the deaths of three hunger strikers from Cork in late October 1920.

Chapter 4

Hatred, Pain and Hunger, 1922 and 1923

'England's terrible works finds Irishmen for its sponsors.'
Mrs Hanna Sheehy-Skeffington, October 1923

George Bernard Shaw once commented, with perhaps uncanny accuracy, that 'If you put two Irishmen in a room, you will always be able to persuade one to roast the other on a spit.' His wry observation was proved accurate by his fellow countrymen during the period from 1922 until 1923, as the Irish Civil War and its vicious reprisals tore the fledgling Free State to bitter pieces. Indeed, it is not surprising that in the midst of the murder mania and its aftermath, the deaths of three hunger strikers have been lost somewhat in the historical ether. The irony is, however, that the deaths of Joseph Whitty, Denis Barry and Andrew O'Sullivan in 1923 were not at the hands of Perfidious Albion, but in a fast for freedom and political status that had been denied by an Irish government. Men in power, who had in previous years been infuriated and provoked into action by the deaths of Thomas Ashe and Terence MacSwiney, fell silent and indifferent as former comrades starved to death. How such a transformation could have taken place within such a short period of time is due, perhaps, to the matter that dare not speak its name in contemporary Irish society, namely the Civil War. From June 1922 until April 1923 Irish republicanism turned its aggression in on itself as the legacy of the War of Independence and the Anglo-Irish Treaty left a political and social scar on the island. It was a truly brutal era that ensured that a nation that had been born in violence would spend its formative years wading through further bitter and bloody tragedy. What is sometimes forgotten though, is that a majority of the most heinous crimes perpetuated in Ireland in the 1920s were by Irishmen against fellow Irishmen. Amid the murder, mayhem, burnings, anarchy and executions it is also easy to forget that men were allowed to starve to death.

In the past the violent reality of the Irish War of Independence has been the subject of much coverage on the big screen. Films such as *The Wind that Shakes the Barley* have succeeded in showing the viciousness of the conflict with the British from a republican perspective. What is perhaps ignored is the viciousness and sheer depravity of some of the acts that took place in the Civil War, which commenced in June 1922 and saw the country plunged into further chaos. This time, however, it was Irishmen against Irishmen. Families split over the pro-British sentiments of the Treaty and each morning brought news of further slaughter in the name of Ireland. It was a conflict that dictated Irish politics for decades, as pro- and anti-Treaty forces settled scores in an orgy of bloodshed that overshadowed the growth of the fledgling Irish Free State. On its conclusion in 1923, the legacy of bitterness that had been created was compounded by further executions, mass imprisonments and yet more deaths by hunger strikers. In essence, the State took on the mantle of an avenging army and showed a disregard for fellow countrymen that has never been fully explained or acknowledged.

The seeds for the murder and madness were sown by the signing of the Anglo-Irish Treaty in December 1921. Michael Collins' famous words that he had, in fact, 'signed his own death warrant' were to prove prophetic, as he too would fall victim to the violence. The split within the IRA and Sinn Féin was made permanent when the Dáil voted narrowly to back Michael Collins and his pro-Treaty stance on 7 January 1922. Despite Collins' belief that the settlement was a 'stepping stone' to the Irish Republic, this notion was rejected by a significant and determined grouping within the Dáil and throughout the country. Just as Collins was to be proved prophetic, it was a speech by Éamon de Valera on St Patrick's Day that gave the clearest indication of how bloody and bitter any civil war would be: 'If the volunteers of the future tried to complete the work that the volunteers of the last four years have been attempting, they would have to wade through Irish blood . . . perhaps through the blood of the members of the Irish government to get it' (cited in Coogan, *Michael Collins*, p. 319).

The seeds of civil war had, thus, been sown and de Valera was soon displaced as 'President of the Irish Republic' by the pro-Treaty Arthur Griffith. As preparations began for the establishment of the Treaty government, so too did the belief that the Free State would need to be secured, or destroyed, by arms. In March 1922 the anti-Treaty IRA held a convention where a new constitution was drafted and the organisation reaffirmed its allegiance to the Irish Republic. By June both Collins and de Valera had agreed a pact, of sorts, and an election was fought by both a pro- and anti-Treaty Sinn Féin, with an understanding that further discussions between the parties would take place after the election. The poll, which took place on 16 June, saw the pro-Treaty Sinn Féin under Collins returned with 58 seats, while de Valera's Sinn Féin trailed behind with 36 seats.

The anti-Treaty IRA was by this stage still unsure as to the tactics it would use to oppose the Treaty. Emboldened by the election result (and given that Winston Churchill had threatened to intervene), Collins, to save face, was prompted into action by the kidnapping, early in the morning of 27 June, of J. J. O'Connell, a general in the newly formed National Army. Soon an order was sent to the anti-Treaty forces under Rory O'Connor that they should leave the Four Courts in Dublin, which they had occupied since April 1922. The order was refused and within an hour the Irish Civil War began with the bombardment of the building from Bridgefoot Street by a British-supplied 18-pound artillery gun. The war that followed was ferocious and, with hindsight, both sides were guilty of serious war crimes: coming events would portray the bloody reality of 'an eye for an eye' many times over. The most prominent fatality during the war was indeed Michael Collins, whose death at Béal na mBláth in August 1922 cut short a brilliant career and robbed Ireland of a dynamic leader.

The anti-Treaty forces suffered a body blow in September 1922 with the introduction of the Public Safety Bill. This bill was to be a trump card and sent out a message that the government was not going to shirk its duty or compromise in the face of the insurrection. In essence, the bill provided for draconian laws to deal with those opposing its power, but more telling was the power the bill gave to the government to impose the death penalty. In early October the Catholic bishops of Ireland published a pastoral letter condemning the anti-Treaty forces and threatening excommunication. It described the anti-Treaty faction as fighting an unjust war and implored the people of Ireland to support the government as their civic duty. The military wing of the pro-Treaty government, under the leadership of General Richard Mulcahy, would soon show a ruthlessness that made the executions after the Easter Rising look tame in comparison. After a short-lived amnesty, the round-up and imprisonment of anti-Treaty suspects began in earnest. On 17 November; the first executions under the Public Safety Bill took place in Kilmainham Jail, where four anti-Treaty Volunteers from Dublin, Peter Cassidy, John Gaffney, James Fisher and Richard Twohig, were shot for possession of weapons. It was an act that shocked Ireland to its core and even the staunchly pro-Treaty *Irish Independent* commented: 'We have the greatest misgivings as to the wisdom of inflicting the extreme penalty for offences as disclosed . . . penal servitude would have been generally regarded as adequate punishment for these four men' (18 November 1922).

A week later Erskine Childers, who had officiated at the negotiations for the Anglo-Irish Treaty, was executed. He had been taken prisoner in Wicklow on 10 November in possession of a pistol, which, ironically, had been given to him by Michael Collins prior to the split in the republican movement. In political terms, Childers was one of the strongest supporters of de Valera and he was tried on 17 November by a military tribunal. As speculation mounted on his destiny, word was released on the morning of 24 November that Childers had 'met his fate' by firing squad in Portobello Barracks. Dorothy McCardle pointed out ruefully in her book *The Irish Republic* that 'Even in England, jurists held this to be a judicial murder.' The Minister for Defence, General Mulcahy, who had escaped narrowly when his house at Portobello Barracks was attacked by Irregulars on 3 November, was plainly in no mood, literally, to take prisoners, and refused to comment on Childer's execution saying, 'our most effective work has always been done with our mouths shut' (Associated Press, 30 November 1922).

While the executions in November were ongoing, the Free State government would show its compassionate side when faced with the spectre of a hunger strike. On 4 November 1922 Mary MacSwiney, sister of Terence MacSwiney, began a fast in Mountjoy Prison that attracted widespread support. In early November a meeting of what was described as an anti-Treaty 'Council of War' in Dublin had been raided by Free State soldiers and MacSwiney had been arrested. Subsequently she refused food and was joined two weeks later by her sister Annie, who had been denied a visit to Mary. Annie's fast was a very public affair and took place outside the prison. Each night there were vigils in support of the two women in the streets of Dublin. On 27 November Mary MacSwiney was released and taken to the Mater Hospital in order to recover. It was a gesture by the authorities that flew in the face of the attitude that prevailed at the time. But perhaps, with the country in a state of convulsion at the ferocity of the backlash against the anti-Treaty forces, in the aftermath of Childers' execution, the death of Mary MacSwiney on hunger strike was something that the government could not countenance.

The madness continued unabated, with both sides determined to outdo each other. Thus the ruthlessness of General Mulcahy was matched by the commander of the Irregulars, Cork man Liam Lynch. Shocked at the execution of Childers, Lynch issued his 'Orders of Frightfulness', which were aimed at members of the National Army and pro-Treaty politicians. In essence all pro-Treaty members of the Dáil, the military and the judiciary were deemed collaborators and threatened with execution. On 5 December George V granted Royal Assent for the establishment of the Irish Free State and Timothy Healy, the valiant advocate at Thomas Ashe's inquest, was installed as the first Governor-General. The day after the official opening of the Dáil on 6 December, Lynch's threat to the members of the new parliament came to fruition when Sean Hales, a TD for Cork who had been a confidant of Collins, and Pádraic O Máille, the Deputy Speaker of the Dáil and the Brigadier General of the National Army, were attacked on their way to Leinster House. The attack took place as both men mounted a jaunting cart and Hales was killed outright, while O Máille was badly wounded. The tragedy of the Civil War was personified in the fact that Sean Hales came from a family that had been divided over the terms of the Treaty. His brother Tom had been commander of the squad involved in the killing of Michael Collins and had, along with Pat Harte, been subjected to torture by the Essex Torture Squad during the War of Independence. This torture, amongst other things, involved the pulling out of fingernails and was the basis for the famous scene in the film, *The Wind that Shakes the Barley*.

The cycle of outrage was now unstoppable. After the assassination of Hales, an emergency cabinet meeting was convened by the Free State government. The response was swift, brutal and callous. On 8 December 1922, the day after the murder of Hales, four members of the IRA Army Executive were executed in revenge. It was at the behest of General

Mulcahy that a court martial was convened on the evening of 7 December and Rory O'Connor, Liam Mellows, Richard Barrett and Joe McKelvey were sentenced to death. They had each been chosen as a representative of the four provinces of Ireland and to send out a message to the republican vanguard that the government was prepared to inflict the greatest penalty. Early the next morning, accompanied by three priests, the prisoners, with the exception of O'Connor, were blindfolded and placed before a firing squad at Mountjoy Prison. Joe McKelvey's last words were 'Goodbye boys and God bless everyone.' Mulcahy, who had introduced the new laws that expedited the executions, defended the killings and described them as a 'solemn warning against those associated with the conspiracy of assassination against representatives of the Irish people.' He pointed out that the threat posed by the rebels was 'more vicious and insidious than Britain had ever employed against the representatives of the government of Ireland' (Dáil Éireann Debates, vol. 2: 8.12.22). However, he failed to acknowledge that, beyond the reprisals for the Easter Rising, Britain had never summarily executed four men out of sheer spite.

In the Dáil, Labour Deputy Cathal O'Shannon accused the government of murder and described the executions as 'the greatest crime committed in Ireland in ten years'. Also adding his condemnation in the Dáil was Dublin County Deputy Thomas Johnson who stated that 'this is not law but anarchy – lynch law once removed, lynch law without mob violence'. The *Daily Chronicle* in London was rather reserved in its observations, however, but supportive of the action that the Free State government had undertaken: 'The summary execution of four republican prisoners in reprisal for the murder of Sean Hales is very startling, but he would be a bold man who would say that the reprisals are not justifiable. And after all, the Irish government must be presumed to be the best judge of its methods.'

The conflict had indeed plumbed new depths as the tactics of fighting terror with terror were adopted by both sides. For the government it was a crass statement of intent, which two days later saw a reprisal when the home of pro-Treaty Dublin TD Sean McGarry was attacked and burned. McGarry, who had been Tom Clarke's bodyguard during the Easter Rising, survived, but his seven-year-old son perished in the blaze. On 19 December the forces of the Free State again showed that it would not baulk at using the death penalty when seven anti-Treaty Irregulars were executed in the Glasshouse within the Curragh Camp. The men, Stephen White, Patrick Bagnel, Patrick Mangan, Joe Johnston, James O'Connor, Brian Moore and Patrick Nolan, had been captured close to the railway line at Moore's Bridge, County Kildare, where attacks had taken place on trains carrying soldiers of the National Army. At the scene of the arrests, Tom Behan was to die after being struck continually by the butt of a rifle. News of the deaths, it was reported, was 'received coolly' in Dublin (and ignored in the Dáil), as opinion had turned against the Irregulars in the aftermath of the death of Sean McGarry's son. The deaths came after a week when speculation had risen regarding possible peace talks between each side; speculation that was cruelly misguided. The insanity continued in early January 1923, when the Free State forces executed five of its own men from the National Army who had been accused of desertion during a clash at Leixlip, County Kildare.

As the bitterness continued unabated, the assassination of Thomas O'Higgins, father of the Minister for Justice Kevin O'Higgins, counted among the republican outrages. However, the act of terror that marked the lowest point of the war came late on 6 March 1923, when nine republican prisoners were taken to the remote Ballyseedy Wood in County Kerry. The prisoners were all tied to a log beside a mine, which was then detonated. Some of the prisoners survived the initial blast but they were fired on, and in the carnage eight prisoners died. Thirty-two anti-Treaty fighters died in Kerry in March 1923, of whom only five were killed in combat. Given the vicious determination of the government, the inevitable defeat of the anti-Treaty forces was announced on 24 May in a proclamation (cease fire and dump arms orders) released in the name of Frank

Aiken, who had succeeded Liam Lynch as Chief of Staff of the anti-Treaty forces after his death in action only two weeks previously. Despite the fact that some Irregulars continued to hold out in isolated areas, the resistance was disintegrating, while more men and women were interned. In July the government introduced the Public Safety Bill, which 'legalised' internment as opposed to the former illegitimate practice of merely 'holding' prisoners that had led to numerous, but unsuccessful, writs of habeas corpus. As autumn approached in 1923 and semi-normality returned, the business of the 11,000 republican internees still needed to be resolved. It was clear that the gates of the prisons and the internment camps would only be opened whenever the government felt that the peace was secured. Despite the fact that prisoners could be set free by renouncing republicanism, very few did and the prisoners were to become bargaining chips for peace in the foreseeable future. However, as time progressed, it became sadly inevitable that a hunger strike for political status and general amnesty would ensue.

There had been cause for optimism in early 1923 that the tactic of a hunger strike could prove to be a potent tool for anti-Treaty republicans. On 14 February members of Cumann na mBan (the League of Women) commenced a hunger strike against their 'illegal arrest and detention'. This protest, this time at Kilmainham Jail, was led by Annie MacSwiney, together with other notables, such as Lily Brennan, Annie O'Neill, Nora Connolly, Dorothy McArdle and, most notably, Nellie Ryan, a sister-in-law of Commander-in-Chief and Defence Minister, Richard Mulcahy. The protest became a carbon copy of the one undertaken by the MacSwiney sisters the previous November; this time, however, it was Mary who threatened to fast outside the prison in support of her sister. When the hunger strikers were denied the sacraments by decree of the Irish bishops, Mary MacSwiney sent a telegram to Pope Pius in Rome, requesting his support:

> Most Holy Father, the younger sister of Terence MacSwiney, who was honoured with the blessing of your predecessor

on his death bed in Brixton Prison is now 11 days on
hunger strike for the same cause . . . The unfair political
action by the Irish hierarchy [bishops] is not harming the
fight for the republic, it is fraught with grave consequences
to the less educated Catholics, who, in resenting injustice,
do not distinguish between individual bishops and the
church.

Associated Press, 26 February 1923

The tone of Mary MacSwiney's telegram was somewhat
condescending to the 'less educated Catholics' and displayed an
overtly optimistic belief in the pope's ability to influence the
Irish bishops in the matter. What she did achieve, though, was
substantial publicity and within two weeks Annie MacSwiney
had been released, while by the beginning of May all of the other
protesters had been released on the 'grounds of compassion'.
Whether General Mulcahy, as the individual ultimately
responsible for the releases, could tolerate the death of women
on hunger strike – and indeed the wife of his brother – may
never be known. However, his action in releasing the prisoners
was, perhaps, an indication of weakness that the republican
internees within the prison camps felt could be exploited in
similar protests.

The idea of mounting a hunger strike within the prisons
was discussed by the IRA Executive on 12 July 1922, but it was
agreed, given the likelihood that the tactic would not be afforded
any sympathy by the Irish press, that the Executive could not
endorse such a step. On the other hand, since a general election
was due to take place on 27 August, the potential to exploit
the prisoners' plight was also recognised; nevertheless, the IRA
leadership felt that any decision to commence a hunger strike
after the election should be left at the discretion of the various
leaderships within the prisons. The reality was that the use of
a fast to protest was inevitable and, unfortunately, death as a
result would be a reality for some. In a letter written on 25 July
to Michael Kilroy, the Officer Commanding of the Mountjoy

prisoners, Frank Aiken pointed out that any man commencing
a hunger strike 'must stick it to the end and − considering
the brutal and inhuman record of the enemy − a number of
them will probably die in the fight' (O'Malley & Dolan, *No
Surrender Here!*, p. 380). The situation was becoming critical and
in early August fifty internees, much to the embarrassment of
the authorities, tunnelled their way out of the Curragh Camp.
But this escape only caused a harsher regime to be imposed on
the remaining internees across Ireland. The conditions within
the prisons deteriorated significantly and appalling stories
soon emanated, particularly from Mountjoy Prison, regarding
the treatment of the prisoners. Cells holding upwards of five
men were commonplace as overcrowding and a lack of basic
hygiene facilities became acute. In August one prisoner, James
Mooney, took ill and was sent to the prison hospital where he
succumbed to tuberculosis. Despite this, the conditions within
the prisons went unreported because the press, on the order of
the government no doubt, remained silent.

The first death attributed to hunger striking in 1923
occurred at the Curragh Camp on 2 August. Joseph Whitty, from
Trinity Street in Wexford town, died from complications brought
about through fasting. Due to the absolute press embargo on
the situation in the prisons at the time, very little is known of
the circumstances of Whitty's death. He was born in 1904 in
County Wexford and was one of seven children born to John
and Bridget Whitty who lived in the village of Whitechurch.
During the War of Independence Whitty served in the South
Wexford Brigade of the IRA and after the signing of the Treaty
he sided with the anti-Treaty forces. In late October 1922 he
was arrested in a round-up of dissidents within the county and
taken initially to Wexford Prison and from there transferred to
the Curragh. His death went unreported and he is buried in
Ballymore Cemetery in Killinick.

The Dáil election in late August saw a victory for the newly
formed and pro-Treaty Cumann na nGaedhael party, which
claimed 63 seats. The de Valera-led and abstentionist Sinn Féin

claimed 44 seats, representing almost 29 per cent of the popular vote. Significantly, eleven anti-Treaty internees were returned to the Dáil and this fact only served to undermine the democratic process. Undeterred, the authorities sought to divide and conquer within the prisons by isolating leaders such as Austin Stack, Ernie O'Malley and Dan Breen from the ordinary rank and file. The government seemed to be sowing further discontent and failing miserably to deal with a situation for which it could identify no solution. There were soon claims that prisoners were kept outside at night and returned in the morning to vandalised and flooded cells. For the republican prisoners, the bottom line was that they were 'uncharged' and merely 'detained' at the pleasure of the government. In the anti-Treaty press the battle to raise the internees' plight was fought with gusto. Stories of beatings, torture, degradation, solitary confinement and inhuman conditions multiplied throughout October. The *Sinn Féin* weekly newspaper labelled as the 'devil's work' any attempt by the government to criminalise the prisoners. In Ballinrobe, County Mayo, Mrs Hanna Sheehy-Skeffington addressed a large crowd at a public meeting in support of the prisoners and asked the crowd, 'Will you demand with all your force and power to get these prisoners out of the hands of their inhuman captors?' To a unanimous cry of 'Yes', she went on to describe the conditions as 'hellish', 'shocking barbarity' and claimed that 'England's terrible works finds Irishmen for its sponsors' (*Sinn Féin*, 27 October 1923). Sheehy-Skeffington's pronouncements were not cries from the wilderness. County councils across Ireland, trades unions, clergy and prominent individuals all called for the release of the prisoners. The government was facing a new crisis; the conflict had now moved to the prisons and public opinion was being tested.

By the middle of October the Associated Press was reporting that a republican manifesto, penned by members of Sinn Féin, was circulating within the prisons. It was reported that this document included a pledge that prisoners were allegedly signing before joining up for the hunger strike. It read: 'I pledge myself in the name of the living Republic that I will not take food or drink anything but water until I am unconditionally released.' Pointedly, the manifesto continued that prisoners should swear an oath, namely 'What I am about to suffer, I offer to the Glory of God and for the Freedom of Ireland.' It was evident that the prisoners were prepared to die. Such a development, the Sinn Féin paper argued, might help the people to be 'shaken from their apathy by a tragedy or a victory unparalleled in the history of the nation.' Whilst the prisoners seemed outwardly to be united in their determination, inside the prisons there was a degree of confusion. According to Austin Stack, 'the whole business of hunger strike, its starting and the swaying of the men was . . . an underground and underhand business'. According to republican activist Peadar O'Donnell, 'no one was ordered on to it, but then no one felt that they could stay off it'(MacEoin, *Survivors*, p. 31).

By 20 October the order had been given to commence a hunger strike. However, just as during the Civil War, the Free State authorities were prepared and determined to remain steadfast when 426 prisoners in Mountjoy began a hunger strike on the evening of Saturday 13 October. A statement released by Michael Kilroy, leader of the Mountjoy internees, stressed that the fast was 'the ultimate weapon of passive resistance' and made the position of the prisoners crystal clear:

> Each of us, to himself and his comrades, solemnly pledges to refrain from food until he is unconditionally released. In taking this grave decision we, as citizens of Ireland, know that lovers of human liberty the world over will understand and respect our decision. Our lives and the suffering we shall endure we offer to God for the furtherance of the cause of truth and justice in every land and for the speeding of the day of Ireland's freedom.

Sinn Féin, 27 October 1923

Frank Aiken sent a message of support and encouragement to the thousands of internees throughout Ireland, which was stark in the extreme. Saying that there was 'work to be done', he asserted that the outcome of the fast would be 'freedom or the grave' (*Sinn Féin*, 27 October 1923).

Despite the commencement of the strike, the main Irish daily papers were largely, and predictably, indifferent to the prisoners' plight, but on the streets of Dublin the hunger strike was a 'live issue'. Meanwhile, republican news sheets such as *Éire* and *Sinn Féin* ran regular commentary on the progress of the hunger strike and the determination of the prisoners; their accounts have been described by historian Michael Hopkinson in his study of the period, *Green against Green*, as full of 'sob stories' that even the prisoners did not read. As had happened three years previously, nightly vigils were staged at the prisons with hundreds taking part. The Sinn Féin Ard Fheis opened in the Mansion House on 16 October and a unanimous motion of support was passed by the party. During her speech Mary MacSwiney suggested, somewhat ambitiously, that republicans across Ireland should, in support of the hunger strikers, abstain from alcohol as a means of impacting on the Free State exchequer – her suggestion was not put to a vote.

By 23 October there were a reported 440 prisoners on hunger strike in Mountjoy Prison. They had been joined by prisoners in the Curragh (3,200) and Gormanstown (1,200) camps, Kilkenny and Cork (420) prisons and at Newbridge Barracks (2,000). In the higher echelons of Free State government the propaganda battle against the prisoners waged on. William T. Cosgrave, who had by this time assumed the title of President of the Executive Council, took a swipe at the prisoners at a public meeting in Dublin, labelling the hunger strike as a 'fraud' and claiming that 'some brown bread and food pastilles had been found in their pockets' (*The Boston Globe*, 22 October 1922). Interestingly, at the same meeting, Minister for Finance, Ernest Blythe, made the prediction that 'the prisoners would not be released, but they will not die' (*The New York Times*, 23 October 1923). Whether this prediction was bravado or sheer confidence was soon to be tested to the extreme as the fast spread.

On 25 October, the third anniversary of the death of Terence MacSwiney, the IRA Chief of Staff, Frank Aiken, issued a statement of support to the prisoners. In referring to a campaign of alleged disinformation that had been waged against the hunger strikers by the Dublin press, Aiken implored the men in the prisons to remain steadfast (see also MacEoin, *The IRA in the Twilight Years*, p. 85):

> Listen to the lies but do not heed them . . . Smile at the threats of the enemy to put you on the lists of the country's historic dead. Smile at their sneers that you will be forgotten by a people who are proud, beyond all else, of being citizens of the Nation for which Tone, Pearse and MacSwiney died. Smile at the threats that God, Whose Son died to save mankind, will punish you for following his example.

Sinn Féin, 3 November 1923

Despite the calls of Aiken, a minority of strikers broke their fasts as dozens of prisoners were released by the authorities. The Ministry of Defence daily announced that further prisoners had given up their fast and conformed, while the battle for support for the prisoners was played out in many district councils. In response to a telegram from Cork County Council, which stated that 'the Council are strongly of the opinion that the political prisoners should be released forthwith,' Richard Mulcahy, Minister for Defence, was equally as blunt in his response:

> Does your Council not consider that it is much more important, from even a humanitarian point of view, to secure for our people that any small section shall not be allowed to call themselves a Government, or organise an army, and direct all efforts of either or both to destroy the State in utter disregard of any consequence to the people? . . . Are our people or prisoners to be our first consideration?

The Irish Times, 10 November 1923

The government seemed to be unanimous in its aim to remain stubborn in the face of the hunger strike. It fell to the Minister for Finance, Ernest Blythe, to outline to the fasting prisoners in Newbridge Barracks the consequences if they did not end their fast: 'We are not going to force-feed you, but if you die we won't waste coffins on you and will put you in orange boxes and you will be buried in unconsecrated ground. So have sense and come off it' (*An Phobacht*, 15 October 1998). Within a decade, perhaps unsurprisingly given the foregoing sentiments, Blythe would become a senior member of the fascist Blueshirt movement.

On 16 November President Cosgrave was robust in his defence of the government's stance and suggested that the ongoing hunger strike could be 'the most gigantic failure' in the history of the anti-Treaty prisoners. In response to criticism from Patrick Baxter (a Farmers' Party TD from County Cavan) that it was Cosgrave's duty to ensure that decency prevailed and that the prisoners were 'treated at least as human beings', Cosgrave responded:

> Hunger strike will not effect the release of any prisoner either now or in the future, and I would like to tell the Deputy who has just spoken that my view of his responsibility in this business is very great indeed. If a single prisoner on hunger strike dies, the attitude of the Deputy who has spoken, and of other people who, by their acts or resolutions or their talk about this gigantic failure, the most gigantic failure that these people who threatened the State ever entered into – this failure of the hunger strike – must not be overlooked. About 300 out of 7,400 are on strike, and there are people in this country waiting to see who is going to die, some thinking it will mean the release of the remainder, and others thinking it will afford an opportunity to the face-savers to call off this hunger strike. They are held according to law, Sir, every one of them.

Dáil Éireann Debates, vol. 5: 16.11.23

Undeterred, the strikers continued with their fast and four days

later Commandant Denis (Dinny) Barry died on the thirty-fourth
day of his fast at the Curragh Camp. Writing to Molly Childers
from his cell at Kilmainham Jail, Ernie O'Malley, assistant Chief of
Staff of the IRA and fellow hunger striker, displayed a somewhat
fatalistic sentiment at the death of Barry. He wrote 'I got the
evening paper and saw Barry's death on it and felt so happy, not
sad, it was like ecstasy. I know he is happy and I'm sure it will help
us follow' (O'Malley & Dolan, *No Surrender Here!*, p. 405).

Denis Barry was forty years old when he died. He had been
a noted hurler, footballer and athlete who was a member of the
famous Blackrock Club that won four Cork titles in a row from
1910 to 1913. In November 1912 he lined out in that year's
All-Ireland Hurling Final where his club represented Cork, only
to lose narrowly to Tullaroan of Kilkenny. In 1913 he joined the
Irish Volunteers, and by 1916 Barry had become immersed in
revolutionary politics in Cork under the leadership of Tomás
MacCurtain. After the Easter Rising he was arrested in Kilkenny
and was interned for a year in Bala in Wales. On his return to
Ireland he settled in Kilkenny city and was for some years a
charge-hand at The Monster House department store on High
Street. He was an excellent organiser and administrator who
was prominent in the campaign that saw the election of William
Cosgrave in Kilkenny city in August 1917. An election poster
at the time implored people to 'Vote for Cosgrave – A Felon
of our Land'; it is ironic that six years later the aforementioned
Cosgrave was the President of the Executive Council of Ireland,
and Barry himself had died in agony in the Curragh.

In 1919 he returned to Cork and joined the Óglaigh na
hÉireann 1st Cork Brigade and won high esteem in his role as
an impartial republican brigade police officer. Barry was also a
respected businessman in Cork and by 1920 he had taken on
the role of intelligence officer within the Cork IRA; during
the truce after the Anglo-Irish War of Independence he was
appointed Officer Commanding of the 1st Southern Division of
the Police by the former IRA Chief of Staff Liam Lynch.

A close friend of Michael Collins, Barry had supervised the

counting of the votes for election to the Cork constituencies in June 1922. However, Barry chose to oppose both Collins and the Treaty and, whilst little is known of his activity during the Civil War, his obituary stated that 'During the latest phase of the war he was still true to his allegiance and fought in his native county up to the time of his arrest.' It was while attending a Brigade Staff Officers' meeting in Meelin, County Cork, that he was arrested and initially held in Cork Prison before being sent to the Curragh Camp in October 1922. Barry's obituary, glowing in its account of the man himself, became scathing when it turned its attention to William Cosgrave and 'his fellow ministers', referring to Cosgrave's assertion that the hunger strikers were 'calling the bluff' of the Irish people, a statement that had been proved hollow:

> Commandant Denis Barry, 1st Southern Division, died on hunger strike in the Curragh Hospital today. It was with mixed feelings of sorrow and pride we heard the fatal tidings that Denis Barry had 'called the bluff' of Mr Cosgrave and his Ministers by giving all that he had – his life – to maintain the living Republic, which has forsaken so many. Thus has our sacred cause been further sanctified by a hero's blood, and Dinny Barry has gone to his eternal rest, where there are no bars or chains to bind his unselfish spirit.
>
> *Sinn Féin*, 24 November 1923

At his inquest, which was held on 22 November, it was found that he had died 'due to heart failure due to inanition caused by his refusal to take food'. In a twist to the tale, the jury noted that the 'deceased received proper attention from those in charge of his case'. In the report carried in the *Irish Independent*, it was pointed out that Denis' brother Bartholomew had visited him on the day before his death and had demanded that he should be fed and administered with medical aid. It was too little, too late. The document signed by Bartholomew Barry also requested that his brother, in the spirit of the 'Cat and Mouse' Act, be moved to a nursing home in order that proper care could be given. This request was forwarded to the office of General Mulcahy who responded with eight terse words: 'No internee can force release with hunger strike.' Denis Barry was condemned to death and died the following day on Tuesday 20 November.

But the death of Barry prompted other politicians into action as the situation worsened. The following day Lord Mayor of Dublin, Laurence O'Neill, requested that he be allowed to address the Dáil on the plight of the hunger strikers, using the 'ancient right' that his office afforded as his justification. However, ancient right or not, President William Cosgrave objected to any such advice on the government's prison strategy:

> On that [receiving the Lord Mayor] I would have to enter an objection, because I do not consider, as I have said before, that any useful public purpose is served by dragging the sufferings of these unfortunate hunger strikers before the notice of the public. It is done with one object alone, and that is to keep the unfortunate dupes still on hunger strike. I think it is cruel, inhuman, and unworthy of any citizen of this State to persist in such action, and as such it would have my most strenuous opposition.
>
> Dáil Éireann Debates, vol. 5: 21.11.23

In the *Irish Independent* on 26 November an article was printed on behalf of a former comrade of Barry who went by the pen name of 'Eire'. The correspondent, who described himself as a friend of Barry's but someone who had agreed to support the pro-Treaty position during the civil war, was scathing of de Valera and the other 'dupes' who had sent the hunger strikers 'to the grave'.

The funeral of Denis Barry was to be a bitter affair. Initially the government, given the propaganda potential, had refused to release his body for burial and it was pointed out in the Dáil on 21 November by Labour Deputy Thomas Johnson that Barry had been 'an untried prisoner and they [the government] had no right to consider him in any other light.' Cork West Labour

TD Timothy Murphy added to the criticism, referring to the traditional right in Ireland to a Christian burial and warning that 'we who have the reputation of being very generous to our dead and of giving them decent funerals will be establishing a bad precedent if we deny our opponents the right to a Christian burial.'

In response, displaying his undoubted indifference to the hunger strikers, General Mulcahy said:

> If later, when the circumstances are such that advantage cannot be taken of a funeral demonstration to prejudice the safety of the State or to jeopardise further the lives of the men who are still hunger-striking in prison, the friends of Barry or any who may die in this wretched hunger strike desire it, facilities will be granted to have the body of any such person transferred from the burial ground at present provided by the Government to any burial ground his friends or family may wish. The Government have to emphasise again the fact that just now, as at any other time during the last twelve months or more when the safety of the State is prejudiced and endangered, it is their duty to safeguard the State.
>
> Dáil Éireann Debates, vol. 5: 21.11.23

Barry's body was interred in the Curragh Prison Camp at a 'site near the glasshouse' at approximately 1.30 p.m. on Friday 23 November. When his family arrived to collect the body they were shocked to discover that the interment had taken place without their knowledge. The family immediately applied to the High Court for the return of the body and, given that the main hunger strike had collapsed and that Barry had not been charged or convicted of a crime, the State relented and Barry's body was exhumed and returned to his grieving family. That night the body of Denis Barry lay in state in the Town Hall at Newbridge, County Kildare.

However, a new obstacle to a Christian burial arose closer to home. Prior to his body arriving in his native city, the Bishop

of Cork, Daniel Cohalan, who had officiated at the funeral of
Terence MacSwiney, issued a letter to the Catholic churches
forbidding them to open their doors to the body of Barry,
saying that the use of hunger striking was 'irrelevant' and 'even
blasphemous'. In a letter to the *Cork Examiner*, published on 27
November, Cohalan outlined his case further:

> Dear Sir,
>
> I am not allowing the religious exercises which constitute a
> Christian Burial, to take place at the burial of Denis Barry.
> I regret very much to feel obliged to adopt this course. I
> knew the deceased; I knew him to have a great knowledge
> of the social and moral question of the dangers that beset
> girls in Cork and all through Munster. I knew him to be
> a good man. But if it were my brother that had taken the
> course that Denis Barry chose to take, I would treat his
> burial in the same way.

He added that in making his decision he was adhering to
and 'enforcing the laws of the Church.' From a man who had
written the following in the same paper on the death of Terence
MacSwiney, it was a stance that was somewhat hypocritical:
'Terence MacSwiney takes his place among the martyrs in the
sacred cause of the Freedom of Ireland. We bow in respect before
his heroic sacrifice. We pray that God may have mercy on his
soul.'

Incensed by the cleric's intransigence, Mary MacSwiney
wrote to the *Examiner* and called Cohalan to task on a number of
issues, especially his reference, at the time of her brother's death,
to his 'unwilling sacrifice'. She wrote, 'his [Bishop Cohalan's]
slander of my dead brother – the attempt to prove that his great
sacrifice was an unwilling sacrifice – is as unpardonable as his
treatment of Denis Barry'. She added:

> Could anything prove more clearly that the Bishop of
> Cork is not acting in accordance with Catholic teaching
> in his treatment of Cdr Denis Barry than the fact that
> all he says about hunger striking in his statement, if true

today, must have been equally true three years ago when he officiated with all the honour that the Church can pay to a faithful son.

In another letter to the *Examiner* that day Sean O'Hegarty said of the Bishop's letter that 'it was difficult to write calmly in reply to a production [Bishop's letter] so devoid of that spirit of Christian charity, so devoid of a respect for the truth, which we may be pardoned in looking for in one in so exalted an ecclesiastical position.'

On reaching Cork city, Barry's body, therefore, lay in state in the offices of the Sinn Féin Executive Rooms where a great number of people filed passed his coffin. On 28 November his funeral procession took place through the streets of Cork city, with former comrades and volunteers and many representatives of the business community in attendance. Led by a pipe band, it was reported that the National Army and Civic Guards stood to attention as the large and dignified cortège passed. When the procession reached the republican plot at the cemetery, darkness had fallen and the ceremonies took place under the light of oil lamps. David Kent, an anti-Treaty TD for Cork East and North-east, led the mourners in the prayers and, in a defiant gesture to Bishop Coholan, sprinkled the grave with holy water. The oration was given by Mary MacSwiney. Given the absence of any clergy at the proceedings, she (despite prior appeals from the Barry family) made a cynical observation about the burial of Barry compared to that of her brother in the same cemetery:

> Three Archbishops and five Bishops and hundreds of clergy paid all the honour that could be paid to any man. All the honour that was given to Terence MacSwiney and the other Irishmen who died for the Republic was equally due to Denis Barry. What was right three years ago was not wrong today . . . that Denis Barry, like Terence MacSwiney, died for the Irish Republic, and while there is a man or woman left in Ireland the Republic will remain.

MacSwiney, *Letters to Angela Clifford*, p. 156

The following morning the death was announced of 38-year-old
Andrew O'Sullivan, who had been on hunger strike in Mountjoy
Prison since 14 October. He had died of acute pneumonia
resulting from his fast. Born in County Cavan, O'Sullivan had
been working for the Department of Agriculture in Mallow,
County Cork, and had been arrested and interred on 5 July
1923. During the War of Independence O'Sullivan had been
the Officer Commanding for Civil Administration in the North
Cork area and later in the 1st Southern Cork Division, where he
had been appointed by Liam Lynch.

On 20 November, a week before he died, it was reported
that O'Sullivan had become ill and had been removed to the
prison hospital where his condition rapidly deteriorated. Given
the dire situation, the authorities took the decision to remove
the prisoner to St Bricin's Hospital, where he was given warm
clothes, hot water bottles and drinking water.

Two days later, on Thursday 22 November, a telegram was
sent to the mother of Andrew O'Sullivan at 160 West End in
Mallow, County Cork. It was a simple and stark message that
read: 'You are advised that Andrew O'Sullivan is dangerously ill
in Mountjoy Prison. Should you wish to see him facilities will be
granted on personal application to the Governor of the prison.'

As his mother was unable to travel, the message was
conveyed to Andrew O'Sullivan's brother Michael, who was
granted permission to see him in the hospital. At first Michael
O'Sullivan did not recognise his brother, who was a mere shadow
of the man he had known, nor indeed did Andrew recognise his
brother. His features were sunken, his eyesight had failed and he
was near death.

At the inquest into the death, the solicitor acting on behalf
of the O'Sullivan family, Mr A. Lynn, expressed his astonishment
that the authorities did not feel it necessary to send the
Governor of Mountjoy Prison to the proceedings. Lynn went
on to encourage the jury to record the primary cause of death
for O'Sullivan as starvation, but that finding would not (or could
not) be allowed. The medical officer present from St Bricin's

Military Hospital reported that the death of O'Sullivan had been due to acute pneumonia in both lungs and agreed that it would have been 'inhumanly impossible' to save him. At the end of the inquest Dr John O'Byrne, on behalf of the State, referred to the changed circumstances that the end of the mass hunger strike had brought about, and indicated that 'the considerations that applied a couple of days ago [in the case of Denis Barry] did not now apply'. Andrew O'Sullivan's remains would be released to his family for burial in Mallow, but O'Byrne would not let the inquest pass without criticising those on the republican side who had encouraged the prisoners to fast to the end: 'The reason for the death of the deceased lies with those people who did not go on strike themselves but got thousands of prisoners to go on hunger strike and kept them on hunger strike until two unfortunate men died' (*Irish Independent*, 22 November 1923).

The distance from Cork city to Mallow is less than twenty miles but, more significantly, it is within the Diocese of Cloyne and therefore Bishop Cohalan's pronouncements on eligibility for a Christian burial had no validity. Instead, under the authority of Bishop Robert Browne, O'Sullivan could be given a Christian burial – but not without a further bout of ecclesiastical skulduggery. Once more into the equation would come Bishop Cohalan: in the *Irish Independent* on 29 November he decided to 'clarify' his position on the entitlement of the hunger strikers to a Christian burial. But, in effect, he muddied the water by stating that if a hunger striker gave up his fast and showed 'sufficient signs of repentance' then he would be afforded burial in consecrated ground. As argument raged over the eligibility of O'Sullivan to receive a Christian burial, it fell to his parish priest to make the decision. The fact that it was reported that unsuccessful attempts had been made to 'feed' O'Sullivan after he slipped into a coma was sufficient in the eyes of Father Patrick Casey to determine that his fast had ended. In essence, the church had still felt it necessary to determine that O'Sullivan did not die 'on hunger strike' before his burial could go ahead.

Andrew O'Sullivan was buried in the New Cemetery in

Mallow on 27 November. His cortège was reported to have been a mile in length and was headed up by sixty members of Cumann na mBan. By the time of his burial, however, the hunger strikes had ended on 22 November. In the *Irish Independent* Josephine Plunkett placed an advert asking for donations of 'chicken and beef tea and the jelly of calves' feet' to be brought to the prisons. It seemed that the momentum of the strike diminished as it progressed. The Free State government stood firm and the release of prisoners soon started in earnest. Within six months, most of the hunger strikers were released on the condition that they 'be loyal to the Irish Free State'.

Chapter 5

De Valera: Poacher Turns Gamekeeper

'We have pledged ourselves to the dead generations who have preserved intact for us this glorious heritage.'

An Taoiseach, Éamon de Valera, 1945

The spectre of the hunger strike retreated somewhat into the Irish political ether after 1923, but would re-emerge with a vengeance with the onset of the Second World War in 1939. Politics in the interim period had changed, and changed utterly with the IRA still marginalised, but this time under a Fianna Fáil government led by Éamon de Valera. In March 1926 de Valera resigned as President of Sinn Féin and formed Fianna Fáil. Six years later de Valera's party was elected into government, an event that seemed to cement the very existence of the Irish Free State – and indeed Partition. The Rubicon had now been crossed by a vast majority of republicans and it seemed that politics, not militancy, reigned supreme. Despite the shifts in Irish consti- tutional politics towards a tacit acceptance of the Treaty and Partition, the IRA, as a dissident faction, remained steadfastly and ideologically opposed to any form of compromise. By continuing to exist, persist and operate at a relatively low level, the movement caused acute embarrassment to the government who, by the late 1930s, felt duty-bound to tackle forcefully the continuing conundrum that was militant republicanism.

During the Second World War and beyond three IRA members would die whilst on hunger strike; the blame for their deaths was placed, by republicans, squarely at the door of de Valera and his hated Minister for Justice, Gerald Boland. Given that the commencement of war in Europe had forced the Irish government to impose a state of emergency, it was evident that any threat of insurrection from within was to be brutally suppressed. Ireland's neutrality was paramount to de Valera and protecting this status meant that the IRA would be afforded neither quarter nor sympathy. The 'greater good', in essence, was the survival of the Irish Free State and, predictably, harsh measures were imposed to fight the IRA. Inevitably, it would all end in strife, death and bitter recrimination. And, just as inevitably, critics would be quick to point to the irony of a Free State government – and a Fianna Fáil one – that, just as its pro-Treaty predecessors had done in 1923, remained seemingly indifferent and tolerant of the deaths of republicans on hunger strike. Nevertheless, the narrow political by-way that was militant Irish republicanism continued to be treated as a malignant sore that needed to be lanced painfully by the democratically elected government of the land. De Valera believed that his policy was right and unquestionable; seen in this light such a draconian policy was logical and for the good of Ireland. But, with hindsight, he and his government showed a degree of ruthlessness to IRA prisoners that broke new ground. It was almost personal.

Periodically throughout the 1930s hunger striking would be used by IRA members to highlight conditions within prisons. In June 1931 two republicans, George Mooney and Seán McGuinness, ended their eleven-day hunger strike in Mountjoy Prison on the request of the then Chief of Staff of the IRA, Maurice Twomey. Mooney, who had been convicted of possession of guns and explosives, and McGuinness, who had received a sentence for acting as a marshal at a republican rally, had been held in solitary confinement for upwards of nineteen months as a punishment for refusing to accept their categorisation as criminals. On 3 June the two men had commenced a hunger strike in protest at the inhumane treatment they were undergoing, which included beatings and being placed in straitjackets. On 5 June a Mayo republican, Patrick Norton, was released from Mountjoy after serving a short sentence for the then misdemeanour of selling Easter lilies. Having witnessed the conditions under which both Mooney and McGuinness were held, he swore an affidavit, which served to publicise the prisoners' plight and drew attention to their hunger strike. In the Dáil on 11 June the Minister for Justice, James Fitzgerald-Kenney, spoke about the government's attitude towards the strike in terms of the greatest possible indifference:

> It is for these young men to continue or cease this hunger strike themselves. If they choose to injure themselves, it is their look out. They are free agents. They are free to exercise as other prisoners are. They are free to go off hunger strike any moment they like. If they do not, the responsibility is theirs. They are not going to shorten the term of their imprisonment by any hunger strike in which they may indulge. Let it be clearly and distinctly understood that they are not going to abridge by one hour the term of their imprisonment by going on hunger strike.

> Dáil Éireann Debates, vol. 39: 11.6.31

The minister's statement caused Thomas Mullins, Fianna Fáil TD for Cork West, to accuse the government of copying the policy of 1923 towards the IRA prisoners, which he labelled; 'Let them rot'. Perhaps, with the bitter memories of the deaths in 1923 still in the collective memory, IRA leader Maurice Twomey sensed that the protest was futile and sent a letter to the prison to advise Mooney and McGuinness of his view:

> We have learned with horror of the brutal assaults and ill-treatment to which you have been subjected by your

> jailers . . . I am instructed to say that we [the IRA] highly
> appreciate your spirited action in resorting to hunger
> strike and realise that it was only under provocation
> that this action was determined on. Nevertheless, after
> consideration of the whole question, we have decided to
> urge you that you should both call off the hunger strike.
>
> *Irish Independent*, 13 June 1931

With that the fast ended as external pragmatism was brought to
bear on the prisoners. There were other token fasts undertaken
throughout the period, but with little success or publicity.
However, the IRA threat increased as the decade progressed
and a serious clash of wills between the government and the
movement became inevitable.

The Irish Free State that de Valera took control of in 1932
was forward-looking but inwardly in turmoil. The painful and
bitter legacy of the Civil War still dictated politics, while matters
were further complicated by the continued existence of the IRA.
Though marginalised, the organisation still remained resolute,
defiant and determined in its opposition to the partition of the
island. However, it was an organisation that was opposed to
the government of the State and, accordingly, despised within
government circles. As Europe lurched inevitably towards war,
de Valera was not in a mood to tolerate a subversive presence
within the country. By the late 1930s rumours persisted, with
basis in fact, that the IRA was attempting to forge links with
Nazi Germany and this indeed caused much consternation on
both sides of the Irish Sea. With the anxiety of a full-scale conflict
on the horizon, the British government was further irritated
when the IRA's Army Council, under the leadership of Seán
Russell, declared war on it on 16 January 1939. In a somewhat
ambitious declaration of intent the IRA, in its self-styled guise as
the legitimate government of the Irish Republic, informed the
Foreign Secretary, Viscount Halifax, that:

> The Government of the Irish Republic believe that a period
> of four days is sufficient notice for your Government to signify

its intentions in the matter of the military evacuation and for the issue of your Declaration of Abdication in respect of our country. Our Government reserves the right of appropriate action without further notice if upon the expiration of this period of grace, these conditions remain unfulfilled.

Coogan, *The IRA*, p. 124

Viscount Halifax did not respond to the declaration, which was signed by Army Council member Larry Grogan, and the 'war' began. With Britain gearing up for a serious conflict with Nazi Germany, the threat posed by the IRA was insignificant in comparison but worrying and embarrassing for de Valera's government. The campaign was ineffective and amounted to a series of low-level attacks, which began in January and saw bombs explode in London, Liverpool, Birmingham and Manchester. However, on 25 August 1939, nine days before war was declared by Britain on Germany, the situation became critical as five people were killed in an attack in Coventry. For the Irish and British governments, the alarm bells began to ring. The bomb, which had been hidden in the carrier basket of a bicycle, sent shock waves across the British Isles and caused a backlash against Irish people living in the English Midlands. De Valera's government knew that in order to preserve its neutral position – and placate Britain – the IRA would have to be dealt with effectively. Whilst O'Connell's old adage that 'England's difficulty is Ireland's opportunity' may have appealed to some in the IRA, the Irish government would not allow it to test the theory. The potential for the IRA to seek help from, and provide aid to, Nazi Germany was an ever-present threat that had to be addressed by de Valera. On the day before the outbreak of the war the Irish government declared a state of emergency and, the following day, introduced the Emergency Powers Act (1939), which allowed the authorities to 'make provisions for securing the public safety and the preservation of the state in time of war and in particular to make provision for the maintenance of public order.' The Act was aimed at securing Ireland's neutrality but, more tellingly, it gave the government the ability to address the problem of the IRA on its own terms. In effect the government was baring its teeth at the IRA and would not be found wanting if provoked.

Despite the staunch and steadfast attitude the government adopted throughout the war years, there were signs in late 1939 that it could still be vulnerable in the face of a hunger strike. In October five republican prisoners, Con Lehane, Patrick McGrath, John Lynch, Jeremiah Daly and Richard McCarthy commenced a hunger strike in Arbour Hill Prison in protest at being detained as a 'precaution' when the war began. To de Valera the greater goal of securing the security of the State at a time of crisis was more critical than the concerns of IRA prisoners. With pressure growing to free the internees, the government released a statement indicating that it would remain unsympathetic to any hunger strike mounted by the prisoners: 'As arrest and detention in accordance with the powers of Parliament are the only means available for the maintenance of public order and security, they cannot permit the State authorities to be deprived of these means by the policy of a hunger strike. The prisoners on hunger strike will, accordingly, not be released' (*Irish Independent*, 7 November 1939).

In the Dáil on Thursday 9 November (by which stage the government had released Con Lehane, who had embarked on a thirst strike in addition to fasting) de Valera repeated his uncompromising message – but, in truth, the government was losing the battle and the prisoners sensed that further concessions would be forthcoming. Using the argument that if the remaining hunger strikers were released the government might have to capitulate in the face of future protests, de Valera spelled out the logic of his position:

> We have sat down and considered every alternative that was possible for us, and we see no alternative, because we have been placed in a position in which there is no alternative. The alternatives we are forced to face are the alternatives of two evils, one to see men die that we do not want to

see die if we can save them, the other, to permit them to bring the State and the community as a whole to disaster. But they have put us in that position – it is not we who have done it – they have put us deliberately in that position . . . We have had to choose the lesser, and the lesser evil is to see men die rather than that the safety of the whole community should be endangered. We do not wish them to die. We would wish – Heaven knows, I have prayed for it – that these men might change their minds, and that the people who are with them might change their minds, and realise what our obligations and our duties are. If we let these men out, we are going immediately afterwards to have every single man we have tried to detain and restrain going on hunger strike.

Dáil Éireann Debates, vol. 77: 9.11.39

The next day it was reported that de Valera had been placed under armed guard in response to two death threats, allegedly from the IRA. One threat was contained in a letter, while the other was reported at a public meeting outside Arbour Hill where a speaker was heard to say that 'if a prisoner dies, then de Valera dies'. Under threat or not, within a week the statement of de Valera in the Dáil was shown to be mere bravado, as the release of the men began. On 15 November McGrath, Lynch and McCarthy, who had been fasting for just over a month, were removed to various hospitals as their conditions weakened. In keeping with the spirit of the 'Cat and Mouse' Act, some observers saw the move by the government as compassionate and a precursor to the honourable resolution of the crisis. However, to others, it was seen as a sign of weakness and soon rumours began to circulate that the prisoners would be released for good. In the Dáil earlier that day it had been revealed by the Minister for Justice, Gerry Boland, that Jeremiah Daly, who had discontinued his fast three days earlier, had been released; but, in a strange contradiction of his logic, Boland also stated that the government's position had not changed. This contradiction was compounded further when, on 18 November, McGrath, Lynch and McCarthy were released from hospital and transferred to private nursing homes. It was an embarrassing climb down by the government, which stood guilty of saying one thing but doing another when it came to the republican prisoners. The embarrassment caused by the prisoners' victory was not to be forgotten by either de Valera or Boland as the 'emergency' progressed. However, Patrick McGrath's release was to prove something of a pyrrhic victory, since he would be executed by a Free State firing squad on 6 September 1940. McGrath, along with Thomas Green, was found guilty of the murder of Detective Richard Hyland during a gun battle at a vacant shop in Dublin's Rathgar Road on 16 August. On the day following the death of Hyland, Sergeant Patrick McKeown died from gunshot wounds arising from the same shoot-out, and both McGrath and Green paid the ultimate price at the behest of the State.

Given the success of the hunger strike, the IRA did not help its own cause back at home, intent as it was on stirring up the proverbial hornets' nest throughout the country. On 1 December 1939, with anger at the releases unabated, the government suffered a further setback in its attempts to control the IRA. This time the reversal came in the High Court. Barrister Seán MacBride's defence of IRA political prisoners had caused increasing consternation in government circles during the Emergency, and he now applied for a writ of habeas corpus on behalf of a County Mayo internee, Seamus Burke, who was being held at Arbour Hill. MacBride outlined his case, in what Judge George Gavan Duffy would describe as a 'very careful and elaborate argument', that part six of the Offences against the State Act was 'repugnant' to the 1937 Irish Constitution. In essence, he argued, the power accorded to the Minister for Justice to intern suspects was something that usurped the power of the judiciary in variance with the Constitution. Accordingly, Duffy released the remaining fifty-two internees the following day when the government accepted the verdict. The IRA, however, was to infuriate the government further on 23 December when the

Irish Army Barracks at the Phoenix Park were raided by the IRA and over a million rounds of ammunition were taken, together with thirteen lorry loads of weapons. The humiliation caused by the extent of the raid, as well as the sheer panic it engendered in government circles, redoubled de Valera's determination to deal effectively with the insurgents.

The government accepted that more stringent legislation was required and on 6 January 1940 the Offences against the State (Amendment) Bill was enacted to deal with the IRA threat. The amendment ensured that the government, learning from its contested policy of interning IRA suspects, would first seek to convict internees in order to justify their incarceration. The government had been spooked by the arms raid at Phoenix Park and it had also become convinced that the IRA would try and stage a *coup d'état* at Easter. Coincidentally, the murder of Garda John Roche on 4 January (in, ironically, MacCurtain Street in Cork at the hands of Tomás MacCurtain, the son of Tomás MacCurtain Senior, the Lord Mayor of Cork murdered in 1920) acted as a spur to the introduction of the legislation. The death of Roche was particularly shocking; three of his police colleagues had given blood in a desperate attempt to save him. However, the IRA in its involvement in the death of Roche had inflicted on itself an almost fatal blow that would have severe consequences over the following years. The amendment to the Offences against the State Act was presented to the Dáil on the day that Roche died in the most robust terms by the 'blunt and outspoken' Minister for Justice, Gerald Boland, and was passed resoundingly by 82 votes to 9 (*The New York Times*, 4 January 1940). In effect, the government (arguing that the very existence of the State, in a time of war, had been put at stake by the IRA) had now been given carte blanche to deal with the insurgents. The potential for an IRA uprising, real or imagined, was an ever-present bogeyman within the State. Boland argued that if the weapons that had been taken in the Phoenix Park raid could not be found, then the government might have to fight the IRA with the 'unrestricted power of internment'. Since further prison conflict was a distinct possibility, Boland was also keen to display his willingness to face down a hunger strike and pointed out that 'hunger strike or no hunger strike, we have got to keep [the IRA prisoners]. Things have gone too far altogether' (*Glasgow Herald*, 5 January 1940). With the government now believing that the State was on the verge of anarchy, its hand was strengthened sufficiently to face down the IRA. And since the prisons would soon to be receiving more republican inmates, it was inevitable that another crisis would develop over a hunger strike and prison conditions.

It did not take long. On 13 January, a stand-off began in Mountjoy when thirty republican internees refused to return to their cells after recreation. The prison authorities, in an apparent show of strength, immediately called in over 200 members of the Gardaí to restore order and, as expected, the situation was brought under control, but the battle lines had been drawn. On 25 February 1940 six prisoners, Seán (Jack) McNeela, Tony Darcy, Tomás MacCurtain, Joseph Plunkett, Joe Lyons and Michael 'Micksie' Traynor, all began a fast in Mountjoy Prison in an attempt to be permitted free association and to have two prisoners, Nicholas Doherty and John Dwyer, moved from the criminal wing to the republican area within the prison. Five days later, on 1 March, the prison authorities attempted to remove McNeela and Plunkett, together with Seamus Mongan and James Byrne, to the Collins Military Barracks to place them before a military tribunal on charges of a 'conspiracy to usurp a function of the government'; namely being members of the IRA. The prisoners would not go without a fight and a barricade was set-up in D-Wing. In the riot that followed, the Special Branch and Dublin Metropolitan Police were brought in to quell the disturbance. Using fire hydrants, the authorities breached the barricade and forced the prisoners into their cells where they were allegedly beaten in reprisal. After order was restored, four of the prisoners were brought before the military tribunal where they were charged. McNeela, Plunkett, Mongan and Byrne had been arrested on 29 December 1939 at a house in Cowper Gardens in south Dublin from where an illegal radio transmitter was operating. The detective sergeant who made the arrests testified that as he entered the house he discovered Mongan in the process of broadcasting into a microphone; he added that the accused was uttering the words 'Good advice to the King of England' when he entered the living room. It was alleged further that Mongan was startled by the raiding party and shouted out 'Cripes Mac'. The prosecution's case centred on the accusation that they had caught an IRA unit red-handed in the process of broadcasting republican propaganda. The military court found the four men guilty as charged and sentenced McNeela and Mongan to two years' imprisonment, while Byrne and Plunkett received eighteen months each. Five days later at the Special Criminal Court both Tony Darcy and Michael Traynor, who had by that stage been fasting for ten days, were sentenced. Both were charged with refusing to give their names and addresses to Gardaí when arrested in Parnell Square and each were given a three-month sentence.

With the control of the media subject to the provisions of the emergency powers, little or nothing was reported on the ongoing fast. Three weeks later, on the eve of St Patrick's Day, all six hunger strikers were removed from Mountjoy to St Bricin's Military Hospital. The propaganda battle, however, was beginning in earnest. Preparations were in full swing for the commemorations associated with the Easter Rising when a letter of protest criticising the government's stance was published; it was signed by the Lord Mayor of Dublin, Kathleen Clarke (wife of Tom and sister to Edward Daly, both executed in 1916), and other relatives of those who had taken part in the Easter Rising. In response, Gerald Boland issued a forthright statement that was blunt in its interpretation of the hunger strikers' cause, yet summed up the government's position that the IRA was an organisation posing a serious threat to a legitimately elected government:

> The right fought for in 1916 – the right of the Irish people to have a government of their own choice – has, in so far as the community in this part of Ireland is concerned, been

completely won. The tragedy is that there should now be
people who so ignore the real character of the struggle in
1916 as to seek to pervert that rising into a justification
of attacks against an Irish Government, and to use it as an
excuse for perpetual disorder.

The Irish Times, 25 March 1940

At Arbour Hill cemetery on Easter Sunday de Valera was jeered
by supporters of the hunger strikers as he laid a wreath on behalf
of the government in honour of the executed leaders of the
Easter Rising. The fast continued out of the sight and minds
of the Irish public with deaths now seeming inevitable. One of
the hunger strikers, Michael Traynor, would in later years recall
vividly the experience of the fast: 'After a bit, I remember, I
couldn't even turn in the bed without help. We had to be rubbed
down each day with olive oil to prevent the bedsores. I could
smell death off myself, a sickly nauseating stench. We would
have died except that we drank a great deal of water each day'
(Coogan, *The IRA*, p. 144).

By early April the government and prisoners began to
accept that deaths were imminent. Indeed, the extent of the
government's desire to manage the prospective deaths of hunger
strikers was so great that some astonishing measures were taken.
It is interesting to note that, in the weeks before the death of
Darcy and McNeela, the Department of Justice prepared a
memorandum proposing an Emergency Order, which was to be
introduced on 15 April. In essence, the order gave the government
the power to prevent inquests on the bodies of deceased hunger
strikers and, as in the 1920s, the ability to bury the same without
the attendance of the deceased's family. It stated, 'It will also be
observed that at the end of the draft Order, power is given as to
the disposal of the body of the deceased. The intention is to avoid
the danger of the burial being made an excuse for inflammatory
demonstrations' (Office of the Taoiseach, file S11828; cited in Ní
Bheacháin, *Lost Republicans*).

On the evening of 15 April Tony Darcy cried out to

Jack McNeela, 'Seán, I'm dying' (*An Phobacht*, 15 April 2005).
Within hours he had been removed to a private ward within
the hospital. At 5.25 a.m. on Tuesday 16 April, Tony Darcy died
on day fifty-two of his fast. He was thirty-four years old and was
married with two boys, aged eight and six, and a daughter, aged
one. He had been the proprietor of a garage and undertaking
business in Largan, a small village three miles from Headford
in County Galway, where he had been born. Darcy was a
well-known republican in the west of Ireland and was a cousin
of Louis Darcy, who had been the Officer Commanding of
the Headford IRA before his murder by Black and Tans near
Oranmore Bridge in 1921. It was alleged that the body of Louis
Darcy had been pulled behind a military lorry from Oranmore
to Roscam where it was dumped in the woods at Merlin Park.
In 1936 Tony Darcy, along with five other Galway men had been
arrested and charged before a military tribunal with possessing
'certain documents' and sent to Mountjoy Prison. By 1938
Darcy had been promoted to the IRA Army Council under Seán
Russell's leadership, but had become a key target for the Special
Branch. The government's announcement that Darcy had died
was short, factual and, perhaps, indifferent: 'Anthony Darcy of
Headford, County Mayo, died early this morning in St Bricin's
Military Hospital, having been on hunger strike since February
25. He was serving a sentence of three months imprisonment
imposed by the Special Court following his arrest at 40 Parnell
Square on February 17' (*The Irish Times*, 16 April 1940).

The inquest into his death was held in the Military Wing of
St Bricin's Hospital, at which it was established that he had died
of inanition and cardiac failure, due to a hunger strike. However,
with the prospect of further deaths a reality, the jury added a
rider to the verdict that called into question the government's
prisons policy, in so far as it related to republican prisoners:
'We are of the opinion that immediate action should be taken
in regard to the five men at present on hunger strike and in a
serious condition, and we desire to express our sincere sympathy
to the widow, relatives, and friends of the late Anthony Darcy in

their bereavement (*Anglo-Celt*, 20 April 1940).

The inquest into the death of Tony Darcy was the first time that a jury had considered a death of this nature in Ireland since the death of Thomas Ashe. It seemed that, as with the Ashe case, the authorities were not going to win any sympathy. The inquest jury pointedly criticised the stance adopted by both de Valera and Boland in refusing permission, on three occasions, for a Carmelite priest, Father O'Hare, to visit the republican prisoners in Mountjoy. Cross-examined by Seán MacBride on behalf of the Darcy family, the priest advised the jury that he 'had every reason to believe that the hunger strike would have been settled a fortnight ago if I had been allowed to visit Mountjoy.' On being asked if he had advised both de Valera and Boland of his view, O'Hare responded that he had, but 'they had no explanation on their refusal. They simply said that they could not give me permission' (quotations from *The Irish Times* over the course of the Darcy inquest). Both de Valera and Boland stood indicted by the jury. It was an embarrassing situation that compelled Boland to deliver a ministerial statement in the Dáil on the matter:

> In connection with the inquest held yesterday into the death of Anthony Darcy, I think it necessary to correct any misapprehension which may be caused by some of the evidence given by Father O'Hare. It will be understood that I am speaking of the evidence as reported in the daily papers – the only version which reaches the ordinary citizen. As so reported, there seems to be a clear suggestion that if Father O'Hare had been allowed to visit the prisoners in Mountjoy, whose treatment was put forward as the reason for the hunger strike, and to report the facts as regards their treatment to the men on hunger strike, the hunger strike would have been abandoned . . . It may well be that Father O'Hare believes he would have succeeded where all others had failed, but there do not seem to be any reasonable grounds for such a belief. It is quite clear that the demand of the hunger strikers is that all prisoners belonging to their organisation, no matter what offence

they commit, should be held in military custody and recognised as members of a military force entitled to be treated as men engaged in legitimate warfare.

Dáil Éireann Debates, vol. 79: 18.4.40

With the crisis deepening and Jack McNeela close to death, Father O'Hare was allowed into Mountjoy Prison on Friday 19 April, undoubtedly due to the adverse publicity arising from the Darcy inquest. The important information that the priest was to relay to the prisoners was an order from IRA Chief of Staff, Stephen Hayes, that the strike was to end. In the recollection of Michael Traynor, the prisoners believed that they had been granted significant concessions and Traynor believed that 'all we had struck for had been granted' (Coogan, *The IRA*, p. 189). According to Father O'Hare, he had visited the prison after extracting concessions from Boland to the effect that the prisoners would be allowed to wear their own clothes, would be allowed free association at work, and would be held separately from the criminal inmates of the prison. Stephen Hayes had written:

To the men on hunger strike in St Bricin's Hospital,

The Army Council and the Nation, impressed with the magnitude of your self-sacrifice, wish to convey to you the desire that if at all consistent with your honour as soldiers of the Republic you would be spared to resume your great work in another form.

We are given to understand that the cause you went on strike for has been won and that your jailers are now willing to concede treatment becoming soldiers of the Republic. In these circumstances, if you are satisfied with the assurances given you, you will earn still more fully the gratitude of the people by relinquishing the weapon which has already caused so much suffering and has resulted in the death of a gallant comrade.'

Saoirse, May 2001

The strike ended officially at 7.00 p.m., within half an hour of the priest's visit; however, on O'Hare's arrival at the hospital, it had already been clear that the life of Jack McNeela was ebbing away as he entered day fifty-five of his hunger strike.

The initiative was too late: on 19 April Jack McNeela died. The intervention of Father O'Hare had come too late to save him. He was twenty-six years of age when he died and from the town of Ballycroy in County Mayo. Hailing from a family of four brothers and two sisters, McNeela had been well known in GAA circles throughout the county. His republican credentials were impeccable and he had been arrested on Easter Sunday in 1937 when trouble had broken out in Newport, County Mayo, after Gardaí had banned a republican demonstration. Two months later, after refusing to recognise a military tribunal, McNeela was convicted of riot and assault and sentenced to twelve months' imprisonment. In April 1938 Seán Russell was appointed as Chief of Staff of the IRA and he appointed McNeela as Officer Commanding in England. A year later he was appointed Director of Publicity for the IRA and oversaw the production of the weekly internal newspaper, *War News*. He had become the Officer Commanding of the prisoners in Mountjoy in February 1940. He was the nephew of Michael Kilroy, a former Fianna Fáil TD for South Mayo, who had led the fasting republican prisoners in Mountjoy in 1923. However, in the interim, his politics had changed totally. As a loyal member of Fianna Fáil, Kilroy had visited McNeela in his final days to urge him to come off the protest. However, during Kilroy's visit he lambasted his nephew for daring to 'embarrass' de Valera, whom he described as the 'heaven-sent leader'. McNeela, not surprisingly, ordered his uncle out of the room.

The inquest into the death of Jack McNeela took place at the Dublin City Morgue where death was recorded as 'due to inanition and cardiac failure'. The jury heard evidence on the apparent maltreatment of Darcy, McNeela and the prisoners throughout the fast. Gerald Boland agreed to face Seán MacBride at the inquest; his decision, with hindsight, was a serious error and proved counter-productive in the extreme. Denying that he had a political axe to grind, MacBride told the minister that he was there as a legal representative and that if he should speak 'with some heat' it was for the 'sake of humanity and tolerance'. Evidently MacBride was relishing his chance to cross-examine the minister and suggested that Boland's refusal to permit Father O'Hare to enter the prison was unreasonable. He followed this with what amounted to an accusation that the minister was directly responsible for the deaths of both Darcy and McNeela: 'I put it to you that out of sheer intolerance you allowed these two men to die. I put it to you that you refused to make any concessions to Father O'Hare until Darcy died and you saw that the Irish Nation would not stand for it.' Boland had been rattled, but was not in the mood to tolerate MacBride's attack. He asked MacBride if he was posing a question or making a political speech to the court. Referring to MacBride's inference that the Irish people 'would not stand' for the death of the hunger strikers, Boland mentioned the prospect of an imminent election and suggested confidently that the electorate would have every opportunity to test such an assertion. Nevertheless, in delivering the verdict, the jury added the following: 'We are of the opinion that permission should have been granted to Father O'Hare to visit Mountjoy Prison at an earlier date. We are further of the opinion that criminal status should not be accorded to political prisoners' (quotations from *The Irish Times* over the course of the McNeela inquest).

In his memoirs Seán MacBride recalled the exchange with Boland and admitted that he had cross-examined the minister 'rather harshly' at the time. However, he pointed out that Boland had never forgiven him for the incident, that he had issued a statement after the exchanges saying that 'this was the last damn inquest that will ever be held in this country' and that he had gone on to order the suppression of inquests into the deaths of hunger strikers in future (MacBride, *That Day's Struggle*, p. 133). The cases of McNeela and Darcy were lost in the historical ether as the war progressed. However, another clash between Seán MacBride and the Irish government on the morality of letting men die on hunger strike would capture headlines five years later.

Chapter 6

Seán McCaughey: If you had a Dog . . .

If you had a dog, would you treat it in that fashion?

Seán MacBride at Seán McCaughey's inquest, 1946

When considering the death of Seán McCaughey on hunger strike in May 1946, it is somewhat difficult to defend the role played by Éamon de Valera in the affair. With hindsight, McCaughey's death bordered on gratuitous. Unlike Jack McNeela and Tony Darcy, who had died when the government deemed there to be a serious threat from the IRA at a precarious time, McCaughey died eight months after the war in Europe had ended. Not that the war could be used as an excuse for the deaths of McNeela and Darcy. But, arguably, McCaughey posed no threat to the State and his fast was truly a protest of last resort. Yet there was something quite predictable and sadly characteristic in the government's indifference to McCaughey's plight. Whether it allowed McCaughey to die out of sheer spite, or whether it was a calculated attempt to finish off a weakened IRA, there can be no escaping the government's callousness in the affair. If it were not for the remarkable exchanges at his inquest, no doubt the depressing plight and the undoubted suffering of McCaughey might have vanished in the political mists of the time. It fell again to Seán MacBride to expose the conditions under which the IRA prisoners had been held throughout the war – and to score a pyrrhic victory on behalf of the deceased IRA leader. In truth, MacBride's skill placed the government in the dock and, memorably, gained an admission that a dog would not be treated in the manner that McCaughey had been treated.

Seán McCaughey did not suffer fools gladly. He could be cruel and sadistic and possessed a vaulting ambition to lead the IRA. He came to national prominence as the fortunes of IRA Chief of Staff, Stephen Hayes, waned and a power struggle for the movement coincided with the failure of the England Campaign in the early 1940s. Throughout its history, the clash between the northern and southern wings of the IRA has periodically created tensions. Mutual distrust, perceived financial discrepancies, ideological and strategic disagreement, or just a plain clash of egos has caused stresses within the ranks. However, during the Second World War a schism developed between the northern and southern leadership of the IRA that was to lead to one of the most intriguing and eye-opening episodes in its history. What began as a power struggle between two individuals, Hayes and McCaughey, ended in a highly publicised court case that brought acute embarrassment to the IRA. The bad blood that led to this case was essentially a power struggle between these two individuals over the direction of the organisation. However, it was also an episode that was to show how spiteful the IRA could be towards its own members, as personal acrimony led to imprisonment and torture. On the northern side of the split was Seán McCaughey, the heir apparent to the then Dublin-based leader, Stephen Hayes. The desire for 'action' from the North had been met, perhaps justifiably in the face of de Valera's clampdown, with a pragmatism in Dublin that had created a gulf between the IRA factions. In the early 1940s a chain of events unfolded that would lead to the disposal of Hayes as leader, and the death by hunger strike five years later of McCaughey. It was a messy affair that bordered on fiasco and saw the IRA exposed publicly as an exceptionally ruthless organisation, consisting of ideological die-hards and riddled with double-agents. In particular, the IRA, while hating the British, the unionists and de Valera, was seen to have reserved its greatest hatred for its own traitors. With the floundering of the England Campaign in the early 1940s, the pressure began to grow for the resignation of Stephen Hayes, whose main critics came from the Belfast-based Northern Command, led by Seán McCaughey. To McCaughey, Stephen Hayes was the main impediment to the republican struggle in Ireland. Inertia, he felt, was strangling the movement from within. The organisation had been compromised severely under Hayes' leadership, with countless volunteers imprisoned, even executed, and weapons, ammunition and revolutionary imagination in short supply. The executions, imprisonments and, most notably, the deaths on hunger strike of Darcy and McNeela had certainly created new martyrs, but this could not hide the fact that the IRA was rudderless in the face of the onslaught of the State. In truth, the IRA was riddled with informers and McCaughey felt, with cause, that Hayes was working for the Special Branch. The Irish government held the IRA in its proverbial pocket and Hayes was seen as ineffectual in leadership, personality and demeanour. With hindsight it is clear that Hayes had brought suspicion on himself and had played into McCaughey's hands. Any coup within the IRA in 1941 was, as far as the Belfast-based leadership was concerned, a matter of necessity rather than greed or ambition. Inevitably a plan to stage a coup was hatched by McCaughey and, by the start of 1941, Hayes' days within the IRA were numbered. Nevertheless, by Easter 1941 Hayes had adopted the old adage of keeping your friends close but your enemies closer still, and had appointed Seán McCaughey as Adjutant General. But this, in itself, had not sated McCaughey's desire to lead the movement, or to rid it of informers.

During the Second World War the IRA had brought upon itself the full wrath of the Irish government and the Garda Special Branch. The bottom line for de Valera's government was to maintain Ireland's neutrality and no quarter was given to the IRA. But it was an audacious IRA plan to assist a German invasion of the North that really set alarm bells ringing in Dublin, London and Belfast. And so, much to the Irish government's distress, it was the ever-present threat of collaboration between the IRA and Nazi Germany that could finally incur the wrath of Britain. Hayes flirted with Nazi Germany and helped devise 'Plan Kathleen', which plotted an IRA-aided German invasion of Northern Ireland. His plan was forwarded to Germany in April 1940 and low-level meetings were held with a German spy in Dublin. However, the Germans were unimpressed with Hayes or the logistics of Plan Kathleen and, coupled with the fact that a copy had been discovered by the Dublin authorities in May, the plan was abandoned.

The IRA was becoming ever more desperate in its search for arms and money to finance a campaign. Hayes' credibility was diminishing and in the summer of 1940 two significant episodes occurred that hastened his demise and exposed his role as a Special Branch agent. The battle between the IRA and the Special Branch was almost personal in nature. On 16 August 1940 a raid took place at a shop at 98a Rathgar Road in Dublin, which the Special Branch had been observing for some time. Inside the shop (which was, in fact, being used as an IRA training centre) Patrick McGrath, Tommy Harte and Tom Hunt were startled but fought back and injured three police officers, two of whom, Sergeant Patrick McKeown and Detective Richard Hyland, died of their injuries. As the IRA men tried to escape they were captured and put before a military court where all three were sentenced to death. Despite appeals and a vigorous defence mounted by Seán MacBride, only Hunt's sentence was commuted while McGrath and Harte were executed by firing squad in Mountjoy on 6 September 1940.

The second episode concerned the death of an alleged IRA informer by the name of Michael Devereux. In the summer of 1940 Devereux had been arrested by the Gardaí but, strangely, was released soon after. Soon after his release, a number of IRA arms dumps were discovered by the Special Branch and, naturally, suspicion fell on Devereux. On 19 Septembers, on the instruction of the IRA GHQ in Dublin, Devereux was arrested by Michael Walsh, Paddy Davern and George Plant. The interrogation of Devereux was a prolonged affair and he was killed on the mountain of Slievenamon in County Tipperary by Plant. When his body was discovered in a shallow grave on the mountain, there was evidence that Devereux had been subjected to prolonged torture. All three IRA men were eventually arrested and their trial opened at the Special Criminal Court on 9 December 1941. The first trial collapsed but all three were re-arrested under an amendment to the Emergency Powers Act, tried again, and sentenced to death by Military Tribunal. However, with the prospect of three IRA martyrs in the offing, the government chose to reprieve Walsh and Davern. George Plant was not so lucky. On the morning of 5 March 1942 he was taken from Arbour Hill prison in Dublin to Portlaoise Prison by military escort and executed.

However, the suspicion that Hayes had exposed the arms dumps to the authorities and that he had ordered the execution of Devereux to cover his own guilt began to take hold within the IRA. It was clear that under his leadership the movement was stagnating and now rumours began to circulate that he was also an informer. To McCaughey, Hayes was an embarrassment with a drink problem who had to be removed. It was this conviction that would lead to one of the most publicised and eye-opening cases in the history of the IRA. On 30 June 1941 McCaughey, together with fellow Belfast men Liam Rice and Charlie McGlade, met with Hayes and former Adjutant General Joe Dougherty in Coolock in North Dublin, with a view to discussing the future of the organisation. However, it soon became apparent that this was to be no ordinary meeting because the Northerners produced weapons and 'arrested' Hayes, removing him for interrogation.

There is no doubt that the prolonged interrogation of Stephen Hayes at the hands of Seán McCaughey was particularly brutal, at times bordering on the sadistic. Initially Hayes was taken to a secluded farmhouse in the Cooley Peninsula in County Louth where he was interrogated and beaten regularly by his three captors. From there he was moved to Dublin where a prolonged interrogation was carried out with McCaughey leading the assault. Seán McCaughey was a ruthless individual who aimed to seal Hayes' fate with a confession that would enable an execution to be carried out. Thereafter, it was believed that McCaughey wanted to dump Hayes' body outside Leinster House as a message to de Valera. Hayes was put through severe psychological torture but he refused to break. A decision was then taken to move Hayes to a safe-house in Glencree, County Wicklow, where McCaughey ordered the 'arrest' of Hayes' brother-in-law, Larry de Lacy, who verified Hayes' evidence and alibis. Still McCaughey would not believe Hayes and it was decided to move the prisoner to 20 Castlewood Park in Dublin for a formal court martial. This would be overseen by an IRA jury consisting of Charlie McCarthy from Cork, Tom Farrell from Connemara and Pearse Kelly from Dungannon. Ominously for Hayes, who had refused to nominate anyone to defend him, the chief prosecutor was McCaughey who, given his questionable and fiery temperament, went about his task with undoubted gusto.

Giving evidence at the trial of McCaughey in September 1941, Hayes described what he had been put through. He had been beaten with a broom handle, tied to a chair and, for long periods, bound face down to a bed. The affair is truly one that could have jumped straight out of the pages of a horror novel, such was the chilling nature of the interrogation and the psychological damage it caused the prisoner. Hayes explained, 'Then one night I was brought out at midnight, blindfolded, bound with ropes, my arms behind my back, and brought to the banks of a nearby river by McCaughey and the other two. I took it that it was their intention to shoot me, and I gave them my pocket book and stuff to give to my people, and asked for time to say a few prayers'(O'Callaghan, *Easter Lily – The Story of the I.R.A.*, p. 189).

For whatever reason, Hayes was spared on this occasion; on his return to Castlewood Park he was presented with copies of statements that he had allegedly made while in the Cooley Mountain hideout. McCaughey then charged him formally with 'treason against the Republican Army and conspiracy with the Free State Government to wreck the Army' (*Ibid.*, p. 190). Hayes was bound while the court martial was carried out, a process that lasted initially for fifteen hours. He claimed that he was ordered to 'come clean' while being systematically beaten by a series of men. On the third day of the court martial, he was handed a Catholic prayer book, which was opened at the section on how to prepare for a confession; he still refused to break. However, the softly, softly approach was soon exhausted and Hayes claimed that McCaughey told him that they 'were tired of beating him' and that if he did not confess he would be hung up on the kitchen wall and left there without food, drink or sleep until he told them what they wanted to hear. Eventually Hayes' will-power was broken and he asked for some paper in order to write a letter to his sister in Wexford. It was believed that this letter was a precursor to a full confession. Hayes claimed that the letter was destroyed and a further beating was given to him, during which a broom handle was, this time, broken over his back. Thereafter, he 'confessed' and began to write his testament – or as Hayes labelled it 'imaginary happenings' – that would run eventually to over 100 foolscap pages and name the Minister for Agriculture, James Ryan, and the Minister for Education, Tomás Ó Deirg, as his Government contacts.

As August drew to a close, McCaughey dithered and the search for Hayes by the Special Branch closed in. The Special Branch was aware that Hayes had been abducted and a manhunt was in full flow across Dublin. Soon confusion and panic became the order of the day as McCaughey was arrested getting off a train at Castlewood Avenue. The game was almost up; but, in the absence of McCaughey, the main concern for the IRA was how to kill Stephen Hayes and dispose of the body without arousing suspicion. In charge of Hayes in the house in Castlewood Park were Jobie Sullivan, Liam Burke and 'Black Dan' O'Toole, but no definite order was received to carry out an execution. Over the following week Hayes was held in chains while he continued writing his 'confession' until, on 8 September, he seized his opportunity. While still shackled, Hayes noted that one of his captors, Liam Burke, had left his gun unattended on the fireplace while he wrote a letter. At the opportune moment, Hayes seized the gun and jumped through a bay window into the street. Still in chains, Hayes struggled along Castlewood Park to the Rathmines Garda Station, where he handed over the gun and gave himself up to the authorities. The IRA men in the house in Castlewood Park were now in a blind panic as they awaited the arrival of the Gardaí. The episode seemed to sum up the farcical organisation that was the IRA in the late summer of 1941.

Soon a detachment of officers, commanded by an Inspector Gill, arrived at the house and a shoot-out ensued, during which Rice was badly injured. All three IRA men were captured and subsequently sentenced for their part in the debacle. In arresting McCaughey the week before, the government had taken a ruthless operator out of circulation. On the day before Hayes' escape, the date for the trial of McCaughey had been set for 19 September. Although he was to be charged only with 'possession of incriminating documents and ammunition without a licence', the fact was that Hayes was now in a position to add, perhaps fatally, to McCaughey's woe. The trial of McCaughey became a media sensation. It exposed the IRA as ideologically and militarily bankrupt, and overseen by individuals who were, perhaps, semi-megalomaniacs. From de Valera's point of view, Hayes, as chief prosecution witness, would be instrumental in bringing the IRA into further disrepute. Hayes was a godsend to the government and his vivid testimony provided some justification for the draconian legislation introduced to combat the IRA.

Despite not having been arrested or tried for murder, McCaughey was sentenced to death by firing squad. Once more the fear of martyrdom, perhaps, saw the sentence on McCaughey

commuted when the Government issued a short statement to
the effect that the alleged Adjutant General would now serve
a life sentence of penal servitude. In some ways, what awaited
McCaughey in prison over the next five years was the lesser of
two evils, but only slightly. Seán McCaughey, like most of the
republicans held during the war, refused to accept categorisation
as a common criminal. He entered Portlaoise Prison on 24 July
1940, and, from then until the autumn of 1944, he was wrapped
in a prison blanket, kept in solitary confinement and deprived of
exercise or fresh air. A fellow republican prisoner in Portlaoise at
the time, Paddy Murphy, described the conditions under which
prisoners who refused to 'conform' were kept:

> Confinement at that time was such that you never got
> outside the cell door, not even to empty slops; that was
> done for you by an ordinary convict escorted by a warder.
> You wore a blanket only with a hole cut in it through
> which your head passed; and a strip of blanket formed a
> belt for the waist . . . You got no letters or papers. You
> got out of the cell once a week to take a bath, when two
> warders escorted you there and back. The only light of day
> you saw was high up through the bars of the cell and there
> was no prisoner in the cell next to you as they purposely
> held those two empty.

MacEoin, *The IRA in the Twilight Years*, p. 532

The fact was that the policy of 'Let them rot' was still the
unspoken reality of the government's position. Seán MacBride,
along with Con Lehane, visited the republican prisoners in 1944
and was shocked by the conditions he witnessed. Convinced
that the conditions would cause permanent damage to the
prisoners' health, MacBride went to see de Valera and requested
that he do something to alleviate the suffering of the prisoners.
After meeting with Gerald Boland, who had never forgiven
MacBride for cross-examining him at Jack McNeela's inquest,
he became convinced that the government had not the will to
improve conditions in the prison. Occasionally the plight of the

prisoners would be aired on the floor of the Dáil, however, the government's line was stubborn and crystal clear. In July 1943, during a debate on the renewal of the Emergency Powers, de Valera outlined his determination to hold IRA prisoners and face down any subsequent hunger strikes:

> We have to maintain our right to restrain people. If anybody goes on hunger strike, then we cannot let him go out as a result of that hunger strike. That is final. I have got − and I hope that by my example other people may learn − a lesson which is enough to teach me for the rest of my life. There are times when it is fatal, absolutely fatal, to give way to representations such as are being made at present. Now, with the example before me, the example which I have given, I have to say definitely, to prevent any other representations coming in, that we cannot release anybody who is on hunger strike. That is definite and final. Those who wish to save the lives of those men, if they have any influence with them, will tell them to get off that hunger strike.
>
> Dáil Éireann Debates, vol. 91: 9.7.43

On 11 April 1944 James Everett, Labour TD for Wicklow, again raised the matter on the floor of the House, on behalf of fellow TD James Pattison; again Boland showed that he was not for turning in the matter:

> *Mr Everett (for Mr Pattison)* asked the Minister for Justice if he has received a copy of a statement made by James Crofton, recently released after serving nearly four years in Portlaoise prison, who makes serious allegations about the treatment of prisoners there; and if he will order an inquiry into the matter.
>
> *Minister for Justice (Mr Boland)*: I have seen the statement. I am familiar with the facts and I see no object in making any further inquiry. As I informed the House on a previous occasion, certain prisoners have made

conditions harder for themselves than they need be by refusing to comply with the prison regulations.

Dáil Éireann Debates, vol. 96: 11.4.44

On 28 June 1944 Oliver Flanagan, an independent TD for Laois–Offaly, raised concerns about conditions in the prisons and got a typically short and abrupt response from Gerald Boland:

> *Mr Flanagan* asked the Minister for Justice if he will permit Deputies representing the constituency of Laois–Offaly to investigate the conditions in Portlaoise Prison which are reported to be most unfavourable towards political prisoners.
>
> *Minister for Justice (Mr Boland):* The answer is in the negative.
>
> *Mr Flanagan:* That was the reply I expected, but I am of opinion that Deputies representing the constituency of Laois–Offaly should be given permission, accompanied by the governor of the prison, to examine the conditions under which prisoners are treated there at the present time.
>
> *Mr Boland:* The Deputy is entitled to his opinion. He can have any opinion he likes.
>
> *Mr Flanagan:* The Minister is responsible for the bad conditions of the prisoners at any rate.

Dáil Éireann Debates, vol. 94: 28.6.44

With that, the Dáil broke up for nine weeks while the conditions worsened. As far as the government was concerned, out of sight, out of mind was the order of the day.

With the end of the war in May 1945, a significant number of the internees were released. However, the situation regarding the convicted IRA men persisted. On the morning of Tuesday 16 April 1946, Seán McCaughey handed a note to Major R. Burrows, Governor of Portlaoise Prison, which stated that if he was not granted his release by Friday 19 April, he would embark upon a hunger strike. Inevitably, the indifference was palpable and McCaughey's fast commenced as scheduled. Five days later, in an attempt to put further pressure on the authorities, McCaughey began to refuse water.

Meanwhile, in Belfast Prison, David Fleming, a 28-year-old prisoner from Kenmare in County Kerry, had embarked upon a fast on 20 March. Fleming had been convicted, along with John Dynan, John Graham and former Chief of Staff Hugh McAteer, of the antiquated charge of treason felony in November 1942. The four men had been arrested at a makeshift printing shop on Belfast's Crumlin Road and had been caught with incriminating materials that outlined a strategy for a renewed IRA campaign in the North. The jury took a total of twelve minutes to convict the men and they were sent to a prison that had witnessed the execution of eighteen-year-old IRA volunteer Tom Williams only two months previously. In January 1943 four IRA prisoners, led by McAteer, scaled the walls of the prison with improvised ropes made with bed linen and escaped into Belfast in waiting cars. It was a sensation that saw the authorities mount the biggest security operation in the city since Partition and a bounty of £3,000 was offered for any information leading to the arrests of the fugitives. For the republican prisoners within the prison the escape signalled the start of a harsher regime and a struggle for political status that would eventually lead to Fleming undertaking his fast during March. Until 26 April he was force-fed by the Belfast authorities, but thereafter his fast continued and his condition deteriorated. As May began the governments, both north and south, were faced with fasting prisoners – and death as the outcome became a real possibility.

Tensions in Dublin rose as McCaughey's strike continued. On 8 May, 380 turf workers based in the Phoenix Park called a one-day strike in support of the fast. Matters came to a head when the workers attempted to charge the car of President Seán T. O'Kelly, only to be held back by about seventy members of the Gardaí. Later that evening a large crowd tried to march on Leinster House and there were ugly scenes as hand-to-hand fighting broke out between protesters and the Gardaí.

During an adjournment debate in the Dáil that day, Oliver

Flanagan sought a statement on the McCaughey case from the Minister for Justice, Gerry Boland. Flanagan, who was perhaps not the most politically correct of individuals, had already caused consternation during his maiden speech in 1943 when he suggested that Ireland could deal with its Jewish citizens in a manner that hinted of events elsewhere:

> How is it that we do not see any of these [Emergency Powers] Acts directed against the Jews, who crucified Our Saviour nineteen hundred years ago, and who are crucifying us every day in the week? How is it that we do not see them directed against the Masonic Order? How is it that the IRA is considered an illegal organisation while the Masonic Order is not considered an illegal organisation? There is one thing that Germany did, and that was to rout the Jews out of their country. Until we rout the Jews out of this country it does not matter a hair's breadth what orders you [Ceann Comhairle or Dáil chairman] make. Where the bees are there is the honey, and where the Jews are there is the money.
>
> Carroll, *Ireland in the War Years*, p. 137

Flanagan's political career did not suffer any fatal blow from his ill-advised outburst. During the adjournment debate he pointed out that McCaughey had been merely convicted of the common assault of Hayes, and he referred to a case reported in the local press in which a man had been fined a shilling for a similar conviction. He added, whilst distancing himself from the IRA, that McCaughey was 'a good Irishman' and the 'cream' of the republicans in Ireland. In response, Boland refused to go over the intricacies of McCaughey's sentence, merely pointing out that the matter had been 'dealt with by a properly constituted court', in other words a military court. He finished his response with indifference to McCaughey and spelled out explicitly the fact that the Government would not intervene to save him: 'I have had some experience of hunger strike and the mentality of men on hunger strike . . . I want everyone to be certain of this, that our last word has been said on the matter. Anyone who wants to be released will not be released as a result of hunger strike – I have no more to say' (Dáil Éireann Debates, vol. 100: 8.5.46).

Given the stance of the government, the death of Seán McCaughey was made inevitable. In the early hours of 11 May, Seán MacBride received a phone call to his home from Maurice Moynihan, who was secretary to Éamon de Valera. In MacBride's words, Moynihan advised him that Taoiseach thought [MacBride] should be informed that Seán McCaughey had just died and that perhaps MacBride should contact the deceased's family. As MacBride had only a brief knowledge of McCaughey, he found it quite strange that he should be contacted. However, the fact that de Valera had been advised so late at night of the death of McCaughey, perhaps showed (in MacBride's view) the extent to which the Taoiseach had been affected by the hunger strike. The historian Tim Pat Coogan records that, on his deathbed, it was said that the body of McCaughey was better imagined than described. Future IRA Chief of Staff Paddy MacLogan recalled how the tongue of McCaughey had shrunk to the size of a thru'penny bit. As news spread, a crowd of several thousand turned out to protest at the Parnell Monument in O'Connell Street in Dublin, while it was reported that impromptu recitals of the rosary were held at street corners.

The inquest into the death of Seán McCaughey was of massive importance because not only were the prison authorities under scrutiny, but also the policies of the Fianna Fáil government in its treatment of republican prisoners. The McCaughey family were represented by Seán McBride, together with Noel Hartnett and Con Lehane, who himself had spent a week on hunger strike in Arbour Hill Prison in 1939. Immediately, a serious issue of contention arose when the Deputy Coroner, Dr T. J. McCormack, refused to allow any evidence to be considered prior to McCaughey embarking on his hunger strike on 19 April. In effect, the conditions in which McCaughey had been held for five years were to be considered irrelevant to his death. Prior to the coroner's ruling, MacBride scored a significant moral victory when he cross-examined Dr Duane, the medical officer at the Curragh Camp. MacBride described Duane as a 'very honest man' who was 'obviously upset' while giving evidence. MacBride began his examination by asking Duane to confirm the conditions in which McCaughey had been held: that he had been in solitary confinement, wrapped in a blanket and on a 'punishment diet'. There followed an extraordinary exchange (all quotations from *The Irish Times* over the course of the McCaughey inquest):

> *MacBride*: Are you aware that during the four and a half years he was here he was never out in the fresh air or sunlight?
>
> *Duane*: As far as I am aware he was not.
>
> *MacBride*: Would I be right in saying that up to twelve or eighteen months ago he was kept in solitary confinement and not allowed to speak or associate with any other persons?
>
> *Duane*: That is right.
>
> *MacBride*: Would you treat a dog in that fashion?
>
> *Deputy Coroner (intervening)*: That is not a proper question.
>
> *MacBride*: If you had a dog would you treat it in that fashion?
>
> *Duane*: No.
>
> *MacBride*: Did you have to attend the prisoner for a nervous breakdown?
>
> *Duane*: He suffered from a nervous condition for a time.
>
> *MacBride*: By reason of solitary confinement?
>
> *Duane*: I don't know.

The damage had been inflicted to the State's case by Duane's admission that *he would not treat a dog* in the manner in which McCaughey had been held. MacBride had skilfully made the doctor play into his hands and the headline-makers present took note of the statement. To the coroner, this line of questioning was irrelevant. He advised MacBride that he would 'allow him any question from 19 April when the prisoner went on hunger strike and when he was in perfect health'. In response, MacBride pointed out that McCaughey had suffered a nervous breakdown in prison prior to his fast and that, in not allowing discussion of this breakdown, the Deputy Coroner was preventing a complete inquiry into the death. McCormack insisted that the issue of the nervous breakdown was irrelevant, but Junior Counsel for the family, Noel Hartnett, suggested that it had been caused by the conditions under which McCaughey had been held and, as such, was pertinent to the case. He then inferred that there was a political cover-up hidden within the Deputy Coroners' refusal to discuss prison conditions during the proceedings:

> It is in the interests of justice that these conditions should be investigated. The Coroner, for some reason best known to himself, has decided to cloak and conceal this matter. That being the case, there is no reason why counsel should appear on behalf of the relatives. I ask you gentlemen of the jury in your verdict to express your reprobation of the covering-up tactics that have been indulged in here today.

In protest, according to Seán MacBride, Hartnett 'created what I regarded at the time as an unnecessary scene in order to attract attention to his role. He then left and slammed the door after him.' Thereafter, the representatives of the McCaughey family retired from the inquest to consider their position. On their return they asked the High Court for a formal adjournment of the inquest in light of the refusal of the coroner to hear the evidence concerning the prison conditions. However, the adjournment was refused and the inquest continued. In the end the jury returned a verdict that McCaughey had died from cardiac failure following inanition and dehydration. However, it added that the death was due in part to the fact that 'the conditions existing in the prison were not all that could be desired according to the evidence furnished'. This was a polite way of saying that McCaughey, to echo the admission of Dr Duane, had been treated like a dog. As the court cleared, Seán MacBride recalled: 'In the midst of the uproar, for some reason, a police chief or superintendent who was present lost his nerve completely and became hysterical. He ordered the military to arrest me at the inquest before it was over! He must have gone berserk. However, I wasn't arrested.'

McCaughey, as expected, was given a hero's funeral. Overnight the remains rested in Adam and Eve's Franciscan Church at Merchants' Quay in Dublin. At Drumcondra Road on the north side of Dublin, the car stopped briefly while crowds stood to attention for the Last Post. At this point a revolver was produced and three shots were fired over the coffin. The hearse was four hours late in reaching Belfast because there were delays caused by the crowds in many towns en route. At Dundalk the cortège had been met by two pipe bands as it processed through packed streets and another volley of shots had rung out.

The funeral of Seán McCaughey took place at Milltown Cemetery in Belfast on 13 May following a requiem Mass at Holy Cross Church in Ardoyne. Wreaths from every part of Ireland were carried by thousands of mourners as the tricolour-draped coffin made its way to the church. As per instruction, the flag was removed outside the church and after the service the cortège made its way, without the flag, through many unionist areas of the city under heavy police escort. Interestingly, it was reported that many members of the Royal Ulster Constabulary (RUC) on duty saluted the coffin as it made its way to the Falls Road where thousands had gathered since early morning. At the graveside a decade of the rosary was recited by Cathal O'Hara, who was a brother-in-law of McCaughey. The oration was given by Harry Diamond, the Republican Socialist MP for the Falls, and his defiant eulogy was as much aimed at the heavy police presence as dedicated to the memory of McCaughey:

> We are here this morning to pay a last tribute to a loyal comrade. Sacrifices such as McCaughey's should no longer be necessary, but we have all been disillusioned . . . On occasions such as this it is not with any feelings of vengeance that we meet, but to pay silent tribute to one more of the dead who have forged an unbreakable link in the chain of

resistance against foreign rule in this country, and to assert that we will carry on this struggle until his [McCaughey's] wish is met. It is a moral struggle because it is an unequal struggle, but as long as young men such as McCaughey are prepared to make such sacrifices in defence of their principles, those principles will eventually triumph.

The Irish News, 14 May 1946

Memories of the death of Seán McCaughey were recorded vividly by Brendan Behan in his book *Confessions of an Irish Rebel*. He recalled the exact moment that he was told of the death of McCaughey and, in typical Behan prose, recounted a tale he had heard about McCaughey during his hunger strike: 'Now I knew a number of things about this young man and one of them was that when he was lying in his bed after ten or twelve days with neither a bite to eat nor a sup to drink, the warder came into his cell and threw buckets of water over him, saying, "Now, you bastard, if you won't take water one way, you'll bloody well take it another"'(Behan, p. 75).

A flavour of the contempt in which Seán McCaughey was held by some in Dublin society came in a letter to *The Irish Times*, published on 15 May, written by a Mr Lennox Robinson from Monkstown. Despite being critical of the State for allowing McCaughey to be held in such conditions, Robinson's thoughts on McCaughey were made crystal clear, if indeed they were somewhat convoluted. In fact, the latter part of Robinson's letter displayed a crass misunderstanding of the principles surrounding McCaughey's prison protest. Indeed, was 'Mr Robinson' merely a joker to so belittle the fast of McCaughey?

Seán McCaughey was an enemy of the State, and he seems to have been cruel. His sentence to penal servitude for life, I am sure, was just ... It is said that McCaughey refused to wear prison clothes and would have taken exercise if permitted. In a Turkish bath everyone goes about stark naked. I think it was Liam O'Flaherty who said that there is not one bathing dress in Russia. And what about sun-bathing?

Just when they thought the McCaughey issue had been put to bed, one individual who incurred the wrath of the Irish government over the McCaughey affair was the Radio Éireann broadcaster Noel Hartnett. The County Kerry native was also the host of the popular *Question Time* radio show and had acted as Junior Counsel to Seán MacBride at the inquest into the death of McCaughey. Indeed, as noted, he had walked out of the proceedings at one stage in protest at the manner in which the State was handling the inquest. Hartnett embellished his criticism of the government in a letter to *The Irish Times* on 24 May, which called into question the credibility of the Minister for Justice, Gerry Boland. Referring to a statement that Boland had made in respect of the McCaughey inquest and the 'improper conduct' of certain people involved (he was referring to Seán MacBride's questioning of Dr Crane), Hartnett stated:

> By his reference to the type of cross-examination to which he [Dr Crane] was subjected, Mr Boland can only mean Mr MacBride's questions were somewhat improper. The questions were simple questions which received simple answers, and were improper in no sense unless it be that any question and answer which tends to embarrass Mr Boland or indeed any member of his party is henceforth deemed improper.

It was a stunning, public and embarrassing repost to the minister, who had evidently been acutely troubled by the turn of affairs at the inquest and, indeed, Dr Crane's admission that McCaughey had been treated in a manner that would not be shown a dog. Within a week, on 29 May 1946, a message was conveyed to Hartnett on behalf of the Minister for Posts and Telegraphs, Patrick Little, that the broadcaster was to be precluded from acting as the host of the radio programme *Question Time*. Obviously there had been a 'discussion' between Boland and Little concerning Hartnett's future as a public broadcaster: the net result being that Hartnett was sacked. Patrick Little's track record in censorship during the war years has been well-documented elsewhere, but the manner in which Hartnett was removed bordered on the spiteful. The ultimatum was stark: if Hartnett refused to go, then the programme would be taken off the air. Inevitably the government got its way. However, the removal of Hartnett was perhaps a question of exacting revenge on an old ally, as far as Boland and de Valera were concerned. Hartnett had originally been a member of the Fianna Fáil National Executive and a key personal advisor to de Valera, but had resigned from the party in 1937 over 'policy issues' at the time of the enacting of the Irish Constitution. Indeed, prior to leaving the party, it was said that Hartnett was the only person who could enter de Valera's office without knocking. Hartnett was, in the words of a future Minister for Posts and Telegraphs, Conor Cruise O'Brien, a 'dedicated republican propagandist' who would go on to serve in the Dáil as a member of Clann na Phoblachta. Yet the manner of his removal showed a particularly Machiavellian streak within Fianna Fáil that ruined a fledgling career in broadcasting. In essence, the decision to remove Hartnett was a case of the government interfering in an individual's right to free speech and it was a veiled attack on the judicial process.

On 9 June a rally in support of Hartnett's right to free speech was held by the Irish Republican Prisoners Release Association in Tralee, County Kerry. The main speaker on the night was Paddy O'Donoghue, who had been the leader of the IRA in Manchester during the War of Independence. His defence of Hartnett was forthright but it fell to Hartnett to outline his own personal position in the matter. Hartnett stated that 'as long as he had a breath in his body he would exercise his right to freedom of speech'. He added that 'he had been punished because he tried to bring to the notice of the Irish people facts he discovered in his professional capacity about the conditions in Portlaoise Prison' (*The Irish Times*, 10 June 1946). Sadly, for Hartnett, his words were in vain and he had become another extraordinary casualty of the government's ideological battle with the IRA during the war.

The case for an inquiry into the case of McCaughey and

the other IRA prisoners in Portlaoise Prison was defeated in
the Dáil on Friday 21 May. The motion asking for an inquiry
into prison conditions had been tabled by Galway TD Michael
Donnellan of the Farmers' Party (Clann na Talmhan). In his
opening address, Donnellan, a former member of Fianna Fáil,
stressed that he had raised the matter in an attempt to make clear
'to the people of Ireland that there should be no ill-treatment
of prisoners'. In short, the Minister of Justice, Gerald Boland,
was the indirect target of the motion and it was he who was
'in the dock' throughout the debate. Donnellan referred to
the verdict of the jury at the inquest into Seán McCaughey's
death, mentioning that they had criticised the conditions under
which the IRA men were held. He pointed out that the jury's
verdict had exonerated both the Governor of Portlaoise Prison
and the prison officials, but had placed a question mark over
the government's policy towards republican prisoners during
the war.

Donnellan played the role of devil's advocate well, disas-
sociating himself and his party from the IRA. His attack was
well aimed and he demanded to know by what authority
the government had, in one case, allegedly sent a man from
Portlaoise Prison to a lunatic asylum and another prisoner
[McCaughey] had been denied fresh air for six years. In the
interests of getting to the truth, Donnellan argued that it was
essential that an inquiry into the prison conditions was held.
In his robust defence, Boland contended that Portlaoise Prison
had been inspected by Dáil deputies and, strangely, a warden
from San Quentin Prison in California. Given that San Quentin
Prison had, in 1937, implemented a policy of gassing to death
its condemned prisoners, this choice of argument by Boland was
not perhaps the most convincing. He then outlined the reasons
why McCaughey and the seven other IRA prisoners who
'had been found guilty of the most serious crimes that could
be committed against the community' had been kept in the
conditions previously mentioned:

These men on being sent to Portlaoise Prison demanded

that they be allowed to wear their own clothes, contrary to the rule that all long-term prisoners shall wear clothes of a uniform make and colour, as prescribed. This demand was rejected, these prisoners refused to wear the clothes provided for them, and instead improvised garments from their blankets. For obvious reasons of discipline, they could not be allowed to appear before other prisoners, or to go out of doors while so attired. On this account also, they have been exempted from the work usually prescribed.

Dáil Éireann Debates, vol. 101: 21.5.46

It is to be inferred from the foregoing statement that, because the prisoners refused to wear a uniform, all else that followed was justified on 'reasons of discipline'. Boland continued, outlining a plethora of IRA outrages and referring specifically to the bomb that was detonated in Coventry in August 1939 killing five people. He then provided an overview of the legislation that the government had used to combat the threat posed by the IRA and explained that it had chosen to resurrect the military court, which Boland labelled as 'drastic powers to deal with the menace'. Using words that could well have been spoken by General Mulcahy two decades earlier, Boland added that the military court was 'a terror court, set up to meet terror'. In referring to the case of Seán McCaughey, Boland reminded the members of the Dáil of the circumstances of the Stephen Hayes case and added: 'Hayes, described as the Chief of Staff of the organisation, said that he had been imprisoned, tortured and sentenced to death by McCaughey because it was alleged that he was a government spy. These are the people whom we were asked to treat, not as criminals, but as respectable citizens who have political differences with the government.'

Boland stood by the government's official stance that the IRA prisoners had been their own worst enemies within the prisons by refusing to conform. In addition, he stated that he believed the government's policy was, in essence, morally correct, that the policy had helped to keep the Free State neutral during the war and, regardless of perception, this was a price that was well worth paying. He added that it was necessary to keep the remaining republican prisoners in prison after the war as these men 'were needed to help with the reorganisation of that organisation [the IRA].' Naming Seán MacBride as 'one of the most dangerous men in the country', Boland finished with a flourish and was aided by de Valera who said that 'the idea of McCaughey or any similar prisoner being held in a dungeon, chained to a wall and cut off from all human intercourse was a figment'.

By the close of the debate the motion was defeated and the matter was closed to further political scrutiny. The attempt of the government to destroy the hierarchy of the IRA during the war left a legacy of distrust, fear and bewilderment within the movement. However, the generation of republicans that were subjected to the excesses of de Valera's regime in the war years eventually became the leadership base for the border campaign that began in 1956. There is no doubt that Seán McCaughey died an excruciating death in a protest of last resort. The determination of the government to remain indifferent made his death inevitable. In 1967 Seamus Robinson wrote a song in tribute to McCaughey. It is a simple, but evocative, memorial to the hunger striker:

> For five long years in that place he had lain,
> Waiting for the coming dawn;
> His body burned and tortured with pain,
> 'Til death gave Freedom to gentle Seán.

In Belfast, the case of David Fleming, who had been on hunger strike periodically throughout 1946, was finally resolved on 29 November. In stark contrast to the attitude displayed by de Valera and Boland, the Minister for Home Affairs Edmond Warnock exercised his discretion and released Fleming from prison. As part of the deal, Fleming was effectively barred from entering Northern Ireland for eight years and travelled to Dublin on the day of his release. Given the events in Dublin seven months previously, the obvious irony of a unionist government using the prerogative of mercy on an IRA hunger striker perhaps illustrates how gratuitous the death of Seán McCaughey really was. The names of Seán McCaughey and Stephen Hayes are now confined to the history books. Their era as leaders of the IRA was a time, perhaps, of catastrophe, which almost destroyed the movement. But the memory of those years also brings recollection of their dedication to a cause that was ultimately to end in failure.

Chapter 7

Short-term Gain, Long-term Pain

'Are you going to let Billy McKee die?
You have about four days to make up your mind.'
Bernadette Devlin, House of Commons, June 1972

With the commencement of the most recent troubles in Northern Ireland in 1969, it became somewhat inevitable that prisons would again witness strife over the issue of political status; and, in turn, hunger striking. With hindsight, the rejuvenation of the IRA, in its most potent form as the Provisional IRA, called into question the very existence of Northern Ireland. Since Partition, the Unionist government had dealt effectively with any perceived threat from the IRA. By the late 1960s, however, the situation had changed drastically. In short, the unionist supremacy was over and the onslaught of the Troubles threw the Northern state into convulsions. By 1971, rather than having to deal with a small, disorganised and poorly armed band of idealists, the Unionist government was faced with an IRA that had transformed itself in a manner that could not have been envisaged a decade earlier. The key ingredients that led to the rebirth of militant republicanism lay in a combination of linked events that reignited latent nationalist anger at the very existence of the state of Northern Ireland. It was a potent cocktail of sectarian friction, the reintroduction of the British Army, internment without trial and Bloody Sunday, amongst many, many other things, that created the Provisional IRA.

Over the years the state of Northern Ireland had never been short of draconian legislation to deal with insurgency. Indeed the most notable piece of legislation that the Unionist government had at its disposal was the 'Special Powers' Act (1922), which, under Section 5, allowed that individuals 'if a male' could be 'privately whipped' when found guilty of an offence. Since the founding of Northern Ireland in 1921, internment had been introduced periodically to deal with the threat of a republican insurrection. By and large this method had succeeded, due to the fact that the IRA had not the popular support of the nationalist populace to sustain a viable campaign. During World War Two, internment had blunted the IRA's ability to sustain attacks in the North, while throughout the Border Campaign, from 1956 to 1962, the early introduction of internment had stopped any significant uprising in Belfast. However, by 1971 all the ingredients that would make internment ineffective as a means to stamp out the IRA had been mixed into a political quagmire, ensuring that, far from eradicating dissent, internment would spark further carnage. The fact was that the situation across Northern Ireland had changed entirely in the decade since the IRA had ceased its Border Campaign in 1962 – there was now enough popular support to sustain the IRA, especially in Belfast, Derry and the rural nationalist hinterlands. In spite of this, the Unionist government, led by Prime Minister Brian Faulkner, still believed that the blunt power of internment could, in August 1971, obliterate republican resistance by taking its perceived chief operators off the streets.

Thereafter things got worse; and there is no doubt that internment was the turning point. The latter part of 1971 would witness a serious escalation of the IRA's campaign. In total thirty-four deaths had been recorded up to the morning of 9 August, but the events of that day contributed to an escalation

of the violence to unprecedented levels. On the morning of 9
August, at the behest of Faulkner, internment was reintroduced.
It was a blunt weapon that gave the authorities the power to
detain suspected terrorists without trial. In all, troops arrested
342 individuals in Catholic areas in a drive against the IRA.
Those interned that day were by no means the key operators in
the Provisional IRA. Intelligence records held by the military
were hopelessly outdated and the vast majority of those detained
were not associated with republicanism at all. Of those arrested
on the morning of 9 August, 116 were released within 72 hours,
while the remainder were held at Crumlin Road Prison or the
HMS *Maidstone* prison ship, which was moored in Belfast Lough.
It was the first time since 1962 that the decision had been taken
to use the power of internment granted by the Civil Authorities
(Special Powers) Act (Northern Ireland), and it was made after
consultation between Faulkner and the then British Home
Secretary, Reginald Maudling. Speaking in 1991, Maudling
admitted that the introduction of internment in 1971 had been
an 'unmitigated disaster', whilst pointing out that the Unionist
government had had little or no other option. He added, 'For
nationalists, internment became an icon of injustice. Statistically
the introduction of internment signalled the opening of the most
violent period of the troubles' (*Independent*, 17 November 1991).

Rather than stopping the trouble, internment acted as a spur
to the IRA. In the latter part of 1971 and throughout 1972,
all indexes by which the strife had been measured previously
became outdated. Scores of people died in outrages that further
hardened attitudes and ensured that a steady line of recruits was
driven towards the paramilitaries. On 30 January 1972 the events
known as Bloody Sunday occurred in Derry City; the killing of
fourteen unarmed civilians by the Parachute Regiment would
act as a massive recruiting sergeant for the Provisional IRA. In
turn, the conflict intensified and the prisons began to receive
prisoners from both republican and loyalist organisations. Since
prisoners convicted of offences related to the Troubles were not
eligible for special treatment, it was inevitable that the strife on

the outside would soon be replicated within the prisons.

The first clash of wills between the IRA and the British government over political status came in May 1972, when the veteran Belfast republican Billy McKee led a hunger strike within Crumlin Road Prison. McKee's impressive pedigree within IRA circles had been gained through decades of involvement with the organisation. He had first become associated with the IRA in the 1930s and had spent most of the war years interned. During the Border Campaign in the 1950s McKee was again imprisoned in Crumlin Road, and on his release in 1962 he became Officer Commanding of the Belfast Brigade. The failure of the Border Campaign set in motion an ideological debate within the IRA. To the consternation of many traditionalists in the organisation, including McKee, some members of the IRA had begun to consider Marxism as a viable alternative to a purely republican philosophy. With the IRA involved in a process of debating its ideological future, the explosion of sectarian violence in Belfast in 1969 found the Catholic areas without the protection of their so-called traditional defenders. The reality of bitter sectarian strife saw the Belfast IRA exposed as toothless, given that it could mount only a token resistance to the loyalist onslaught. Soon the wry observation on the gable walls of Belfast that the IRA stood for 'I Ran Away' became a festering wound in the Belfast IRA. According to the faction led by Billy McKee, the failure of the IRA to defend the nationalist areas of Belfast in 1969 lay with the then leader of the Belfast IRA, Liam McMillen and, by association, the Dublin-based leader, Cathal Goulding. In September both McKee and fellow IRA member Joe Cahill announced that they would no longer recognise McMillen's leadership in Belfast. This was a precursor to the split in the IRA in December 1969, when the Provisional and Official wings of the movement were born. To a traditionalist like McKee, who became the first Officer Commanding of the Provisionals in Belfast, the philosophy of the Provisional IRA would be straightforward: in essence, the defence of the nationalists in Belfast would be fundamental to an evolving strategy that would see the Provisionals go on an all out offensive against the state of Northern Ireland within two years.

In June 1970 Billy McKee had written himself into the annals of IRA folklore when he led the defence of St Matthew's Church in the Short Strand area of Belfast. The situation in Belfast that day threatened to eclipse the violence of the previous August, as sectarian rioting broke out initially in the Whiterock area and spread throughout the city. In east Belfast the vulnerable Catholic enclave of the Short Strand came under attack from loyalists and, with the security forces stretched across the city, the possibility existed that there could be serious loss of life in the area. On hearing of the trouble, McKee took a number of volunteers to the area and took up position within the grounds of St Matthew's Church. By the following morning three people, Protestants Robert Neill and James McCurrie, together with IRA man Henry McIlhone, had been killed in the ensuing gun battle. St Matthew's Church, however, had been saved by the action of McKee and this, in itself, made him a hero amongst Belfast republicans. McKee's tenure as IRA leader in Belfast was not long. In April 1971 he was arrested, charged, and sentenced to five years' imprisonment for possession of a gun. The Belfast leadership of the Provisional IRA fell to Joe Cahill but, with McKee now in prison, it was inevitable that the struggle for the political status of prisoners would soon become a burning issue.

In March 1972 the British government took direct control of the affairs in Northern Ireland by suspending the parliament at Stormont and imposing direct rule. In real terms, it had sacked Brian Faulkner and stood down the Unionist administration. For some in the IRA this move was considered a sign of the weakness of Heath and his government, indicating that the existence of Partition was again up for negotiation. For the first time since 1922 the Irish Question was top of the British political agenda. Faced with a situation that it had, at best, ignored for fifty years, the British government was somewhat bemused by the eruption of violence on its own doorstep. In the previous thirty months there had been almost 300 deaths attributed to 'civil unrest' and conditions were deteriorating on a daily basis. Westminster's ignorance in the face of explosive realities is best illustrated by the attitude of Conservative Home Secretary Reginald Maudling who, after visiting Northern Ireland in 1970, was to comment on the plane back to London, 'For God's sake bring me a large Scotch . . . what a bloody awful country.' Two years later, after the events of Bloody Sunday, Maudling was assaulted in the House of Commons by Mid-Ulster MP, Bernadette Devlin, as he tried to make a statement claiming that the Parachute Regiment had acted in self-defence. With the situation spiralling out of control, the British were forced to act and, in the aftermath of the suspension of Stormont, William Whitelaw was made Secretary of State for Northern Ireland. At the age of fifty-four Whitelaw had been handed, in political terms, a poisoned chalice and was charged with finding a solution. Perhaps the situation that presented itself was beyond the comprehension of a man who, while politically astute, was the archetypal pleasant but bumbling old Tory duffer. In July 1972 he took a political gamble and organised face-to-face talks with the Provisional IRA. However, this situation came about only through delicate negotiations, during which the lives of hunger strikers were the key to creating good faith. The most prominent hunger striker was Billy McKee and the British government generated the conditions in which talks could take place by granting political status in the face of his protest.

Prior to the commencement of the hunger strike the government had refused to recognise that the troubles that blighted Northern Ireland were political in nature. Outwardly, this was an official position that belied the historical facts underpinning the creation of the State. As far as the government and the prison system were concerned, there had been no *political* conflict since 1969. As a result of this stance, no prisoner could have applied for special treatment on the grounds that their crime was considered to be 'political' – the prisons simply did not recognise this status. However, by May 1972 there was complete agreement between both loyalist and republican prisoners that they were entitled to be treated as prisoners of war. Despite the apparent harmony in the prison, the *Loyalist News* felt it necessary to appease its devoted readership by pointing out that the Ulster Volunteer Force (UVF) prisoners were not, in fact, in league with the 'rebel scum'. On 7 May the Belfast-based *Sunday News* carried a report that both factions within Crumlin Road had forged this unlikely alliance to demand political status. The following day both sets of prisoners refused to wear official issue prison uniform and thus began to wear civilian clothes, which had been brought into the prison by relatives. That was merely the start of a campaign of disobedience. Matters came to a head on 12 May when a full-scale riot broke out in the prison's recreation area and, subsequently, a stand-off developed. Diplomacy eventually prevailed and the inmates agreed to return to their cells as troops in full riot gear waited, no doubt eagerly, to restore order. The situation, however, had reached breaking point and a work strike soon commenced in the prison. Inevitably, the next stage of the protest was to be a hunger strike and, accordingly, it was announced that a group of IRA prisoners led by McKee would commence a fast on 15 May. For the loyalist inmates the idea of hunger striking seemed to be a step too far. Holding the line against the hunger strike would be the newly appointed Secretary of State, William Whitelaw, whose opening gambit was set out in a statement on 12 May, which declared emphatically that granting the status of political prisoner to those on strike was 'out of the question'.

The IRA fast in Crumlin Road Prison commenced on 15 May, when five prisoners – Robert Campbell, Kevin Henry, Martin Boyle, Malachy Leonard, led by 49-year-old Billy McKee – refused food. The word from within the prison, and on the streets, was that the hunger strikers would 'take it to the death if necessary' in an attempt to gain political status (*Irish Independent*, 15 May 1972). From the beginning the pressure began to mount on Whitelaw to find an amicable solution. Across Northern Ireland violence was increasing to a frightening degree and the problems in the prisons threatened to escalate this further.

On 22 May Tony O'Kane, John Cowan, Malachy Cullen, Billy McGuigan and Paddy Monaghan all joined the fast, while six men began to refuse food in Armagh Prison. As ever, the 'slow burn' nature of the tactic led to a significant growth in support for the inmates. Outside the prison a pressure group garnered support, undertaking vigils, petitions, marches and 'sympathy fasts'. On 30 May Kevin Henry from Newry, who had been one of the first to refuse food, was forced to end his protest through ill-health. Within the jail, however, the mood among the republicans remained defiant. A statement released on 30 May by the Officer Commanding of the IRA prisoners, Proinsias MacAirt, reiterated (in somewhat pompous terms) the undoubted determination of the prisoners to win political status:

> They [the hunger strikers] have sacrificed much in the past, these men who today hunger for justice. They have opposed all the injustices of a corrupt and evil regime. They have fought to uphold the inalienable rights of their people. They have been tortured, slandered and finally jailed because they believe in the right of self-determination for their people. Now they seek justice for themselves and their comrades. Must they sacrifice their lives to obtain it? . . . Today, we humbly commit the lives and future of our comrades to Almighty God who gave our fathers the courage and determination to persevere through long centuries of ruthless tyranny. We ask His Devine blessing on the struggle we have pledged ourselves to carry us through to victory.

> *Irish Independent*, 31 May 1972

The extravagant statement and biblical sentiments expressed by MacAirt were in line with those expressed during the hunger strikes fifty years earlier. The idea of calling for the intervention of 'Almighty God' took the protest, literally, to a higher plane. The notions expressed amounted, in short, to a belief that the hunger strike was a case of republican good against British evil. As an argument, it was as unsophisticated as it was flawed. The crude religious ideals belied the reality of everyday life at the time. In the two weeks since the commencement of the hunger strike, twenty-eight people had lost their lives as the conflict intensified. The most notable loss of life came on 28 May when eight people were killed by an IRA bomb that exploded prematurely in a house in Anderson Street in the nationalist Short Strand district. Four of those killed were members of the IRA's 2nd Battalion; it was an accidental blast, or, as such events were known colloquially, an 'own-goal'. As deaths escalated, the prospect of all-out civil war began to grab the headlines, relegating the hunger strike to the inside pages of the local papers. Within the prisons the quest for political status may well have been a black and white issue, but the continuing violence on the streets and the pressure against conciliatory moves exerted by Unionist politicians ensured that no simple solution could be found to the hunger strike.

In the background, however, there was a bigger picture at play and that was the attempt to secure an IRA ceasefire. Such an achievement would have been of benefit to Whitelaw in two ways: firstly, it would have created a valuable breathing space to assess the situation; and secondly, it would have been a political coup for the Secretary of State. By late spring of 1972 the British government felt that tentative talks might take place with the IRA on the feasibility of a truce. On 29 May the Official IRA declared a ceasefire, while in the same month the British Army recorded a total of almost 1,300 shooting engagements. In announcing their ceasefire, the Officials stated that 'The overwhelming desire of the great majority of all the people of the north is for an end to military actions by all sides.' Whitelaw responded by noting that the ceasefire was 'a step in the right direction'. With the Troubles now at their height, June 1972 would prove to be a month of delicate and secretive negotiation in the face of a hunger strike.

On 6 June the condition of McKee and Robert Campbell, who was serving a sentence for armed robbery, worsened significantly and the authorities decided to move Campbell to the Mater Hospital (next door to the prison) for observation. It was reported that relatives of Campbell had pleaded with him to end his fast, since by then he had lost four stone in weight. The following morning, incredibly, Campbell managed to escape by jumping from a ground-floor window of the hospital and was whisked to safety by friends in a waiting car. The escapade proved to be a massive embarrassment for the prison and hospital authorities. Immediately, republican areas of Belfast were swamped by troops in a search for Campbell and, in an ensuing gun battle in Andersonstown, Charles Coleman of the Royal Artillery was killed. One theory that gained prominence in Belfast at the time was that IRA leader Martin Meehan, who had escaped from Crumlin Road Prison in December 1971, had masterminded the escape of Campbell; and indeed drove the getaway vehicle. Campbell's wife, 28-year-old Marie, told the *Irish Independent* that she was 'delighted' to hear of her husband's escape and would visit him in Dublin as soon as feasible. Back in the prison, the prisoners' condition was becoming critical. It was reported that three of the inmates, McKee, Leonard and Boyle, were 'dazed' and unable to receive visitors to their cells. Despite this, Máire Drumm, Vice-President of Sinn Féin, who had been allowed access to the jail, said that the prisoners were determined that the fast would continue. On the outside, moves towards a ceasefire were now advancing and the hunger strike would become integral to the negotiations. In the House of Commons on 12 June Bernadette Devlin summed up the situation:

> How can the Secretary of State talk peace to the House and the mass media? Because of what is happening in the Crumlin Road Prison, people make up their own minds about what he means by peace. Does peace mean that because nobody can see Billy McKee die of hunger, that because he does it slowly, quietly and painfully, believing in a principle and his right to be treated as a political prisoner, it is a peaceful way to die? I have a straight question which I hope the Minister who winds up the debate will answer. It is not a question of blackmail or initiatives. It is: 'Are you

going to let Bill McKee die?' You have about four days to
make up your mind. If Billy McKee dies, peace initiatives
will be for nothing, because the understanding of peace
will be that it will be the pre-1968 peace. It will not be
justice but the concept that peace exists when nobody
complains.

Hansard, HC (series 5) vol. 838, cc1148–222 (12 June. 1972)

In the IRA-administered 'Free Derry' on 13 June, Chief of
Staff Seán Mac Stíofáin outlined the Provisionals' terms for a
permanent ceasefire. There was to be no 'stepping stone' to a
united Ireland, and the British were advised that the IRA
expected a full British withdrawal as a pre-condition for a
cessation of violence. By offering to meet Whitelaw in Free
Derry to discuss the issue, Mac Stíofáin was placing the Tory
stalwart in a somewhat impossible position. However, in the
background, Whitelaw had also sought the assistance of both
John Hume and Paddy Devlin of the Social Democratic and
Labour Party (SDLP) to act as intermediaries between him
and the IRA. Both Hume and Devlin accepted that the IRA
was genuine in its desire to call a ceasefire. In early June the
British government released a number of internees and this act,
it seemed, signified that the British were prepared to be generous
if the situation arose. Since the granting of political status to the
IRA prisoners was at the top of the IRA's 'good faith' wishlist,
both Hume and Devlin felt that Whitelaw would be prepared to
make such a concession if the IRA was prepared to act. Later on
the afternoon of 13 June, with the strike in its twenty-eighth day,
reports circulated throughout Belfast that Billy McKee had died.
Rioting began in republican areas of the city before the rumour
was quelled. The hunger strike was now entering its end game
and the removal of McKee to the Royal Victoria Hospital on 19
June seemed to force Whitelaw's hand.

The talking had continued in the background and both
Hume and Devlin had made contact with IRA leaders Seán
Mac Stíofáin and Dáithí Ó Conaill to advise them of Whitelaw's

position, and that they believed he would be genuine and generous. In fact, behind the scenes, Whitelaw was preparing to accede to the demands of the hunger strikers – using the face-saving term 'Special Category Status' – and to allow the release of further internees, including Gerry Adams, as a precursor to talks. Unaware of the delicate ongoing negotiations, Adams, when advised that he was to be released, feared that it was a trap. It was only after he had consulted his uncle, Liam Hannaway, who told him bluntly to 'get out', that the advanced nature of the negotiations became apparent (Coogan, *The Troubles*, p. 173). It seemed that agreement on political status might already be a fait accompli. On 20 June John Hume stated that he 'hoped' that the granting of the prisoners' demands would act as a precursor to a full political amnesty in the event of talks (*Irish Independent*, 20 June 1972). Still, the timing of a move was of utmost importance to both sides – the hunger strike continued regardless. With these talks still in process, it was evident that the public position of the British government and its private stance were distinctly at odds. In the House of Commons Whitelaw tried to appease Unionist unease since rumours of a government capitulation were rife. He stated, 'I am not the sort of man who responds to ultimatums, or a loaded pistol to my head. Nor am I the sort of man who makes secret deals with anyone.' However, in realising that the goal of a ceasefire was tantalisingly close, he added that 'a ceasefire would provide a new opportunity for us all; sanity and common sense must prevail before it is too late' (*Fortnight*, July 1972).

On 19 June the choreography that would lead to the ceasefire commenced. The Secretary of State ordered the removal of republican prisoners from Belfast to Long Kesh in a move that signalled the government's willingness to compromise. In addition, the prisoners – both republican and loyalist – would be moved to their own private wings where they would be permitted to wear their own clothes, refrain from hard labour and be granted other special privileges. By the following day the hunger strike was, in effect, over. Whitelaw himself said that the move was an attempt to 'relieve tension' in Crumlin Road but the indications were that there had been a capitulation. Frank McManus, the independent nationalist MP for Fermanagh and South Tyrone, criticised Whitelaw for letting the fast continue so long as 'it was fairly well-known at Westminster for the last ten days that something of this nature was contemplated.' Despite these developments, there had been a significant oversight, in that nobody had informed the striking prisoners that a deal had been struck. Relatives of the hunger strikers complained that they were getting no cooperation from the authorities when they enquired of the prisoners' welfare. It fell to Paddy Devlin, incensed by the 'callous' inaction of Whitelaw's deputy Lord Windlesham, to phone Whitelaw at his home and request that he contact the governor of the prison to advise him that the situation had changed.

It was, on the face of it, a victory for the IRA and the hunger strike. The two demands that had been made by the IRA as preconditions for talks – namely the granting of political status and the right to choose their own deputation – had been met. At Long Kesh Gerry Adams was released as the fast ended and the next stage of the process would be face-to-face negotiations. The British government could be seen as pragmatic in pursuit of a greater goal: the political gamble was that the concession of special category status would be reciprocated by the establishment of a ceasefire. Another interpretation could be that the onslaught of the Troubles had shaken the government and the concession of special category status and negotiation with the IRA was a sign of weakness. That this was the reality would be borne out by the policies of subsequent governments who fought tooth and nail to claw back special category status.

Despite the fact that special category status had been given to both loyalist and republican prisoners, there was considerable criticism of Whitelaw from the Unionist benches in the House of Commons. James Kilfedder, MP for North Down, summed up the Unionists' concerns:

Is my Rt Hon. Friend aware that in Northern Ireland a

great number of people – this is not restricted to the loyal community – feel concerned about the status of political prisoner being granted to a number of men in Belfast Prison? Will he let us know whether the Government intend to give the same special privileges to members of the Angry Brigade or to the man now in prison who threw a tear gas bomb into this Chamber?

> Hansard, HC (series 5) vol. 840, cols 741–2 (6 Jul. 1972)

Since he was the man who had, in the House of Commons less than a week previously, described the tactic of hunger striking as 'blackmail', Whitelaw was on a proverbial 'hiding to nothing'. Years later Whitelaw came to believe that he had made the wrong decision in June 1972:

> In the circumstances of that moment the decision seemed a fairly innocuous concession, although I was clearly warned by my officials of the dangers vis-à-vis the prison system throughout the United Kingdom. Alas, though, it did establish a practice which caused my successors considerable trouble. I conclude today that its immediate impact was limited and it was later found to have been a misguided decision.
>
> Ryder, *Inside the Maze*, p. 103

The actual terms for the IRA ceasefire were discussed face to face by Dáithí Ó Conaill and Gerry Adams, in the company of the British diplomat, P. J. Woodfield, at the home of Michael McCorkell, a former British senior public servant, on the afternoon of 20 June 1972. McCorkell's home was in County Derry, close to the border with Donegal. This was a historic meeting as it was the first authorised contact between repre-sentatives of the IRA and the British government. The talks provided a basis for an IRA ceasefire that would commence on 26 June. History records that, on 7 July 1972, an IRA deputation consisting of Gerry Adams, Martin McGuinness, Seamus Twomey, Ivor Bell, Dáithí Ó Conaill and Seán Mac Stíofáin travelled to London for face-to-face talks with the British government. The talks took place at the Cheyne Place home of Paul Channon, a junior minister in the Conservative government and were attended by William Whitelaw and other officials from the Northern Ireland Office. The talks came to nothing and it seemed that both parties had been brought together with irreconcilable agendas. For the IRA, led forcefully by Mac Stíofáin, a declaration of British intent to leave Ireland was the bottom line; for Whitelaw, the will of the people of Northern Ireland (the unionist majority) had to be respected. According to British Cabinet papers, the meeting left Whitelaw feeling emotionally exhausted and 'clearly depressed', adding that the Secretary of State had found the experience of meeting and talking to Mr Mac Stíofáin 'very unpleasant' (PREM 15/1010, released 1 January 2003). The talks came to nothing and the ceasefire broke down two days later in the Lenadoon Estate in Belfast. An attempt to move displaced Catholic families into vacant houses was stopped by the army and serious gun battles broke out. It was a resumption of violence that would lead to July 1972 becoming the bloodiest month in the history of the Troubles.

Despite this, special category status was not withdrawn by the government. It had been a concession that was easier to give than to take away. Such a move in the summer of 1972 would have been disastrous. Perhaps Whitelaw and the Northern Ireland Office had lost the stomach to engage in a prolonged prison dispute with Northern Ireland on the brink of anarchy. Nonetheless, the issue would not be forgotten; the British perceived the concession as a loss of face by the government at the hands of the Provisional IRA. That would be addressed vigorously by later administrations.

Six months after the granting of special category status in the North, the government of the Irish Republic stood firm in the face of a hunger strike by IRA Chief of Staff, Seán Mac Stíofáin. Mac Stíofáin had been convicted of IRA membership, and had not helped his case when an interview with him was broadcast on RTÉ Radio on Sunday 19 November. Since Mac

Stíofáin was the only member of the Provisional IRA to speak with a Cockney accent, his admission that he was in a 'position of authority' within the movement was, perhaps, not advisable. He was sentenced to six months' imprisonment and embarked on a hunger and thirst strike, announcing melodramatically at his trial that he would be 'dead within six days'. After four days he agreed to take liquids – including soup and sweetened tea. Mac Stíofáin continued to refuse food for fifty-seven days. Characteristically, he also refused to sign a form confirming his objection to intravenous feeding as the form was not in Irish. On his own admission, he was 'ordered' off the fast by the IRA leadership and on his release he was charged with 'bringing the IRA into disrepute'. Since he had lost his 'rank' on admission to prison, Mac Stíofáin never regained any credibility in the movement and was sidelined. His fast was construed as a publicity stunt by a man who perhaps could not draw a line between reality and myth.

Chapter 8

Take Me Home to Mayo

*'I die proudly for my country and in the hope that my death will
be sufficient to obtain the demands of my comrades.'*

Michael Gaughan

A s 1972 ended the writing on the walls in the republican areas
of Belfast bore the stark message that 1973 would finally
see a British withdrawal from Northern Ireland. The situation
had festered further, with deaths, shootings and bombings all
increasing exponentially as the political vacuum was filled with
violent terror. As 1973 dawned the IRA believed that if its
campaign were to be further intensified the will of the British
to remain would finally crumble. In its New Year message, aimed
specifically at members of the British Army, the IRA said, 'you
are the imperialist foreigners, lording it over this last part of your
inglorious and infamous empire . . . we guarantee that you will
be fought with even greater vigour in the coming year.' Despite
the confident prediction, the army would not be making an exit
from the streets of Belfast and beyond. A constant flow of young
men and women, both loyalist and republican, was processed
through the courts, sentenced and designated as special category
prisoners. The rights won by the hunger strikers of June 1972

became an accepted benefit for paramilitary prisoners. However, in a society that, on an official level, was trying to deny that a 'war' was taking place, the images and stories emanating from the prisons provided cause for concern. The notion that Northern Ireland's prisons were used as training grounds for paramilitary recruits caused the right-wing Conservative MP, Lieutenant-Colonel David Mather, to state in the House of Commons in April 1973:

> These special category prisoners have used their position in a scandalous way and scandalous abuses have taken place. Prisoners have only to make a simple statement at the time they go before the court that they do not recognise it to be given a political category akin to that of a prisoner of war. In the camps, in Crumlin Gaol and in Long Kesh they ape the Colditz Story. Escape tunnels are built. A successful escape took place through one of these tunnels, which was 40 yards long. The prisoners practise drill, weapon training and section training and a fearsome armoury of model weapons – and some more lethal weapons – ammunition, training manuals, and so on, have been seized. I heard it said by a company officer from the battalion responsible for looking after Crumlin Gaol that inside the gaol was a formed body of men actually training for war.
>
> Hansard, HC (series 5) vol. 855, cols 275–392 (17 Apr. 1973)

After the failure of the talks in July 1972, the British government, in the absence of a devolved administration, was determined to pursue a purely political solution to the northern Irish question. In the early autumn of 1972 attempts were being made to encourage the constitutional parties – including the moderate and nationalist SDLP – to agree a way forward for a settlement. At the end of October the government published a discussion document entitled, quite unimaginatively, *The Future of Northern Ireland*. This paper reiterated Britain's desire to preserve the Union for as long as a majority of citizens in Northern Ireland wished it to remain. To this end, a referendum on the existence of the border – the 'Border Poll' – was scheduled to take place on 8 March 1973. The outcome of this exercise was, given the unionist majority in the six counties, a foregone conclusion. That being the case, nationalist or republican aspirations for Irish unity that might be reflected in the vote were bound to be ignored. In addition, the government's paper suggested that some form of assembly could be established to replace Stormont and that a very limited 'Irish' dimension, involving the Dublin government, could be explored. It was evident that the British government had had its proverbial fingers burnt by its initial contact with the Provisional IRA. It now seemed determined to overlook the paramilitaries and seek a solution with the mainstream parties. In the face of the relentless violence, it was the political equivalent of a circus high-wire act.

Within the space of six months the IRA had been sidelined. In effect, it had gone from face-to-face talks with the British government to being ignored. Both sides had dug in during the interim period and it was predictable that the IRA would reassert its strength: and, in broadening its campaign, London became the prime location for a strategic attack. As Richard English notes:

> There was, from the IRA's perspective, certain logic in taking their war to England as they did in the 1970s. Attacks in England gained far more publicity than tended to be the case with actions in Ireland. British bombs were intended to put pressure on London, via popular British opinion, to accede to republican demands. In a sense, this fits a wider pattern already identified, whereby British state action intended to deal with subversion in fact backfires and generates propaganda own-goals.

> English, *Armed Struggle*, p. 170

There had, of course, been historical precedents for such a step. In 1939, the IRA's England Campaign had begun with a series of low-level attacks. In late August that year a bomb planted on a bicycle in Coventry exploded and killed five innocent bystanders in the process. The revulsion at this attack effectively ended the

IRA campaign and the anti-Irish feeling in Coventry, and across the English Midlands, rose to unprecedented levels. Thirty-three years later, though, it seemed that the lessons of the Coventry debacle had been lost on some within the republican movement. In February 1972, in what was supposed to be direct retaliation for Bloody Sunday, the Official IRA exploded a bomb at the headquarters of the Parachute Regiment in Aldershot. It was a tragic and unmitigated disaster as the massive bomb destroyed the officers' mess, killing five women cleaners, a gardener and a Catholic chaplain in the process. The outcry was immediate. Brigadier Rowley Manns, acting General Officer Commanding of South-East district, said at a press conference: 'whatever part, or faction of the IRA, claims this battle honour, it is completely negated, is it not, this war as they call it, that has been waged against a chaplain and innocent women?' Indeed, such was the outcry at the attack that within the Official IRA a debate on the futility of violence began, which would lead to the calling of the open-ended ceasefire at the end of May 1972.

By February 1973 the initial media interest in the Northern Ireland situation had inevitably waned, and it seemed to the Provisional IRA that bringing the campaign to England would reignite wider interest in the conflict. On 8 March they launched their London offensive when a team of eleven recruits, including Marion and Dolours Price, Hugh Feeney and future prominent Sinn Féin member, Gerry Kelly, were involved in a bombing attack on central London. Given that the Whitelaw-inspired Border Poll was taking place in Northern Ireland on the day of the attack, the symbolism was obvious: regardless of the outcome of the poll, the IRA was still at war with Britain. Four bombs were transported for the operation from Belfast to Dublin, then onwards to Liverpool and London. Dolours Price, who was the leader of the group, flew in to London and met up with Hugh Feeney and her sister Marion at the Pimlico Hotel on the night before the attacks to coordinate the operation. The following day, two bombs exploded – one at the Old Bailey and the other at the Ministry of Agriculture – while two others were defused. In all,

180 people were injured, while a sixty-year old man, Frederick Milton, who was employed as a caretaker at Hillgate House beside the Old Bailey, died in the attack. A meeting between the Prime Minister, the Home Secretary and various high-ranking security officials was immediately convened and demands were made that the 'the strictest possible controls' be placed on the entry of Irish people to Britain. *The Daily Mirror* was defiant in its editorial on 9 March: 'If the IRA – or anybody else – imagine that loosing terror on London will get them anywhere, they are wrong. Bloody wrong. Just as Hitler discovered, the British people turn very stubborn when attacked.'

In reality, given that the Border Poll referendum was being held that day, the British authorities had been expecting some form of IRA attack; but the ferocity and extent of what had taken place shocked everyone. As Dolours Price was to comment, the purpose of the attacks on 8 March was to deliver a 'short, sharp, shock' to the British Establishment. Soon a massive follow-up operation was under way and ten of the eleven members of the IRA unit were arrested in a swoop at Heathrow Airport. In fact, such was the intelligence of the police, there had been detectives monitoring the Irish check-in desks in the airport from early morning on the day of the attacks. The ten people arrested and charged, who had an average age of twenty-one, were Roisin McNearney, Billy McLarnon, Robert Walsh, Gerry Kelly, Martin Brady, Billy Armstrong, Hugh Feeney, Paul Holmes and sisters Dolours and Marion Price. Dubbed the 'Belfast Ten', their ensuing court case became one of the most high-profile legal events of the 1970s. Each day throughout the ten-week trial, the strictest security was implemented at Winchester Crown Court as the evidence unfolded of the plot to bomb London. On 15 November the verdicts were handed down to the defendants who were surrounded by at least forty police and prison officers in a courtroom that was bolted shut. The first sentence, however, was a not-guilty verdict on eighteen-year-old Roisin McNearney from Belfast, who is believed to have helped the police identify the other conspirators. As she left the dock in tears, the other defendants hummed the 'Dead March (from Saul)', while one prisoner tossed a coin in her direction and told her 'take your blood money'. She was taken into police protection and given a new identity. Another defendant, William McLarnon, had admitted his part in the attacks on the first day of the trial and was given fifteen years' imprisonment, while the other eight conspirators all received life sentences. The prisoners left the dock in a defiant mood, giving clenched-fist salutes to their relatives. In Dublin the severity of the sentences was noted by the IRA, which commented in a statement, 'In due course retribution will be exacted from the people who exacted such callous punishment on Belfast youth.'

Special category status was not extended to the prisoners and they were dispersed to prisons throughout England. More importantly, their transfer to Northern Ireland was deemed inappropriate – and, with that, the scene was set for a prolonged and bitter hunger strike that would capture world headlines. The crux of the matter – again – was the British government's desire to label IRA members common criminals. The will of the prisoners to fight for political status through fasting was matched by the government's determination to remain steadfast. A decision had been made at the very highest level to face down the IRA within the prisons. In late November force-feeding was introduced to combat the hunger strike. By 5 December four of the eight fasting IRA prisoners had stopped their protest, leaving just the Price sisters, Gerry Kelly and Hugh Feeney to continue the protest.

It is clear now that the publicity surrounding the republican hunger strike of late 1973 and 1974 was dominated by the fast of the Price sisters. What they endured was indeed shocking, but for Gerry Kelly and Hugh Feeney the experience of isolation, hunger and force-feeding was equally as horrific, if not worse. The British government, and the prison authorities, seemed determined to defeat the hunger strikers through force-feeding. The authorities would ensure that the loss of face involved in granting special category status to Billy McKee and his fellow hunger strikers in 1972 did not repeat itself. The decision to force-feed was made almost as the hunger strike began. Despite the public's surprise that the prisoners were being force-fed, the practice was still widely used in prisons in England and Wales. Indeed a total of twenty-five prisoners had been subjected to force-feeding during 1973, on the grounds that it was 'essential in order to prevent irreparable damage to a prisoner's health'. Why, in 1973, the British government thought it sensible to force-feed such high-profile prisoners – a situation that could potentially end in a public relations disaster – is a conundrum in itself. The answer lies in the fact that the authorities felt they could 'break' the will of the prisoners to see their protest through to the death. Inevitably, the process became a daily battle of wills between the prisoners and the authorities. Quite simply, the aim was to force a vitamin-rich solution containing glucose (usually dissolved in the nutritional supplement Complan) into a prisoner's stomach using a rubber tube. On paper it seems a straightforward operation; that is, of course, if the prisoner cooperates. Advocates of the practice believed that, if force-feeding was administered successfully, it was possible to provide a prisoner with 1,700 calories a day, enough to stave off starvation. The logic behind this theory was that a prisoner would tire of the process before the authorities. As Gerry Kelly, who was force-fed in Wormwood Scrubs, recalled:

> We had decided beforehand that if sentenced that we would ask for a transfer and if this was not granted then we would go on hunger strike to the death. We did not see ourselves as common criminals and we definitely had the determination to follow it through. A hunger strike though is an action of last resort. It is a highly personalised and public statement for an individual to embark on a fast against the might of the British State. It is also a very lonely form of protest. It becomes a physical and psychological battle and I was determined to resist all attempts to force

feed me. They certainly decided from an early stage that they would force-feed me and the rest of the prisoners. It was, I feel, a political decision in the Home Office to embark on this policy.

We had been aware of the history of force-feeding, especially the case of Thomas Ashe. Each day, the food was left in the cell and at some point the governor would come to check on me. He obviously knew of the Ashe case and would wind me up about the whole force-feeding procedure. As I was young he felt that I was, therefore, breakable. On the process itself the medical staff would come in and, basically, giving me a half-hour warning that they intended to force-feed me. I was naked in the cell so I tried to barricade myself inside, waiting on them to arrive. They eventually burst through the door but I was determined and I fought back with all my might. They held me down and the governor came in and I believe that he was shocked that the process was so violent, and given my resistance. The wardens then pinned my arms and legs down and forced my head over the back of the bed, so they could somehow get me in such a position so as the feeding could be attempted. I just clenched my teeth tight in resistance and they tried to force my mouth open by leaning on my chin and prising my lips apart, but I was not going to open my mouth without a fight. The next thing they produced was an instrument that looked like a big pair of forceps and they rubbed these up and down my gums until, eventually, I gasped and they then jammed the forceps into my mouth while another warden forced a wooden bit into my mouth. This 'bit' had three different sized holes in it and into one they put a rubber tube that was lubricated with liquid paraffin. I can still recall vividly the horrible sensation as it was being forced down my throat. Once they were content that the tube was in my stomach they started to pour down the mixture.

Author interview with Gerry Kelly, 5 August 2010

While Kelly and Feeney were enduring this treatment (Kelly was force-fed a total of 170 times during his 205-day fast) the plight of the Price sisters captured world headlines. Dubbed the 'Vereremos Sisters' (from the Spanish word meaning 'we shall overcome'), their high profile in the early 1970s was perhaps in keeping with the age. It was an era throughout Europe when feminism was in vogue; and a time of left-wing, anti-imperialist protest into which the sisters blended perfectly. Both girls were young, attractive, well-educated and fitted none of the accepted stereotypes associated with pre-conceived notions of a guerrilla army. Both had become involved in politics in the late 1960s when the Civil Rights movement captured the imagination and politicised many young nationalists. They were also the daughters of the veteran republican Albert Price who, along with twenty other internees, had tunnelled his way out of Derry Prison in 1943. Ideologically, their credentials were impeccable. When Gerry Adams was released from Long Kesh in June 1972, in advance of the talks with the British government, he was greeted outside by the Price sisters. In fact, it was revealed during her trial that Dolours Price had travelled to Europe to give lectures from a republican perspective on the political turmoil in Northern Ireland. Marion and Dolours Price were the first female Irish republican prisoners to undergo force-feeding and this, in itself, placed them in the media spotlight. Most notably, however, the fact that they were in Brixton Prison, where Terence MacSwiney had died in 1920, was a historic irony not lost on the Irish people. As Gerry Kelly recalled, the prominence of the sisters during the fast was both a positive and a negative factor: 'the Price sisters, no doubt, caught the public imagination and that was an advantage. They were young, photogenic students and in my view the British used this fact to isolate them from the other hunger strikers.'

The Price sisters themselves seemed quite happy to embrace the almost mythical position that they were assuming within republicanism. In a letter to her mother, Marion Price wrote of her plight: 'Sometimes we can achieve more by death than we could ever hope by living. We've dedicated our lives to a cause and it's supremely more important than any one individual's life' (*Time*, 17 June 1974). They became the subject of songs and poetry throughout their ordeal, and that also tended to elevate them to 'living legend' status. One such example was the song 'Bring them Home', containing the lyrics:

> T'was the love of dear old Ireland
> Brought them to a prison hell.
> But the ghosts of Pearse and Connolly
> Filled their lonely prison cell.
>
> So I pray you men of Ireland
> Don't betray our daughters true.
> Proudly stand beside our heroes
> Lest they die for me and you.

Another example of this was a poem by IRA prisoner Sean Murphy, which was penned on Christmas Day 1973:

> I knew them when as girls at school,
> They welcomed me as a friend.
> I watched them come to womanhood,
> Watched as they cast aside the joys of youth,
> And set out on the bitter path that challenged English rule.

The plight of the Price sisters prompted some in the Belfast IRA to fraught measures to force the British government to give in to their demands. On the evening of 27 December 1973 an IRA gang entered the home of German industrialist Thomas Niedermayer on the outskirts of west Belfast and took him captive. The original plan had been to hold Niedermayer as hostage and to barter his freedom for the transfer to Northern Ireland of the English-held prisoners. However, on the third day of his captivity, Niedermayer, who was the West German consul to Belfast, fought back against his captors and in the ensuing struggle he was killed by a blow to the head with an automatic pistol. Niedermayer's body was buried secretly in a shallow grave at Colin Glen overlooking Belfast where it was discovered by workmen in 1980.

In February 1974 a British general election was called by Prime Minister Edward Heath in an attempt to face down the trades unions. In west Belfast the election was seen as an opportunity to garner support for the plight of the hunger strikers. Accordingly, Albert Price declared his intention to run as an independent, who would campaign for an end to internment and to see his daughters and the other prisoners transferred to jails in Northern Ireland. Albert Price was, in all but name, a Sinn Féin candidate. However, he polled only 5,562 votes, while the sitting MP, Gerry Fitt, eventually retained his seat with a two-thousand majority over the Democratic Unionist candidate, Johnny McQuade. In Westminster, the Heath government was replaced by Labour under the leadership of Harold Wilson. The Northern Ireland portfolio transferred from William Whitelaw to Merlyn Rees but outwardly the stance of the government remained the same.

As the fasting and force-feeding continued, on 31 March a second hunger strike was begun by IRA men Michael Gaughan, Paul Holmes, Hugh Feeney and Frank Stagg in Parkhurst Prison on the Isle of Wight. In December 1971 Michael Gaughan, who was born in 1949 in Mayo but had lived in England since 1966, had received a seven-year prison sentence for his part in an armed robbery of the Midland Bank in Hornsey, Greater London. On passing sentence on Gaughan and his fellow accused, Jack McElduff, James Moore and Frank Golden, the judge told the men that he 'was not concerned with the political views of any of you four, nor your political activities. I am concerned with this particular criminal offence' (*The Irish Times*, 24 December 1971). Gaughan, who had originally been involved with the Official IRA, was imprisoned in Wormwood Scrubs, Albany and Parkhurst Prisons but not afforded political status. The Parkhurst hunger strike opened up a secondary front in the protest and was sparked by the long periods of solitary confinement that Gaughan and Stagg endured in their quest for political status. Considering that Ian Brady, the Moors murderer, was also in Parkhurst at the time and was bracketed in the same category as the IRA prisoners, there were, with hindsight, considerable grounds for protest. On 10 April both Gaughan and Stagg were transferred to the prison hospital for observation and two weeks later, on medical advice, the authorities began force-feeding the pair.

However, the political situation in Northern Ireland soon eclipsed the hunger strikes because May would once again witness political and violent strife on the island of Ireland. During the latter part of the month Northern Ireland was to be paralysed by the mass stoppage of the Ulster Workers' Council, which sought to bring down the power-sharing Executive established by the Sunningdale Agreement in 1973. By 28 May the resolve of Harold Wilson's government to face down the loyalist action had been undermined, as Brian Faulkner resigned as Chief of the Northern Ireland Executive in protest at Merlyn Rees' refusal to meet with the leaders of the strike. It was a humiliation for Wilson's government. But more sinister events coincided with the workers' strike: two bombs exploded in Dublin and Monaghan on Saturday 17 May. A total of thirty-three people were killed in the explosions; it was perhaps one of the bloodiest outrages of the Troubles and was to be blamed on the UVF. The events had set back the political process and the future looked bleak. Meanwhile in the English prisons, the hunger strikes were about to reach their climax.

On 18 May the force-feeding of the Price sisters ended abruptly when the Home Secretary was advised that medical officers had decided that, in view of the degree of non-coop-eration the sisters had displayed during the previous few days, to continue with force-feeding would be too dangerous. The sisters were surviving on liquid alone and facing death. The government was now in a dilemma, since a violent reaction in the wake of the death of one or other of the sisters was certain. In a letter to her mother in late May, Dolours Price seemed sure that she would die. Of the British government she wrote, 'They will never live down the stigma that they let four people die on hunger strike rather than transfer them to another prison. How ridiculous they will look to the rest of the world. I am only sorry that I will not be there to see it' (*Glasgow Herald*, 31 May 1974). It is interesting to note that the Price sisters seemed to be oblivious to the fact that a separate republican fast was in progress and also reaching a critical juncture. Indeed, although the situation of the Price sisters, Kelly and Feeney was precarious as June began, it was the unexpected death of Michael Gaughan on 3 June that sent shock waves across Britain and Ireland. Despite having been force-fed seventeen times during his fast – the last on Sunday 2 June – he died on the sixty-fourth day of his strike. In his final hours it was reported that fellow hunger striker Frank Stagg had visited Gaughan and asked him to accept medical intervention. He refused and died primarily of pneumonia at 7.25 p.m. on the evening of 3 June. He was twenty-four years old and weighed less than six stone. His final message to his fellow-prisoners is said to have read:

> I die proudly for my country and in the hope that my death will be sufficient to obtain the demands of my comrades. Let there be no bitterness on my behalf but a determination to achieve a New Ireland for which I gladly die. My loyalty and confidence is to the IRA and let those of you who are left carry on the work and finish the fight.

The death of Michael Gaughan was met with widespread condemnation throughout Ireland and the blame was placed squarely on the British government. Sinn Féin President, Ruairí Ó Brádaigh, described the death as 'callous, brutal and premeditated murder'. Commenting that the previous week the British had 'capitulated' in the face of the Ulster Workers' Council strike, Ó Brádaigh pointed out that 'they [the British government] refused to grant a simple transfer for these strikers to Irish jails'. Frank Maguire, the former MP for Fermanagh and South Tyrone, was forthright and described the British government as 'murderers in the eyes of the world'. John Gaughan, a brother of Michael, described seeing his brother who looked 'like something out of Belsen' and, given his anger, opted wisely not to pass comment on the family's opinion of British Home Secretary, Roy Jenkins. In Dublin the Minister for Justice, Patrick Cooney, was not so sympathetic and rounded on the IRA, claiming that 'they wanted a martyr and this unfortunate man was picked'. The minister made a further attack on the Provisionals, adding that 'they involved him in crime in England and then involved him in the hunger strike . . . the same people who professed sorrow at his death had it within their power to keep him alive' (all quotations from the *Irish Independent*, 4 June 1974).

An inquest into Gaughan's death found that the cause of death had been pneumonia due to malnutrition. However, the Gaughan family were not satisfied and requested a second inquest as rumours circulated that Gaughan's lung had been punctured during force-feeding and that this had led to his death. Speaking at the inquest, prison doctor Dr Brian Cooper, who was present at the time of death, said of Gaughan that he was 'a very brave man' and added that 'his political motives overcame his natural fear of death'. Dr Cooper, though, showed little sympathy when he described Gaughan as a 'rational man' who knew well what the consequence of his hunger strike would be.

In keeping with republican tradition, the National Graves Association, who oversaw the burial of IRA members, indicated that they would be providing a coffin for Gaughan and that the very tricolour that had been draped over Terence MacSwiney's coffin would be used at the funeral. On 7 June the body of Michael Gaughan, flanked by eight men in berets and dark glasses, arrived at the Sacred Heart Church in Kilburn in North London. A crowd of almost 3,000 observed the procession, while inside the church almost 1,000 were in attendance to hear Mass, which was said in both Irish and English. Afterwards the coffin was opened and thousands filed past in silent tribute. The following day further controversy ensued when a cousin of Gaughan's, Father Michael Connolly, who was the parish priest of St Joseph's Church in Wolverhampton, addressed the crowds as the coffin emerged from the church. Connolly was no stranger to controversy and had been given a 'final warning' two years previously by the Archbishop of Birmingham, George Dwyer, for his outspoken views on Ireland: on the previous occasion in 1972 he had urged the Irish government to 'hand over guns which are going rusty to the freedom fighters in Northern Ireland'. When he addressed the crowd in Kilburn, he said of Gaughan's death that 'the price of freedom has been very high' and Irishmen were 'always prepared to pay that price to the full'. Whilst this remark, especially within the highly emotional context of a funeral, could be construed as innocuous enough, the Archbishop of Birmingham reacted immediately and suspended Connolly from his position. The Archbishop stated that it was Connolly's 'intemperate utterance on Irish affairs which can only foment bitterness and division' that had made him act (all quotations from *Irish Independent*, 12 June 1974).

Gaughan's body was flown from Heathrow Airport to Dublin on Saturday 8 June. The IRA provided a guard of honour for his body and it lay overnight in Adam and Eve's Franciscan church by Merchants' Quay. The funeral was to be a publicity coup for the IRA, as many thousands turned out the following morning to witness the journey of the coffin across Ireland. Gaughan's body was taken onwards to St Muredach's Cathedral, Ballina, and he was buried later in Leigue Cemetery in the republican plot. In his homily, local curate, Father Michael Keane, made an impassioned plea for peace and unity. Outside the cathedral, before the cortège made its way to the cemetery, three volleys of shots were fired over the tricolour-draped coffin. Among the mourners were prominent members of IRA leadership, including Dáithí Ó Conaill, but the Gardaí made no attempt to arrest him. The affair was an embarrassment to the Cosgrave government. An attempt to stop similar scenes in February 1976 would result in a battle of wills between the IRA and the Irish government over the remains of Frank Stagg.

Negotiations around the time of Michael Gaughan's funeral would soon bring an end to the fasts of the remaining hunger strikers. In the wake of the government's failure to face down the Ulster Workers' Council strike, Roy Jenkins released, on 1

June, a statement concerning the Price sisters that seemed to offer a chance of progress. Jenkins commented that he would be concerned if the lives of the sisters were 'needlessly lost'. However, he continued by saying that the government 'objected to giving a promise under duress or threats of violence'. He added that it was 'reasonable' that the sisters would serve 'the bulk' of their sentence 'nearer their home', but that he could not act 'at present', no matter 'how harrowing the consequences' (*Sunday Times*, 2 June 1974). It was obvious that the Home Secretary was suggesting that if the hunger strike was suspended – and with it the associated threat of IRA retribution – then the issues at hand could be addressed. Apart from being a blow to the ongoing negotiations, the death of Michael Gaughan two days after the Home Secretary's statement on the Price sisters' case gave added impetus to the search for a solution; unfortunately, to avoid loss of face, there could be no instant or absolute answer. On 5 June Jenkins received a deputation on behalf of the sisters. The deputation consisted of the left-wing Labour peer, Fenner Brockway, Jock Stallard MP and Paddy Devlin of the SDLP. While reiterating that there could be no negotiation with the Price sisters, Jenkins outlined a theoretical timescale for their transfer, which he said could be considered as long as 'there was no great outbreak of violence'. With Frank Stagg now close to death on the Isle of Wight, the sisters received a visit from Lord Brockway, who was acting as an unofficial go-between. Brockway impressed upon the sisters his belief that they would be granted a transfer to Armagh Prison in the near future. Further discussions took place within the Price family and on 7 June, as Mass was being said for Michael Gaughan in Kilburn, news broke that the women had ended their fast. It was reported that the sisters were allowed by the Home Office to telephone both Kelly and Feeney and, accordingly, after 205 days all the fasts were over. In Parkhurst Prison Frank Stagg ended his fast in the belief that he also would be given a transfer in due course. He was wrong.

Following the prolonged hunger strikes the government agreed, in July 1974, that the practice of force-feeding would end. It seemed that the case of the Price sisters had forced the hand of the government because the international outcry had caused embarrassment. On 23 May, five days after the authorities had stopped force-feeding the Price sisters, Roy Jenkins made a statement in the House of Commons on their welfare and was asked the following question by the Labour MP Renee Short:

> May I ask my Rt Hon. Friend, as a reforming and compassionate Home Secretary, whether he does not think that forced feeding should now be banished completely from our penal system? Is he aware that over 50 years ago we were force feeding suffragettes and that it is astonishing that this process still takes place in our prisons? Will he therefore, irrespective of pressure in this particular case, consider whether he should decide that since this is a distasteful procedure – distasteful for prisoners and for doctors and prison officials who have to administer it – it should be banished from British prisons?

> Hansard, HC (series 5) vol. 874, cols 599–602 (23 May 1974)

Accordingly, Jenkins agreed to look into the alternatives to force-feeding and report back to the House of Commons, which he did on 17 July. The crux of the problem, from the point of view of medical ethics, was that it was deemed unfair to ask a doctor to force-feed a prisoner who was resisting violently. The Home Secretary clarified the position of a doctor faced with a hunger-striking prisoner, indicating that he or she was, in effect, only answerable to their professional conscience and to their duty at common law. In future, he said, a doctor would not be required as a matter of prison practice to feed a prisoner artificially against the prisoner's will. The Home Secretary then outlined the new procedure that was to be followed:

> On 23rd May, I said that I would review the position regarding compulsory feeding and the traditional view that a prison medical officer would be neglecting his duty if he were not prepared to feed artificially a prisoner

on hunger strike, if necessary against his will, in order to preserve his health and life. Accordingly, the future practice should, in my view, be that if a prisoner persists in refusing to accept any form of nourishment, the medical officer should first satisfy himself that the prisoner's capacity for rational judgment is unimpaired by illness, mental or physical. If the medical officer is so satisfied, he should seek confirmation of his opinion from an outside consultant. If the consultant confirms the opinion of the prison medical officer, the prisoner should be told that he will continue to receive medical supervision and advice and that food will be made available to him. He should be informed that he will be removed to the prison hospital if and when this is considered appropriate. But it should be made clear to him that there is no rule of prison practice which requires the prison medical officer to resort to artificial feeding, whether by tube or intravenously. Finally, he should be plainly and categorically warned that the consequent and inevitable deterioration in his health may be allowed to continue without medical intervention, unless he specifically requests it.

Hansard, HC (series 5) vol. 877, cols 451–5 (17 Jul. 1974)

The bottom line was that if a doctor was convinced that the prisoner refusing food was of sound mind, then there would be no attempt at force-feeding. The statement set out the position that the authorities would adopt when faced with future hunger strikes and clarified the moral obligations of the prison officials. Responsibility was now firmly in the hands of future hunger strikers. There would be no intervention and any future fasts would be construed by the government as suicide.

None of the prisoners who ended their fasts in early June would be granted a transfer to Northern Ireland during 1974. The security situation in England had worsened seriously with the Birmingham pub bomb in November, which killed twenty-one people, impacting on the Home Secretary's ability to act compassionately. In February 1975 Jenkins refused to grant the Price sisters compassionate parole to attend their mother's funeral in Belfast. However, on 18 March both Marion and Dolours Price were transferred to Armagh Prison. The Home Secretary said that he had taken the decision 'in full consultation' with his counterpart in Northern Ireland, Merlyn Rees. Unionists were incensed, and South Belfast MP Robert Bradford said that the transfer of the sisters was like 'putting a python in a paper bag'. In April both Gerry Kelly and Hugh Feeney were transferred back to Northern Ireland. Frank Stagg, as a citizen of the Irish Republic, was denied a transfer back to Northern Ireland.

On 30 April 1980 Marion Price was released from Armagh women's prison on humanitarian grounds. She had been suffering from anorexia nervosa and was granted the Royal Prerogative of Mercy in an attempt to save her life. On 22 April 1981, with Bobby Sands entering the fifty-third day of his fast, the British government released Dolours Price, again because she was suffering from anorexia. At the time, unionists felt that the move was a signal to the IRA that the government was prepared to address the hunger strikers' demands. Medical advice had indicated that Dolours Price, like her sister, would most likely die if she remained in prison.

Michael Gaughan was remembered in a song penned by the Belfast songwriter Seamus Robinson. Entitled 'The Ballad of Michael Gaughan' (or, more commonly, 'Take me home to Mayo') it has become a republican standard:

> My name is Michael Gaughan, from Ballina I came.
> I saw my people suffering and swore to break their chains.
> I raised the flag in England, prepared to fight or die.
> Far away from Mayo beneath an Irish sky.
>
> Take me home to Mayo across the Irish Sea,
> Home to dear old Mayo where once I roamed so free.
> Take me home to Mayo there let my body lie,
> Home at last in Mayo beneath an Irish sky.

My body cold and hungry, in Parkhurst Gaol I lie;
For loving of my country, on hunger strike I die.
I have just one last longing, I pray you'll not deny
Bury me in Mayo, beneath an Irish sky.

Chapter 9

Frank Stagg: Death and Humiliation

'It was not Mr Stagg's wish that he should die; it was his wish that his request be met.'

Michael Sachs, Stagg family solicitor

With the transfer of the Price sisters, Hugh Feeney and Gerry Kelly back to Northern Ireland, a precedent had been set that enabled the British government to transfer republican prisoners to Northern Ireland. However Frank Stagg (a citizen of the Irish Republic), who had almost died while fasting in June 1974, was not to be afforded the same treatment. In all, Frank Stagg partook in four hunger strikes. At the time of his death in February 1976, the chain of events surrounding the burial of his body caused anguish and revulsion. The dispute within the Stagg family and between the republican movement and the Irish government over who had the right to oversee the burial of his body was deep and bitter. It was a sad chapter that detracted from the ordeal that Frank Stagg had endured. However, his apparent dying wish – to be buried beside Michael Gaughan – would become a reality.

Frank Stagg was the seventh of thirteen children born in Hollymount, a small village between Claremorris and Ballinrobe

in County Mayo, in 1941. He was educated in the Newbrook
Primary School and later at the Ballinrobe Christian Brothers'
Secondary School. The economic conditions in the Ireland of
the late 1950s and early 1960s forced Stagg to travel to Britain,
where initially he found work as a bus conductor and later as a bus
driver. In England he also married Bridget Armstrong, a fellow
County Mayo native. His republican sympathies drew him into
politics and in the aftermath of Bloody Sunday he joined Sinn
Féin in Coventry and soon was an active member of the IRA. In
April 1973 police in England and Scotland mounted a concerted
offensive on IRA cells operating in major cities. In the Midlands
seven men were arrested and charged with planning a major
arson campaign in the Coventry area. Among the seven were
Frank Stagg and Fr Patrick Fell, who at the time was a curate
at All Souls Church in Coventry. Father Fell was an enigma
in IRA circles. Born in England in 1940, he had converted to
Catholicism and joined the priesthood, becoming involved in
IRA activity. Despite the lack of serious incriminating evidence,
all seven men were tried in November 1973 at Birmingham
Crown Court. At the end of the trial Fell and Stagg, who were
described as the unit's commanding officers, were given ten- and
twelve-year sentences respectively. Thomas Rush was sentenced
to seven years and Tony Lynch was given ten years. Despite
the relatively low level of the offence under which Stagg was
imprisoned, his absolute and total ideological commitment to
the cause of the republican movement was displayed throughout
his incarceration.

Initially, Frank Stagg was sent to Albany Prison on the
Isle of Wight and refused to cooperate with the authorities
because he was being treated as a 'common criminal' and was
attempting to gain transfer to a prison in Northern Ireland. As
a result he spent most of his time in solitary confinement, a
punishment that seemed only to harden Stagg's resolve. In April
1974 Stagg joined the hunger strike led by the Price sisters,
Gerry Kelly and Hugh Feeney. He was to spend sixty-eight
days on the fast before the death of Michael Gaughan, with

whom Stagg had shared a cell in Parkhurst, brought an end
to the hunger strike. As that strike ended, Stagg's plight was
largely overlooked by the authorities, although doctors battled
to save his life in the aftermath of the trauma his body had
suffered. Frank Stagg's recovery from this initial hunger strike
was to be hindered because his body rejected food and his jaw
had been dislocated by less than sympathetic attempts at force-
feeding. Less than two weeks after the end of his fast, Stagg's
eldest brother, Joseph, reported that Frank would begin refusing
food again if he was not transferred from the Isle of Wight.
According to the British Government, the problem in granting
this transfer was that Stagg was a citizen of the Irish Republic
and there was no reason to transfer him to Northern Ireland.
It was an argument that bordered on the petty. After his second
short strike had ended, Stagg was transferred to Long Lartin
Prison and subjected to solitary confinement for refusing to
do prison work. Defiantly, he began a further hunger strike in
protest against the strip-searching of himself and his visitors.
After twenty-six days the governor of the prison agreed to stop
the practice and Stagg's hunger strike ended. Nevertheless, Frank
Stagg's health had suffered and he was now bedridden for long
periods due to an acute kidney complaint. He was transferred
again, to Wakefied Prison in Leeds and, on 15 December 1975,
Stagg began what would be his last hunger strike. The catalyst
for the fast came when a further request for repatriation was
turned down by the then Home Secretary, Roy Jenkins, who
had overseen a plethora of republican hunger strikes since 1974.
In keeping with the policy of the time, Stagg was advised by the
prison doctor, Geoffrey Pollitt, that force-feeding would not be
administered during the strike: Stagg, however, was fully aware
of the consequences of his actions. Besides accepting pain relief
on a number of occasions, Frank Stagg's hunger strike continued
and on 22 January 1976 he was placed on the 'dangerously ill'
list in the prison hospital. Asked by Dr Pollitt if he would accept
any medical intervention in the event that he lapsed into a
coma, Stagg insisted that no steps should be taken to revive him.

Outside the prison a vigorous campaign was being orchestrated in his support.

On 5 February a rally in the Falls Road area of Belfast in support of Frank Stagg was addressed by Sinn Féin vice-president, Máire Drumm. In what was a blunt speech, Drumm drew on all the iconic imagery possible as she predicted mayhem in the aftermath of Stagg's death. She stated that Stagg's hunger strike had been inspired by 'the greatest of them all, great Christ, who died for us on Calvary'. Having touched on the religious aspect of his demise, Drumm added that 'Frank Stagg's death will be revenged as all our martyrs' deaths have been by the soldiers of Óglaigh na hÉireann [IRA].' She finished on a crescendo that left no room for confusion: 'If they send Frank Stagg home in a coffin I would expect the fighting men of Crossmaglen would send the SAS home in boxes. If Frank Stagg lives or dies the fight goes on. England is the hangman of the world, [Roy] Jenkins is her undertaker aided and abetted by the renegades of Ireland' (McKittrick, Kelters, Feeny & Thornton, *Lost Lives*, p. 626).

The sabre-rattling of Máire Drumm drew criticism from a wide audience. In Coventry Frank Stagg's sister, Veronica Phillips, summed up the plight of the Irish in England at the time when she said 'we have to live here and a lot of Irish people, especially in Coventry, are really frightened by this kind of talk.' In the House of Commons, the Unionist MP William Ross raised the content of the speech and Drumm's remarks were, in turn, investigated by the Director of Public Prosecutions. Six weeks after her speech three British soldiers lost their lives in a landmine attack in Belleeks, County Armagh. Their deaths prompted the then Secretary of State, Merlyn Rees, to single out Drumm for criticism. In comparing her to the character Madame Defarge from Dickens' *A Tale of Two Cities*, Rees said 'she is rather like the woman at the guillotine during the French Revolution – she is knitting and enjoying what is going on.' Máire Drumm was shot dead by loyalist paramilitaries in Belfast's Mater Hospital on 28 October 1976.

Given the megaphone diplomacy that was ongoing as Frank

Stagg's hunger strike progressed, it was inevitable that there would be division created within his family. By the fifty-third day of his fast doctors advised his relatives that his organs were closing down and that the family had one last chance to save his life. In keeping with Stagg's wishes, no medical intervention was sought. Prior to his death Stagg also suffered the public indignity of not being permitted to hear Mass within his prison cell. This had been determined by the Auxiliary Bishop of Leeds, Father Gerald Moverley, who turned down the request on the grounds that the prisoner had 'no pastoral necessity' to hear Mass. Ironically, it was discovered that a predecessor of Moverley's, Cardinal John Heenan, had paid a special visit to Wakefield Prison in the 1950s to see IRA leader Cathal Goulding, who was serving time for his part in the abortive republican arms raid in England (reported in the *Sunday Independent*, 8 February 1976). With the last rites administered to Stagg, Home Secretary Roy Jenkins offered his own slice of compassion, reiterating that he would let the hunger striker die rather than transfer him to a jail in Northern Ireland. Jenkins justified his cold logic with a simplistic argument: 'I cannot see any basis on which somebody not born in Northern Ireland, without his family in Northern Ireland, who committed a crime in this country should go to Northern Ireland.' Despite the fact that a precedent had been set in transferring a loyalist, Belfast-born prisoner, Albert 'Ginger' Baker, from a jail in Belfast to England, Stagg's transfer was refused. However, it would later come into the public domain – not least through his own admission – that Baker, a British Army deserter, had worked for British Intelligence and had been given carte blanche by that organisation to oversee a sectarian murder campaign in Belfast during 1972 and 1973.

Frank Stagg died on the sixty-second day of his hunger strike on 12 February 1976. His death was greeted with widespread violence across Northern Ireland. Rioting and gun battles erupted in Belfast, Derry and Newry as the tensions that had been building over the previous weeks erupted on the streets. In Belfast Sinn Féin organiser Seamus Loughran told the media that 'Frank Stagg's death will not go unavenged', because, as he put it, there was a 'debt of honour beholding the whole republican movement to repay the death of Frank Stagg'. Máire Drumm, in dramatic style, said that 'if I could change places with someone, I would change it with Frank Stagg in his shroud', adding that it was 'a wonderful thing for someone to be able to give their life for their country.' In Dublin British-owned shops were attacked and the foyer of the Shelbourne Hotel, close to Leinster House, was reduced to rubble in a bomb attack. Meanwhile, in London, the city braced itself for a backlash and on Friday 13 February a 20-pound briefcase bomb was diffused on the main concourse of Oxford Circus underground station. The consequences had this bomb exploded were summed up by the actor Michael Palin who noted in his diary that 'it could have been the bloodiest explosion yet'.

Prior to his death Frank Stagg had requested through his solicitor that his body be taken to Dublin and onwards through the midlands of Ireland to his home town of Hollymount, County Mayo. After Mass his body would travel to Ballina where he would be buried beside Michael Gaughan. At the inquest the jury determined that he had killed himself. Medical evidence provided gave the actual cause of death as cardiac atrophy due to malnutrition. Representing the Stagg family, Manchester solicitor Michael Sachs pointed out that 'It was not Mr Stagg's wish that he should die; it was his wish that his request be met.' After the Coroner of Wakefield had finished his deliberations, the body of Frank Stagg was placed in the care of Sinn Féin's Derek Highstead, who was a party organiser in England – but further obstacles waited.

At Leeds Airport British Airways staff had banned the handling of IRA remains after the Birmingham bombings of November 1974. In Ireland, on the other hand, the government and the republican movement were on a collision course over the funeral arrangements. There was a united front across Irish politics, voiced by opposition leader Jack Lynch when he blamed the IRA for Stagg's death. At the Fianna Fáil Ard Fheis

Lynch accused the IRA of being 'only too willing to sacrifice
the lives of their young insubordinates', saying that 'they [the
IRA leaders] disgrace the name of Ireland'. Caught between
the two opposing forces was the hunger striker's widow, Bridget
Stagg, who was clearly reluctant to allow her husband's death
to become an occasion for political point-scoring. The kind
of funeral that she considered appropriate and dignified was
at odds with what the IRA desired and, as Garret FitzGerald,
Minister for Foreign Affairs at the time of the crisis, recalled, the
situation had been complicated further by the unofficial stance
of the British:

> [Mrs Stagg] was threatened by the IRA with being shot
> through the head if she pressed her view [regarding her
> husband's funeral]. We were told that the authorities in
> Britain had refused to accord her a police guard on her
> home and had entered into a deal under which it was
> agreed to ignore her rights to her husband's remains and to
> hand them to the IRA in return for an agreement that the
> IRA confine their demonstrations to our island. They [the
> IRA] proposed to parade the coffin through Dublin and
> various other towns before bringing it to Ballina, County
> Mayo, for interment.

> FitzGerald, *All in a Life*, p. 280

The British government outwardly, it seems, made contact with
the IRA to avoid paramilitary displays in Britain: if Stagg's body
was handed over to the IRA, any public demonstrations of
paramilitary strength would be saved for Irish soil. FitzGerald
was furious and contacted Jenkins to say that he would call a
press conference 'to announce that the British government was
collaborating with the IRA.' The net result of this exchange
was that the Irish government assumed control of the funeral
arrangements and expectations of a stand-off grew.

To make matters worse, the government was also to find
itself caught in the midst of a disagreement between Bridget
Stagg and the rest of Frank Stagg's family, some of whom felt

that his widow wanted to ignore his own last wishes as to the funeral arrangements. The government chose to intervene on the widow's behalf. With the prospect of an IRA show of strength that would, in all probability, have lasted a full weekend, the order was made that the plane carrying the coffin of Stagg be diverted from Dublin to Shannon Airport in County Clare. This decision, which was taken while the plane was in mid-air, caused uproar in IRA circles, with cries that the body had been 'hijacked' and 'stolen'. The decision to divert the plane that carried Stagg, whilst perceived as a crass act by republicans, also drew subtle criticism from the more conservative press. The *Connacht Sentinel* noted in its editorial of 27 February that while 'the representatives of the government of the Republic have handled some delicate situations with tact . . . it is unfortunate that they should be seen to err somewhat on this occasion.' FitzGerald contends that Mrs Stagg was prepared to permit the IRA to oversee the actual burial of her husband. However, the organisation's 'stage management' of the body's return to Dublin and beyond was not acceptable to her.

The 'official' funeral of Frank Stagg took place on Saturday 21 February in Leigue Cemetery, Ballina. As there was little dignity in death for Frank Stagg, there was certainly no dignity in his burial. The Irish government, as per the wishes of Mrs Stagg, was determined that the funeral would not become an occasion for a paramilitary display. The body of the deceased hunger striker was to be buried beside the Stagg family plot according to the instructions of his widow, rather than next to his comrade Michael Gaughan in the republican plot, as he himself had wished. The Stagg family was no doubt torn by the situation, as the agony of their grief must have been further compounded by the unseemly disagreement over the funeral arrangements. On the plane from Birmingham to Dublin Mrs Stagg sat uncomfortably within yards of the other relatives of the deceased hunger striker; on landing in Dublin, she was taken by Irish government officials and placed in a hotel.

The family was split over the government's handling of the

affair. At the graveside were his 28-year-old widow together with his brother, Emmett, his sister Veronica Philips, and a number of cousins. Frank Stagg's mother and the rest of the family boycotted the event in protest at the State's intervention. In the end, the thirty-eight mile journey of the hearse from Robeen Church – where Stagg had been baptised – to Ballina was uneventful. The town had effectively been taken over by police and soldiers in an attempt to thwart any IRA show of strength. When the almost surreal ceremony ended, it was reported that Mrs Stagg was placed under the protection of the Gardaí for her own safety. To add to the finality of the occasion, six inches of concrete were poured over the grave to frustrate any efforts by republicans to move the body. For this final act the then Minister for Justice, Patrick Cooney, would earn himself the unenviable nickname of 'Concrete Cooney'. Later, in 2008, the President of Sinn Féin, Ruaraí Ó Brádaigh, would remark ironically that the Irish government had, in effect, provided Frank Stagg with what amounted to a massive military send-off. With hindsight, he was correct in his assertion, although at the time of Stagg's funeral he had stated to the media at Dublin Airport that the government were 'body snatchers'.

The following day, the police and army returned to the cemetery to oversee a republican commemoration in honour of Stagg. From early morning a ring of steel surrounded Ballina as cars were searched. However, over 8,000 people made their way through the town to Leigue Cemetery where both Stagg and Michael Gaughan were honoured. Periodically, scuffles broke out along the route between mourners and Gardaí, and soldiers fired rubber bullets at a group of youths who had attacked them with stones. Forty yards from Frank Stagg's grave, Belfast IRA leader Joe Cahill addressed the crowd: 'I pledge that we will assemble here again in the near future when your [Frank Stagg's] body will yet lie side by side with that of fellow hunger striker Michael Gaughan in the republican plot.' In words that sounded quite clumsy, Cahill spoke to Stagg and made a promise: 'Let there be no mistake about it, we will take it [Stagg's body],

Frank, and we will leave it resting side by side with your great comrade, Michael Gaughan' (*The Irish Times*, 23 February 1976). Present at the ceremony were Mrs Mary Stagg, Frank's mother, together with most of his brothers and sisters. The Last Post was sounded amid the drone of a hovering helicopter and the crowds dispersed. It had been a weekend fraught with tension and sadness in Ballina, and it had cost the police over £250,000. To uphold the decision of Bridget Stagg, Gardaí mounted a 24-hour vigil at Frank's grave to ensure that it would not be interfered with. This costly measure lasted for six months until the vigil was lifted and a further three feet of concrete was poured onto the grave.

The bitterness created by the funeral of Frank Stagg was deep and personal. Regardless of the tension that it undoubtedly produced within the wider Stagg family, republicans and the Irish government, Stagg's interment became a depressing clash of egos over who ultimately ruled the country. In Belfast a statement purporting to come from the IRA was issued describing the Irish government as 'fiends' and stating that 'never has so much pain and humiliation been heaped on one man alive or dead in the history of humanity'. A direct threat was then made to the government for the part it had played in the funeral – it was an abject lesson in diplomacy: 'We as republicans will not forget the fiends of the Free State government for what they have done to our comrade and as republicans our debt of honour to Frank Stagg will be exacted in full from those who have so horribly maligned him in life and death. We will not forget'(*Sunday Independent*, 22 February 1976).

In the aftermath of the Stagg funeral, other individuals were caught up in the ideological battle between the government and the IRA. Sergeant Martin Hogan, a 41-year-old friend of the Stagg family, was suspended from duty after attending the Sunday commemoration for the deceased hunger striker. With the prospect of being dismissed from the force a real possibility, Hogan went to the press to talk about the 'agony' he had endured since his suspension. Stating that he had been in Ballina at the event as he had been 'a friend and neighbour of Frank Stagg when we were growing up', Hogan felt that his twenty-year career in the Garda Siochána stood in doubt. He was advised by Garda authorities that he had one month to provide an explanation as to why he had attended the funeral. After a prolonged period, and a lengthy appeal, Hogan was reinstated.

The matter of the 'hijacking' of the body of Frank Stagg, and the subsequent state-sponsored burial, remained a festering sore in the republican psyche. In essence, Stagg's last wish to be buried beside Michael Gaughan had been disregarded by his widow with the, perhaps, all too willing assistance of the government. The plot in which Frank Stagg was buried had been purchased by the Irish government and the grave had been dug by members of the Gardaí. Who would have the final say over where Frank Stagg was buried became a legal conundrum. Moreover his body was to become central to a clash of egos between the Fine Gael/Labour coalition government and the republican movement. The events surrounding the interment of Stagg in February 1976 had gone according to the wishes of the government of the time, however, the matter was not at an end. In July 1977, with Fianna Fáil, the *republican party*, now in power, a campaign was mounted to have Stagg's body exhumed and returned to his mother for burial. Galway, Roscommon and Monaghan county councils all passed notices of motion that the Minister for Justice, Gerry Collins, should agree to implement the last wishes of Stagg and ensure that his body was buried beside Gaughan. With hindsight, given the legal position of his widow, the split within the Stagg family and the fact that Stagg's last will had been made outside Ireland, the power of the Minister for Justice to intervene was negligible. It was evident that the body of Frank Stagg would be moved legally only after a prolonged, costly and divisive court case. Others, however, could and would not wait.

In the early hours of Sunday 6 November 1977 the body of Frank Stagg was exhumed from its resting place in Leigue Cemetery and reinterred in the republican plot. The last wish of

Frank Stagg to rest beside Michael Gaughan had been granted by the IRA, and Joe Cahill's promise at the commemoration event in February 1976 had been honoured. A short religious ceremony, presided over by an unnamed priest, took place as the removal of the coffin occurred. It is believed that two groups of IRA men arrived at the cemetery and one group opened a new grave in the republican plot, while the other removed Stagg's body. The grave adjoining the Stagg family plot had been purchased by Stagg's brother George in 1977 and, by digging eight feet down in this empty grave, the removal of the coffin from below its layer of concrete had been made possible. It was thought that the operation took three hours to execute and it was only at dawn the following morning that the removal of the body was discovered. Apart from the Gardaí interviewing a few local IRA sympathisers, there was nothing to suggest that the matter would induce shock or scandal amongst the local populace. It was, for many, a case of justice finally done – an inevitable end to a sad episode. Sinn Féin President, Ruairí Ó Brádaigh described the development as 'an act of simple justice', while government officials indicated that there would be no further move to relocate the body of Frank Stagg. It was cold revenge for the IRA over the National Coalition government of Liam Cosgrave.

The republican contention that the Cosgrave government acted illegally in hijacking the body of Frank Stagg in 1976 was supported by State papers released in 2010. The fact was that Stagg, in his final will, had made it clear that his funeral was to be overseen by the republican movement. Against the wishes of Stagg, most of his family and republicans, the Cosgrave government had diverted the plane carrying his body and had carried out a politically expedient burial in Ballina. Papers reveal that the Cosgrave government knew of Stagg's will and were advised to follow it but refused to do so.

Chapter 10

Beating the Terrorists?

'You turn if you want to. The lady's not for turning!'
Margaret Thatcher, October 1980

By the mid-1970s the Troubles in Northern Ireland had become engrained in everyday life and there would be no quick solution. Political progress had stalled with the collapse of the Sunningdale Agreement and the power-sharing Executive in 1974, while the worst excesses of the IRA's bomb campaign in England had caused serious consternation in government and security circles. In fact the British government was at a stalemate with the IRA. However, out of this apparent impasse, private talks between Northern Ireland Office officials and the IRA secured an unlikely truce in February 1975. The truce, to the distaste of the mainstream parties, gave quasi-recognition to the IRA and Sinn Féin in monitoring the ceasefire within republican areas, yet it also caused much confusion within the ranks of the republican movement. The fact was that certain elements within the IRA mistook the truce as a precursor to a phased British withdrawal and, as a result, placed faith in Secretary of State for Northern Ireland, Merlyn Rees, as an honest broker. In the absence of a military campaign, the British government felt that the IRA's ability to reignite its war would be diminished. In the short-term, however, the IRA witnessed progress as the British Army retreated to barracks and so-called 'on the runs' were allowed to return home unhindered. Throughout 1975 the IRA was to be drawn into internecine and bloody feuds with the Officials and a bitter sectarian battle with the loyalist paramilitaries. In November 1975 Merlyn Rees announced that he would implement the findings of the prison-related Gardiner Report and that anyone convicted of terrorist crimes committed after 1 March 1976 would not be accorded special category status. His statement of 4 November confirmed the British government's position that the IRA and the loyalist paramilitary were no more than gangsters:

> The past week illustrates some facets of the position even more sharply. There have been 74 shooting incidents, the vast majority of which were concerned with the feud between the Official and Provisional IRA. This is in addition to the five people killed and 64 injured during the week. The dead include a six-year-old child and the injured three women who were shot in the knee. Indeed, during 1975 no fewer than 168 people have been knee-capped. This compares with the figure of 127 for the whole of 1974 and 74 for 1973 . . . This is gangsterism. There is no other word for it. It can and will be dealt with by effective policing with the full support of the Army. The people responsible must be arrested and brought before the courts.
>
> Hansard, HC (series 5) vol. 899, cols 233–94 (4 Nov. 1975)

With hindsight, it seems obvious that the British government had hidden its hand during the IRA ceasefire negotiations in early 1975. Ten days prior to the calling of the open-ended ceasefire on 10 February, Merlyn Rees had presented the Commons with the findings of the committee chaired by Lord Gardiner, known as the Gardiner Report. The committee had met initially in June 1974 with a remit to consider measures for the 'preservation of civil liberties and human rights' within the context of 'terrorism and subversion in Northern Ireland'. The introduction of the report gave a clear indication that the British were intending to stay in Northern Ireland for the foreseeable future, and indeed were gearing up to take on the IRA:

> They cannot bludgeon the British out of Ireland and, as the events of November 1974 [the Birmingham and Guildford bombings] have proved, the extension of terrorism to Britain simply increases the resolution of the British. They can offer no gifts to the people of Northern Ireland by way of greater freedom, security, or prosperity which the people cannot now attain by legal and democratic means. Moreover, they command the support of only a small fraction of either the minority or the majority community in Northern Ireland.

> *Report of a Committee to Consider, in the Context of Civil*
> *Liberties and Human Rights, Measures to Deal with Terrorism*
> *in Northern Ireland (Gardiner Report) p. i*

Crucially, the report also concluded that an end to special category status was an absolute necessity for future prison policy. The report continued, 'The prison system plays a most important role in the maintenance of law and order; it is not fulfilling that role adequately at present, and certain aspects of the prison situation are considered to be appalling.' According to Gardiner, special category status was a 'serious error' and must end 'at the earliest practical opportunity'. In its place, it was suggested that the government should identify sites for a permanent prison to house 400–500 inmates and that the design of prison compounds should be of a cellular nature. The Gardiner Report was a sign that the government was prepared to advance the cause of normalisation by re-criminalising the paramilitaries.

The phasing out of special category status was part of an overall government policy that evolved at this time and came to be known as 'Ulsterisation'. The aim of this policy was to distance the British government from the Troubles by placing the Ulster Defence Regiment (UDR) – local police and soldiers – back in the front line of the conflict. In the political arena, a devolved solution would be sought between the 'moderate' faces of unionism and nationalism (in other words, the Ulster Unionist Party and the SDLP), while the megaphone diplomacy offered by Ian Paisley's brand of unionism, embodied in the Democratic Unionist Party (DUP), stood defiant but on the margins. The problem of the paramilitaries would be tackled by new tactics; in essence the gloves were off. The process was straightforward and had three facets. Firstly, the number of British troops would be scaled back to enable the RUC and the Ulster Defence Regiment (UDR) to take primacy in the fight against the paramilitaries. Secondly, the arrest, detention and interrogation of terrorist suspects in specialised detention centres would become crucial in the 'breaking' of suspects: indeed, up to 80 per cent of all convictions were subsequently based on self-incriminating statements made by prisoners, many of whom were assaulted during interrogation. Thirdly, the prison system would provide the final piece in the Ulsterisation process.

After the proposed changes to the prison system had been digested, Sinn Féin President, Ruairí Ó Brádaigh, said that 'the republican-sentenced prisoners have said that they will resist any such move'. In what would prove to be an understatement, he added that 'Mr Rees will find himself with a fight on his hands if he attempts to degrade the men of Long Kesh, Magilligan and Crumlin Road, as well as the women of Armagh Jail.' The republican prisoners smuggled a communication out of Long Kesh, which declared that 'Mr Rees is completely blind if he believes that we will sit back and accept this typical British "divide and conquer" while even one of our comrades is to denied political status.' The scene was now set for the politicisation of the prison issue, with the IRA adding that it would 'fight every inch of ground' and assuring Merlyn Rees that 'the removal of political status will not happen'.

The whole judicial process in Northern Ireland had been amended since the early 1970s to deal with the subversive threat posed by the paramilitaries. However, the IRA prisoners considered themselves in no way criminals. They felt that they were the products of a dysfunctional society that had created the circumstances in which they had been imprisoned. They were arrested and charged under specialist legislation, interrogated in specialised holding centres and tried by a single judge before a juryless 'Diplock' court. The IRA could see no logic in the government's stance, and the term 'criminal' was not going to be accepted lightly.

The man who was seen as the captain steering the course of the good ship 'Ulsterisation' policy was Secretary of State for Northern Ireland, Roy Mason. He capitalised on the work carried out by Rees with gusto and changed the situation utterly. Labelled 'Mason the Mighty Midget' on the walls of nationalist Belfast, the former Barnsley miner was to become a hated foe of republicanism, noted for his no-nonsense approach to finding a solution to the Troubles. He arrived in September 1976, having been appointed by Prime Minister James Callaghan in his first Cabinet reshuffle. He was described as 'bombastic and pugnacious, theatrically affecting the style of a paternalistic colonial governor, appearing for photo-opportunities clad in a tweed safari suit'. Gerry Fitt, on the other hand, found the Belfast vernacular more descriptive and said of Mason that he was 'an Irish-hating wee get'. He did not seek nor win friends easily; indeed Ian Paisley after one meeting was to say of Mason 'the sooner that wee Yorkshire man goes back to the pits the better for the people of Northern Ireland'.

The Northern Ireland Mason found on his arrival was suffering from its worst bout of strife since 1972. By the end of 1976, 295 people would have lost their lives, although that figure was to drop significantly in the following three years as Ulsterisation took its course. However, a constant battle was being waged in the prisons and on the streets as the campaign to restore 'political status' grew. Mason, however, was a tough and uncompromising politician who seemed utterly convinced that the government's approach would break the paramilitaries. By August 1976, with the IRA's campaign again at full tilt, the new Maze Prison still awaited its first inmate. At a rally in Belfast to commemorate the fifth anniversary of the introduction of internment, Sinn Féin Vice President Máire Drumm spoke on the proposed ending of special category status. In forthright style she told the crowd that if the British tried to criminalise the IRA, then 'Belfast would come down stone by stone, and if necessary other towns will come down, and some in England too.' In mid-September Kieran Nugent became the first prisoner to be sentenced under the new legislation and refused to wear prison clothes, thus beginning the 'blanket protest'. In turn, a propaganda battle commenced, and Nugent's plight was publicised worldwide by a reinvigorated republican media machine. Soon the numbers 'on the blanket' grew, as did the campaign on the streets, and a separate protest was begun by women in Armagh Prison.

However, stalemate was reached and in March 1978 the protest was escalated when the prisoners, who were refused permission to leave their cells dressed in blankets, introduced the no-wash campaign. This was the beginning of what became known around the world as the 'dirty protest', during which prisoners began to dispose of their excreta by smearing it on the cell walls. In April Don Concannon, a junior minister at the Northern Ireland Office, wrote to Bishop Edward Daly of Derry, who had raised concerns about the escalation of the protest and had suggested that some form of 'emergency status' could resolve the situation. Concannon replied, 'I must make it plain that there are going to be no concessions on the question of special treatment for prisoners, no matter how such treatment may be described.' On the issue of prison clothing, the minister was equally adamant, 'Convicted prisoners can wear their own clothes of an appropriate type during recreation periods. This is as far as we are prepared to go' (*The Irish News*, 30 December 2008). The following month, in a briefing note for Roy Mason dated 23 May, it was stated that 321 prisoners were currently refusing to wear prison clothes or to work in protest at the removal of special category status. The situation was heading towards crisis.

It is almost impossible to imagine the physical and psychological conditions under which the protest was maintained. Isolation was a key problem for the prisoners, as essentially they were cut off from the outside world and without access to papers, books, television and radio. Cells soon became infested with maggots and fleas, and the ever-present smell of excreta all contributed to a surreal existence. Pat McGeown, who was also to partake in the 1981 hunger strike, recalled the conditions, 'There were times when you would vomit. There were times when you were so run down that you would lie for days and not do anything with the maggots crawling all over you. The rain would be coming in the window and you would be lying there with the maggots all over the place' (Bishop & Mallie, *The Provisional IRA*, p. 352). McGeown died of a heart attack in October 1996 at the age of forty. He had survived forty-two days on hunger strike before lapsing into a coma – his family intervened to save him. His death was attributed, in part, to the effects of hunger striking and he is still recalled as the eleventh fatality of the 1981 fast. However, the government's bottom line was that the conditions were self-imposed and that the prisoners were totally to blame for their plight. In short, it could not appreciate the point of principle at stake.

On Sunday 30 July 1978 Tomás Ó Fiaich, future Primate of All Ireland, paid a visit to the H-Blocks; he was shocked and felt compelled to issue a statement on what he had seen. In words that were a throwback to the exchanges at the Seán McCaughey inquest in 1946, he said:

> Having spent the whole of Sunday in the prison, I was shocked at the inhuman conditions prevailing in H-Blocks three, four and five, where over 300 prisoners were incarcerated. One would hardly allow an animal to remain in such conditions let alone a human being. The nearest approach to it that I have seen was the spectacle of hundreds of homeless people living in the sewer pipes in the slums of Calcutta.

Coogan, *The Troubles*, p. 265

It was a widely reported comment that prompted much debate. In response, the Northern Ireland Office hit back with a strong statement of its own. Suggesting that the government was 'surprised' by the Cardinal's attitude, it maintained that nobody was to blame for the prisoners' conditions but the prisoners themselves. The government's attitude was largely defensive, but also bullish: allegations of prisoner ill-treatment were said to contain 'no truth', and the protest was labelled just another 'propaganda campaign' by the IRA:

> These criminals are totally responsible for the situation in which they find themselves. It is they who have been smearing excreta on the walls and pouring urine through the cell doors. It is they who by their actions are denying themselves the excellent modern facilities of the prison. It is they, and they alone, who are creating bad conditions out of very good conditions.

> Northern Ireland Office press release, 1 August 1978

What must be remembered when discussing the tensions within the prisons at the time is the fact that the IRA and the Irish National Liberation Army (INLA) had, in April 1976, begun a campaign to assassinate prison officers and officials. In all fourteen murders were carried out by paramilitaries in a three-year period ending in December 1979. In truth, the campaign detracted severely from any sympathy that the prisoners' peaceful protests might have won. The most prominent member of the prison service to die was the Deputy Governor of the Maze, Albert Myles, who was killed in November 1978. Ten months later the Assistant Governor of Belfast Prison, Edward Jones was killed. He died when he was shot from another car while waiting in traffic less than 100 yards from the prison. Although the IRA claimed that prison officers were 'mercenaries of British injustice', the killings contributed to the absolute hatred between guards and prisoners. This, in turn, led to the brutalisation of individuals at the hands of guards. The deaths on the outside were, by and large, gratuitous acts that only exacerbated an unmanageable situation.

By the beginning of 1980 the IRA had begun to accept the folly of their campaign and the attacks dwindled as the situation lurched towards a hunger strike.

In the winter of 1979 an H-Block/Armagh committee was formed to campaign on behalf of the prisoners. The establishment of this committee was an attempt to widen the appeal of the campaign by allocating specific roles for youth, trades unions and a wide spectrum of human rights groups and political parties within the organisation's structure. The key demands of the campaign were identified as:

1. The right not to wear a prison uniform;
2. The right not to do prison work;
3. The right of free association with other prisoners, and to organise educational and recreational pursuits;
4. The right to one visit, one letter and one parcel per week;
5. Full restoration of remission lost through the protest.

In May 1979 Margaret Thatcher was elected prime minister. While Roy Mason had wallowed in his ability to remain staunch and unyielding, the prisoners were now faced with an enemy who had absolutely no sympathy for their plight. After three years of high-profile protests throughout Ireland, Britain and the United States, the campaign had failed to extract any concessions. There was only one other option available, namely, the protest of last resort.

The initial fast for political status, begun in October 1980, was not the first hunger strike to capture the public's attention during that year. In May 1980 IRA veteran Martin Meehan, against the wishes of the IRA leadership, began a hunger strike in the Maze Prison in protest that he had been 'framed' for the kidnapping of a British Army informer. Meehan was sentenced in March 1980 to twelve years and immediately joined the 'no-wash' protest in the Maze, switching to the side of the 'conforming' prisoners when he embarked upon his hunger strike in May. Despite being requested by IRA leaders in the jail to come off the strike, Meehan refused and his condition deteriorated significantly. By late July Meehan had lost over 50 pounds in weight and had been transferred to Musgrave Park Hospital where he was afforded the last rites. In a haunting portent of what was to take place in the following months, nightly marches and vigils were held in nationalist areas of Belfast while news of Meehan's condition was awaited. As tension grew and widespread rioting was anticipated, Meehan ended his fast on its sixty-sixth day, thanks to the intervention of Cardinal Tomás Ó Fiaich and Amnesty International. The reality, however, was that Meehan's fast had given the Northern Ireland Office a 'dummy run' of what was to be expected later in the year and his fast impinged somewhat on the delicate plans for the hunger strike which were ongoing.

History has a strange knack of throwing up coincidences that, with hindsight, seem inherently linked. On Friday 10 October 1980 the Conservative Party ended its annual conference at Brighton. In her keynote speech Prime Minister Margaret Thatcher delivered one of her most famous lines in response to widespread pressure on her government to change its economic policies, which had seen unemployment rise to unprecedented levels. Borrowing the title of the 1948 Christopher Fry play *The Lady's not for Burning*, Thatcher told the conference, 'To those waiting with bated breath for that favourite media catchphrase, the U-turn, I have only one thing to say: You turn if you want to. The lady's not for turning!'

It was a line written by the Prime Minister's speech-writer, Ronnie Millar, and, despite the fact that the Iron Lady reportedly failed to understand the humour in the pun, it defined perfectly the political essence of Margaret Thatcher. Perhaps this was an inopportune time for the IRA leadership in the Maze to announce that a hunger strike would commence on the morning of Monday 27 October:

> WE, the Republican Prisoners of War in the H-Blocks, Long Kesh, demand, as of right, political recognition and that we be accorded the status of political prisoners. We claim this right as captured combatants in the continuing

struggle for national liberation and self-determination.

We refute most strongly the tag of 'criminal' with which the British have attempted to label us and our struggle, and we point to the divisive partitionist institutions of the six counties as the sole criminal aspect of the current struggle . . .

We declare that political status is ours of right and we declare that from Monday 27th October, 1980 a hunger strike by a number of men representing H-Blocks 3, 4 and 5 will commence.

English, *Armed Struggle*, p. 192

It was anticipated that seven men, representing a wide geographical cross section of Northern Ireland, would begin fasting with others joining at appropriate times. Accordingly, the psychological game between the prisoners and the Northern Ireland Office began. A statement issued on behalf of the 400 prisoners on the no-wash protest stated that every channel open to them had been exhausted: 'We now commit ourselves to a hunger strike,' the prisoners declared, 'it will carry us through to the bitter climax of death, if necessary.' Immediately, the Northern Ireland Office hit back, saying that the government's position would remain unchanged, and that it was not prepared 'to create gradations of crime. There will be no compromise on the principles of political status.' In rather clichéd words that sounded as if they might have been a direct quote from Margaret Thatcher, the statement ended 'Murder is murder wherever it is committed' (*The Irish Times*, 11 October 1980).

One individual who did, however, make Mrs Thatcher 'turn' with the threat of a hunger strike was the President of Plaid Cymru, Gwynfor Evans. In April 1980 he issued a statement announcing that he would 'fast to the death' unless the government kept its pre-election promise to establish a Welsh television channel. Evans had been upset that the government, and Mrs Thatcher in particular, had reneged on its promise and gave notice that he would begin fasting on 6

October. Due perhaps to the 'slow-burn' build up to Evan's strike and the widespread detestation of Thatcher in Wales, his proposed protest was acknowledged on 20 September when the Home Secretary William Whitelaw gave Channel 4 Wales the go-ahead. In effect, Thatcher had made a 'U-turn' and this fact had not gone unnoticed by the prisoners in the Maze. The threat of hunger strike from a shy and introverted Welsh nationalist over the establishment of a television station was one thing to Margaret Thatcher. Quite a different matter entirely was the prospect of a hunger strike by militant representatives of a philosophy that, in 1979 alone, had been responsible for the deaths of Thatcher's confidant Airey Neave, Lord Mountbatten and eighteen members of the Parachute Regiment close to Warrenpoint, County Down – she took this latest threat, perhaps, almost personally. Pat Sheehan, who went fifty-three days on the 1981 fast, explained that the knowledge of Thatcher's stubbornness, at that stage, had not been factored into the prisoners' thinking:

> In essence, we had little or no access to the media and our knowledge of Margaret Thatcher was limited. While we accepted that she was stubborn, we felt that we would be equally as stubborn and determined to see the fast through. Political status had been won in 1972 through a hunger strike and we were sure that the British would again be forced to act. There was a momentum within the prison at the time and the movement towards a hunger strike was, we felt, our best tactic. We believed that we had no option as everything else had been exhausted.

> Author interview with Pat Sheehan, 11 November 2010

Outside the prison Sinn Féin sources were telling the press that the party was unanimous in its support for the fast. Underneath this bullish exterior many republicans doubted the effectiveness of a hunger strike, given that the position of the government seemed to be set in stone. The hunger strike was a final act of defiance that would test the courage and determination of both sides. However, since there were two weeks left until the fast was due to commence, hopes were still high that diplomacy might provide a solution. Within a week Cardinal Tomás Ó Fiaich and Bishop Edward Daly of Derry issued a joint statement asking the prisoners to 'think again', adding perceptively that 'hard line attitudes on one side will be met by hard line attitudes on the other'. Prior to the commencement of the hunger strike, the British government announced that it was to permit, on a limited basis, all prisoners in Northern Ireland to wear 'civilian-style' prison garb. This concession followed a plea by the then Chief Constable of the RUC, John Hermon, who feared that the security situation on the ground could spiral out of control. This may have seemed like a concession to the government – to the prisoners it was a petty gesture: too little, too late.

Battle was engaged when seven prisoners refused food on 27 October. The hunger strikers were led by Brendan Hughes, who had been the Officer Commanding of the prisoners, although he was succeeded by Bobby Sands as the fast began. The group consisted of IRA members Brendan Hughes from Belfast, Tommy McKearney from County Tyrone, Raymond McCartney from Derry City, Tom McFeeley from County Derry, Sean McKenna from County Down, Leo Green from County Armagh, and INLA member John Nixon from Armagh City. The number seven was chosen symbolically because seven men had signed the Easter 1916 Proclamation of the Republic.

In the House of Commons, Secretary of State for Northern Ireland, Humphrey Atkins, was coming under attack from both Ian Paisley and Enoch Powell for attempting to 'buy-off' the IRA with concessions over clothing. In response, the Secretary of State was equally as blunt and confirmed that 'they [the government] cannot or will not concede on an issue of principle'. Elsewhere in the Palace of Westminster, Mrs Maura McKearney, the mother of hunger striker Tommy McKearney, addressed the media at a press conference in one of the building's committee rooms. Speaking as a guest of the Labour MP Ernie Roberts,

Mrs McKearney appealed to the government to 'end its stupid and illogical attitude towards the prisoners and to end its policy of trying to criminalise them'. She added ominously that 'she was proud that her son had the guts to die for his people, if it came to the point that he had to do so'. On 30 October Vatican officials handed Mark Heath, then Britain's Minister to the Holy See, a personal message to Margaret Thatcher from the Pope, which read:

> I am receiving disturbing news about the tension in the Maze prison in Northern Ireland, where a number of prisoners have begun a hunger strike. I would express my deep concern at both the tragic consequences which the agitation could have for the prisoners themselves and also the possible grave repercussions upon the whole situation in Northern Ireland. I would ask you to consider personally possible solutions in order to avoid irreversible consequences that could perhaps prove irreparable.
>
> *The Independent*, 30 December 2010

It was, in the nicest possible terms, a plea from the Pope for Thatcher to make some form of concession. In characteristic style, the Prime Minister wrote back to the Pope explaining that to make concessions would be 'utterly wrong', and asked the Pontiff to support her stance:

> To do so [make concessions] would be to accept that political motivation in some way excuses such serious crimes; it would encourage the use of violence as a means of obtaining political objectives; and it would be likely to provoke a violent confrontation between the two communities in the North . . . You may be sure that we very much welcome the efforts of the clergy in Northern Ireland to persuade the prisoners both to give up the strike and to end their protest; and I hope you will be able to give your full support to this objective.
>
> *Belfast Telegraph*, 8 January 2011

The Sinn Féin Ard Fheis in early November was dominated by the ongoing hunger strike. Party president Ruairí Ó Brádaigh spoke in stark terms, saying, 'They have thrown their frail bodies in front of the juggernaut of imperialism as a last resort to challenge British policy towards Irish people.' He was followed by Vice President Gerry Adams who pleaded for mass demonstrations across Ireland to highlight the demands of the prisoners. In a pragmatic speech, he added, 'These men aren't into blood sacrifice . . . I know them, and they don't want to die. But we cannot stop that happening without major organisation. We don't want big funerals, we want big protests' (*The Irish News*, 3 November 1980).

On the streets of Belfast and beyond direct action was in vogue as local committees were established, marches took place, rosaries were said, and pickets were mounted. The pot was boiling and into the mix was added a controversial speech by Fianna Fáil TD Síle de Valera, granddaughter of Éamon de Valera, who, at a party conference in Donegal, described Margaret Thatcher's attitude towards the hunger strikers as 'callous, unfeeling and self-righteous' (*The Irish News*, 3 November 1980). Given the role that her grandfather had played in the deaths of three hunger strikers in the 1940s, there was an obvious irony in Ms de Valera's outburst. However, memories were short, as dozens of telegrams of appreciation were sent to her on behalf of numerous anti-H-Block committees. Indeed, the South Down Committee, proud of being the 'former constituency of Éamon de Valera', congratulated his granddaughter that 'at least one voice [in Dáil Éireann] [was] raised on our behalf' (*The Irish Times*, 13 November 1980). De Valera's speech was disowned by an embarrassed Charles Haughey, who was busy throughout the period trying to cultivate a working relationship with Margaret Thatcher.

The world did not stop as the hunger strike continued. In the United States Ronald Reagan was elected to the White House, while millions of mundane lives were dominated by a conundrum that was resolved finally when it was revealed, to record audiences on Saturday 22 November, that J. R. Ewing had, in fact, been shot by a former mistress Kristen Sheppard. Two other factors that added to the complexity of the situation were at play in the background as the fast progressed. The first was that the IRA and the INLA both scaled down operations to a minimum in order to focus events on the prisons. On the same day that the fast was announced, 10 October, a part-time UDR member, James Hewitt, was killed by a booby-trap explosion under his vehicle in County Armagh. His death was to be the last at the hands of republicans in Northern Ireland for a month, until Owen McQuade, a soldier in the Argyll and Sutherland Highlanders, was shot dead at Altnagelvin Hospital in Derry City on 11 November. In addition to the fast for political status, 25-year-old Seamus Mullan, from Garvagh in County Derry, had begun fasting in late September in an attempt to get a retrial for his conviction for blackmail. His hunger strike would last for fifty-eight days until his lawyers were granted permission to bring the case to the House of Lords as it 'raised a point of public importance'.

At Westminster the member of parliament for West Belfast, Gerry Fitt, was signing his own political suicide note within his constituency. Fitt's politics, shaped by his mild republican and Labour background, had remained steadfastly opposed to violence, but by 1980 his detestation of the IRA had become even more palpable and almost fanatical. For his stance, Fitt's home had been targeted on numerous occasions since he had come out as one of the IRA's staunchest opponents. In his speech on 10 November Fitt, despite having lobbied for the introduction of political status in 1972, implored the government not 'to make the mistake' of giving in to the prisoners. His stated logic was that granting 'special category status' in 1972 had not stopped the violence. Referring to what he perceived as a new hierarchy of victimhood, Fitt added, 'A propaganda war has begun and we are hearing emotive phrases such as "do you want to see coffins coming out of Long Kesh?" My answer is no, but I am ever mindful of the thousands of

Catholics and Protestants, in little villages and towns, as well as Belfast, carrying the remains of the men of violence.'

From the militant republican standpoint, the condemnation of Fitt and the calls for his resignation were swift. Sinn Féin suggested that Fitt should put his opinions to the electorate of West Belfast, where the party suggested that 'provided with an alternative choice our people will positively and overwhelmingly reject Gerry Fitt's Unionism.' Bernadette McAliskey (née Devlin) described his speech as 'murderous', adding that Fitt was a mere 'shadow of a man'. However, the MP remained defiant, pointing out that the hunger strikers had the choice of life, while over 2,000 people since 1969 had had none. (*The Irish News*, 12 November 1980).

Each evening brought protestors on to the streets as the temperature on the ground rose considerably. In late November, the then still legal Ulster Defence Association (UDA) warned its members that they must be prepared for a war against the IRA. In Armagh Jail the twenty-eight republican women prisoners agreed in principle that they would join the fast. The three chosen to lead the fast were Mairéad Farrell, Mairéad Nugent and Mary Doyle, all of whom came from the Belfast area. Tragedy had not been a stranger to the family of Mary Doyle. In March 1975 her mother, Marie, had been killed in a UVF bomb attack on Conway's Bar in Greenisland. In Dublin forty-five relatives of republican prisoners began a 48-hour strike outside Leinster House in an attempt to force the Taoiseach to speak out in support of the demands. At a massive rally in Dublin on 23 November, during which the Union flag was burned, Bernadette McAliskey predicted that 'if the British let one man die, there will be an all-out confrontation'. In Brussels Queen Elizabeth's trip to the ballet was disrupted as she was greeted by noisy protesters carrying a banner which read 'ElizaBrit Go Home'. In *The Irish Times*, columnist Fionnuala O'Connor noted that 'there are fewer people in the middle ground than at any time during the Troubles,' while, typically, the *Protestant Telegraph* labelled the hunger strikers as 'two-legged rats'. In

Clough Orange Hall, Ian Paisley was sabre rattling and advising 'I solemnly warn this government that enough is enough; if they backtrack on the H-Blocks issue they will have a real problem on their hands.' Positions were being cast in stone. During the entire period the condition of the hunger strikers worsened, with the critical period predicted for mid-December (*The Irish News*, 29 November 1980).

Margaret Thatcher, who famously would ban Sinn Féin from the airways in 1988, was, however, more than likely apoplectic on the evening of Monday 24 November, when ITV's *World in Action* examined the issue of the hunger strike. On the evening in question, Thatcher was meeting with Pope John Paul II to whom, after their initial crossing of swords, she was explaining the government's position. Included within the footage was an interview with a bearded and gaunt Raymond McCartney from his bed within his hospital cell. Rather than conforming to the government's accepted view that the IRA were thugs and criminals, McCartney's composed and almost Christ-like demeanour became a powerful propaganda tool for the hunger strikers. The documentary was entitled 'The H-Block Fuse' and 26-year-old Derry man McCartney stated, 'We are prepared to die to prove that we should be treated as special category prisoners. Our five basic demands are just.' Recalling the event thirty years later, Raymond McCartney was clear in his memory:

> The director of the programme at that time was the film maker Paul Greengrass and he took an interest in me in that we were both the same age and had come from working class backgrounds. The authorities had told him that they could ask one question of me and, as I had never been interviewed before, there was a certain degree of nervousness on my behalf. I was very conscious that I needed to say the right thing in a clear and concise manner. The message I wanted to get across was that we were prisoners of the conflict and that we should be treated differently. I feel, however, that the most important thing about that interview is the image that it portrayed and

in some ways the message was secondary. In many ways people remember the hunger strike by the images that the programme showed. People understood more clearly how stark the situation was and the symbolism of that interview provided the fast with a big publicity boost.

Author interview with Raymond McCartney, 9
November 2010

Despite a last minute plea by Official Unionist leader, James Molyneaux, to Mrs Thatcher for the programme to be banned, the programme was broadcast. The government had obviously gambled that the prisoners would lose out in the propaganda battle over the programme. Appearing also on the *World in Action* report was the minister responsible for prisons, Michael Alison MP, who said that government would not accede to the Five Demands and added that 'the prisoners were banging their heads against a brick wall'. The sight and sound of the Eton-educated minister denouncing a man starving for his political principles only garnered further sympathy for the prisoners' cause. In the House of Commons the following day the row continued, with Mrs Thatcher talking of her distaste at 'seeing convicted murderers on television' and pointing out that the government felt that the programme would help counteract the IRA's propaganda machine (*The Irish News*, 26 November 1980).

Rumours that the government were prepared to negotiate over the prisoners' demands began to circulate in early December. Secretary of State Humphrey Atkins, in a meeting with John Hume, stated that the government remained willing to discuss with anyone interested the humanitarian aspect of Northern Ireland's prisons. Hume felt that this statement represented a breakthrough and appealed to the prisoners to call off their protest in order that the issue could be addressed 'in an atmosphere devoid of tension'. Rumours that Hume could be appointed as an intermediary were soon dismissed by the Irish Republican Socialist Party (IRSP), who stated that the only person who could negotiate with the government on their behalf was the INLA Officer Commanding in the Maze Patsy O'Hara. However, the prisoners knew that if they ended their fast before the discussion of any substantial concessions, they would be giving the government the upper hand. In the House of Commons Atkins elaborated on the government's stance, commenting that it aimed to create an 'enlightened and humane' regime within the prisons. He went on to list the privileges that conforming prisoners would be granted: limited association, books, newspapers, a gymnasium, additional visits and the right to wear their own clothes at certain periods. Unfortunately, in outlining his perceived view that the prison regime in Northern Ireland was fair and liberal, Atkins made it obvious (just as Mrs Thatcher had done) that the Conservative Government did not understand the real issues. The dispute in the prisons was based on a principle that was engrained in the republican psyche: the prisoners were not, in fact, as British as the residents of Mrs Thatcher's constituency, Finchley. At a press conference on 8 December, following a summit meeting with Charles Haughey, Mrs Thatcher spelled out her position again: 'Murder is a crime. Carrying explosives is a crime. Maiming is a crime . . . Murder is murder, is murder. It is not and never can be a political crime. So there is no question of political status.'

With the situation heading towards critical, Ireland and the world were shocked on the morning of 9 December when news broke of the assassination of John Lennon in New York the previous evening. In the early 1970s Lennon had been rumoured to have pledged his support for the IRA and the issues of Irish unity. As a mark of respect protests planned for that evening were called off across Ireland. On Wednesday 10 December the call by the National H-Block Committee for a half-day work stoppage across the country received a decidedly lukewarm response. Only in Belfast and Derry were there notable numbers in attendance, while marches elsewhere were poorly attended. In the Republic it was estimated that less than 2,000 people actually left work to join protests. In response, the organisers claimed that the day had been a 'significant success'.

In the Maze itself, the news was grim. Real concern was expressed over the condition of Newry protester, Sean McKenna. The 25-year-old, in the fiftieth day of his fast, was deteriorating rapidly and in danger of losing his eyesight. McKenna, who had been arrested at the border by the SAS in March 1976, was serving a total of 303 years concurrently for a spate of offences carried out over a five-year period. Within hours his name became the most prominent of the hunger strikers and the worst was feared. In Belfast all Christmas leave was cancelled in the RUC and the RUC Reserve. In Armagh a protest led by Bernadette McAliskey was prevented by the police from reaching the city's prison. A sit-down protest was staged and addressed by McAliskey who told the crowd that 'Time is running out for Britain as sure as it is running out for the prisoners.'

The end game was now approaching as news of the condition of Sean McKenna was awaited. The seven hunger strikers in the Maze were joined by twenty-three others in the prison on the morning of 15 December, which brought the total number fasting to thirty-three, including the three women fasting in Armagh Prison. A statement issued by the prisoners on the escalation of the protest was perceptive and realistic concerning the attitude of the British government:

> While creating the appearance, indeed the illusion of movement, while using transparent statements of concern about the health of our comrades, Margaret Thatcher, Michael Alison and Humphrey Atkins have remained coldly resolute in their determination to break us ... Only the British Government, which has wasted and cast aside so many opportunities to resolve this issue, can prevent our deaths.

> *The Irish News*, 16 December 1980

Mrs Thatcher, though, was unmoved by the developments. In response to a telegram sent by Cardinal Ó Fiaich asking her to intervene, she stated, in a line which confirmed her ignorance of Ireland beyond doubt, 'I believe that there is now almost universal agreement in Ireland that men of violence can have no right to political status.' In the Commons, in response to a question asking whether the Taoiseach, Charles Haughey, had asked her at a recent summit to grant the prisoners political status, she responded, 'I cannot answer specifically for the Taoiseach. I have not been requested to give the hunger strikers political status by anyone except the hunger strikers themselves. There is no question, either now or at all, of giving them political status.'

As the morning of Thursday 18 December broke, the family of Sean McKenna was advised by the prison authorities to 'be on stand-by'. The H-Blocks Information Centre in Belfast stated that McKenna's family had resigned themselves to the fact that he would die. The family of County Tyrone hunger striker Tommy McKearney was told that their son was 'deteriorating further', while the parents of John Nixon were 'shocked' at his condition, having been told that he was also in danger of losing his eyesight. At a rally in Ballymurphy, Gerry Adams told the crowd that the British were acting with the same stupidity as they had in 1916 when the leaders of the Easter Rising were executed. The words intransigence, stubborn, abyss, martyrdom, prayer and death were in vogue. In the darkness of mid-December, time was running out as the inevitable end approached.

★

And then – it was over. On day fifty-three of the fast, on the evening of Thursday 18 December, the hunger strike was called off. At the end of a frantic day of behind-the scenes diplomacy the prisoners' leader, Brendan 'The Dark' Hughes, decided to place his tentative trust in Secretary of State Atkins. The decision to end the fast was taken solely by Hughes, who was awaiting delivery of a document on 'prison procedures' that Atkins was due to announce in the Commons the following day. This document was to be delivered to Redemptorist priest Father Brendan Meagher by Foreign Office official Michael Oatley, code-named 'Mountain Climber'. Meagher had visited Hughes early on the morning of 18 December to advise him that he had

seen a summary of the document and that there might be the
basis of a settlement there. Both Bobby Sands (who had become
the prisoners' Officer Commanding) and Hughes wanted to see
the document and Fr Meagher was advised by the British to
go to Aldergrove Airport where a 'man wearing a pin-striped
suit with a pink carnation' would give him a copy. It was now a
waiting game. With Sean McKenna, who was in the process of
being transferred to the Royal Victoria Hospital, not expected to
last the night, Hughes gambled. As McKenna was being wheeled
out of the prison hospital, Hughes was advised by the prison
medic, Dr Ross, that he was almost dead. Hughes was placed on
the spot. Before McKenna had slipped into a coma, Hughes had
promised him that he would not let him die. The document was
on its way and, at 9.00 p.m. on the fifty-third day of the strike,
Hughes gave the order that Sean McKenna was to be fed.

It was a leap of faith that would come back to haunt the
prisoners. But there was to be no division or blame game over
the failure of the first fast. In essence, all involved would see
that Brendan Hughes had been duped and his decision to end
the fast was therefore respected. As Raymond McCartney
recalled:

> The Dark [Brendan Hughes] had been advised by Father
> Meagher, in whom we had the greatest trust, that he felt
> that there was a basis for a solution [in the document].
> Brendan was faced with a dilemma in that Sean McKenna
> literally had hours to live and he took the decision to
> end the strike. At that stage we felt that there was to
> be a settlement and when the document arrived it was
> ambiguous and on a bad day you could have possibly
> 'driven a bus through it' as Bobby Sands said. Yet, it was in
> the subsequent days that the thing unravelled completely.
> There were rumours of course that some officials within
> the Northern Ireland Office and the Prison Officers'
> Association would walk if the government implemented
> any changes. However, on the evening of 18 December,
> there was only one possible decision that Brendan Hughes

could have made and that was to end the fast.

Author interview with Raymond McCartney, 9
November 2010

A statement was issued on behalf of the prisoners and it seemed that there had been a real breakthrough, but the distrust was evident for all to see. They placed the ball firmly in Atkin's court: 'In ending our hunger strike we make it clear that failure by the British Government to act in a responsible manner towards the ending of the conditions that forced us on to hunger strike will only lead to inevitable and continual strife within the H-Blocks' (*The Irish News*, 19 December 1980).

In Ireland a violent Christmas had been predicted, but relief swept across the country with the end of the fast and the prisoners' statement – it seemed that a solution, of sorts, had been found. It was, however, to be a false dawn: the prisoners and the government were poles apart. In essence, Thatcher had not crumbled and the whole matter would soon unravel. In the House of Commons on 19 December Atkins made his eagerly awaited statement. He began by reiterating the government's position, confirming that 'their [the prisoners'] demand for political status is not going to be granted', and went on to point out that the government had taken action on a number of prison regime issues that the European Court of Human Rights had drawn to its attention. He stated that, since the hunger strike had ended, the government was to provide the prisoners with a clean cell. Thereafter 'civilian-type clothing' would be issued for use during the working day – it was therefore taken as read that prison work would be expected. In addition, eight letters, four parcels and four visits would be permitted on a monthly basis. Association would be allowed in the evenings and at weekends, but the extent of this was not elaborated upon. On lost remission, Atkins stated that each case would be considered at the restoration of 'good behaviour'. With hindsight, the position outlined by Atkins might have been considered a starting point for the extraction of further concessions. The prisoners, in turn, issued a statement: 'Dependent on a sensible and responsible attitude from the British Government in implementing their proposals, the Blanketmen will make a positive response. We are satisfied that the implementation of these proposals will meet the requirements of our Five Demands (*The Irish News*, 20 December 1980).

In the H-Blocks confusion reigned. Outside the prison, supporters thought that the government had crumbled and given the prisoners assurances on the Five Demands – they were wholly misled. Over the course of the next few days, the conservative press in London was inclined to see the situation as a miscalculation on the part of the prisoners and 'pure luck' for the government. *The Times* correspondent in London, Fred Emery, in a considered piece on 20 December, noted that confusion had reigned and that Atkins' ambiguous response to the cessation in his subsequent Commons' statement had added to the prisoners' sense of bewilderment. Emery added that Charles Haughey and the Catholic hierarchy had talked the prisoners off the strike and noted that the aforementioned duo 'may have made promises to the prisoners that the British government cannot endorse or deliver'. Tellingly, he suggested that the prisoners may have 'asserted an influence in Ulster affairs that will not easily be regained'; it was a power that Enoch Powell suggested would have to be 'clawed back' by the government.

Bobby Sands was one of the first men to read the document for which they had all been waiting and his immediate response was 'We got nothing' (O'Rawe, *Blanketmen*, p. 108). Sands added that 'there was nothing concrete' and that he could have driven a bus through the document (Taylor, *Provos*, p. 235). Sands wanted the fast to recommence immediately, but was persuaded to hold back by Sinn Féin Publicity Director, Danny Morrison, to see if the British position changed over the following days. Cardinal Ó Fiaich greeted the end of the fast with a fervent 'Thank God', adding that he hoped the government would respond to the move with 'flexibility'. Yet the reality was that the British had, in fact, duped the prisoners. Humphrey Atkins pointed out to the media on 19 December that the government 'had not moved' and that 'no secret deals had been done'. He added, with patronising gusto, that 'they [the prisoners] must have grasped the fact that they were not going to get what they had asked for'. Stressing that the Maze Prison was 'one of the best in the UK', he added that the government would look at the prison regime to ensure that it was 'humane and fair'. It was quite evident that political status was not on the agenda and that the prisoners' position had been weakened (*The Irish News*, 19 December 1980). Later, Margaret Thatcher would say that any claim that concessions had been made were only 'to excuse [the prisoners'] defeat' and added that the 'non-existent concessions failed to materialise'.

Within days of the end of the protest, Sean McKenna's condition improved and he was taken off the critical list. However, by Christmas 1980 nothing had changed. Angry confusion reigned within the prison. Prison chaplain Father Denis Faul, who spoke with the inmates on 22 December, noted that the prisoners had not given up the blanket protest and would only do so when honour was restored. It was a waiting game, as the government procrastinated and distrust built up again. At a rally on the Falls Road Gerry Adams spelled out the situation and advised the marchers that 'the ball is now firmly in the British court' and that a solution lay only in the government's ability to act in a 'sensible manner' (*The Irish Times*, 22 December 1980). As the New Year approached, with 446 republican prisoners still on the no-wash protest, the word emanating from the Maze was that a new fast was a real possibility. Father Faul reported that the frustration of the prisoners was such that five men, including their leader Bobby Sands, had threatened to go on hunger strike from 1 January. Pointedly, the cleric laid the blame for the impasse at the door of the prison authorities due to their 'crass stupidity and lack of humanity, generosity and plain commonsense' (*The Irish Times*, 29 December 1980).

The year 1981 dawned and the deadlock continued throughout January with renewed speculation that another fast was imminent. The republican vocabulary of the time was rich in words such as 'double-cross', 'bad faith', 'reneging' and 'deceit'. Among the republican prisoners, however, morale and determination remained high. Bernadette McAliskey, spokeswoman for the National H-Blocks Committee, in announcing on 3 January that a new campaign would be mounted in support of the Five Demands, predicted that any new protest would be 'even more bitter' than the first hunger strike. Two weeks later McAliskey's prominence within the H-Block campaign was to lead to an attempt on her life that would leave both herself and her husband in a critical condition. Three loyalists were arrested by the army in a follow-up operation and the McAliskeys were, ironically, flown by military helicopter to the Mater Hospital. The attempt on Mrs McAliskey's life was just one of a number of attacks made on prominent figures within the national H-Blocks campaign: in 1980, five campaigners had been shot dead by loyalists – Miriam Daly, John Turnly, Peter Valente, Noel Lyttle and Ronnie Bunting. In the context of the time, the shooting of Bernadette McAliskey was just another statistic, since Ivan Toombs, a major in the UDR, was killed in Warrenpoint on the same day.

Indeed, the month of January would end with one of the more shocking murders of the decade. Norman Stronge, the 86-year-old former Speaker of the Stormont Parliament, and his 48-year-old son James, were assassinated by the IRA at Tynan Abbey, County Armagh. It was a truly horrific episode, which saw the two pillars of the unionist establishment shot in the head and their 250-year-old stately home burned out. The IRA claimed that they had struck at the 'hated symbols of Unionism' as a response to the recent attacks on nationalists by loyalists. Norman Stronge and his son were (like the Brookeborough dynasty) part of the unionist hierarchy of Northern Ireland, and they were killed because they were easy targets. But, in effect, the IRA had murdered the Queen's personal representative in County Armagh. The Stronge family requested that government representatives stay away from the funeral service, due to what the family called the government's lack of will to deal with the terrorist threat along the border. At the funeral service, the Church of Ireland Bishop of Armagh, John Crooks, reiterated Margaret Thatcher's mantra that 'murder was murder' and that 'agents of sin with the mark of Cain' had carried out the deed. It was an abject end to a month of bitterness and recrimination. On 27 January, in the midst of the spirit of revulsion surrounding the murder of the Stronges, talks between Bobby Sands and the prison governor of the Maze, Stanley Hilditch, broke down without agreement. There seemed to be no common ground and the fallout was inevitable: protesting prisoners proceeded to wreck their cells. The situation had disintegrated and soon it was announced that the second hunger strike for political status would commence on the fifth anniversary of the ending of special category status – 1 March 1981.

Chapter 11

1981: It's Gonna Happen

'Watching your friends passing by,
going to sleep without blinking a blue eye.'

Fergal Sharkey, The Undertones, *Top of the Pops*, May 1981

The announcement that the second fast was to commence was made on Thursday 5 February 1981. This time, the general opinion was that there were sure to be deaths arising from the resumption of the fast. In the days running up to the announcement, meetings of local support committees took place as plans to mount further street protests were agreed. In the St James' area of Belfast on 4 February a meeting addressed by Fergus O'Hare of the National H-Blocks Committee advised attendees that all forms of support and pressure groups must be 'reorganised and strengthened immediately'. The prisoners' announcement was forthright and angry in tone, and it spread the blame for the failure of the 1980 fast over many culprits. It stated that the first fast had ended because the hunger strikers had been 'morally blackmailed by a number of people and politicians who called on them to end the fast and allow a resolution'. It was evident that the prisoners were not in a forgiving mood, and their statement continued:

It needs to be asked openly of the Irish Bishops, of Cardinal Ó Fiaich and of politicians like John Hume: What did your recommended ending of the last hunger strike gain for us? Where is the peace in the prisons which, like a promise, was held before dying men's eyes? And who but the British are responsible for our state which is worse now than it ever was?'

The Irish News, 5 February 1981

The date for the hunger strike was set, symbolically, for 1 March 1981 – the fifth anniversary of the withdrawal of special category status. The man who would lead off the fast was Bobby Sands. Sands was born in 1954 in Rathcoole, a new 'model estate' that had been built on the outskirts of north Belfast in the 1950s. By June 1972 the area had become a loyalist stronghold and the Sands family were intimidated into leaving their home in Doonbeg Drive. They moved to Twinbrook on the edge of west Belfast, which had become a refuge for nationalist families driven by intimidation from all areas of the city. At the age of eighteen Sands joined the IRA and was arrested and charged with possession of weapons. He spent three years as a political prisoner in Long Kesh, where he furthered his education and taught himself fluent Irish. On his release in 1976 he became involved in community agitation and battles over social issues in Twinbrook. In October 1976 he was arrested after an IRA bomb attack on the Balmoral Furniture Company in Dunmurry and was brought to Castlereagh Detention Centre where he was subjected to a prolonged and brutal interrogation, during which he refused to speak. He was sentenced to fourteen years' imprisonment in September 1977 and immediately he joined the blanket protest. Sands quickly rose through the ranks of the republican prisoners and, as Officer Commanding, volunteered to lead the new hunger strike. He insisted on starting two weeks before the others so that, in the event of his death, a solution could be found to secure the Five Demands and save further loss of life.

Death was in the air. Two weeks prior to the commencement of Bobby Sands' fast, death would visit Twinbrook when two men from the area, Bobby Hillock and Jim Millar, perished in the Stardust nightclub in Artane in Dublin. The fire that broke out that St Valentine's night claimed the lives of forty-eight people, as flames, smoke and mass panic spread throughout the packed building. The horrific stories of what had happened, coupled with pitiful images of the injured and the subsequent mass funerals, shocked Ireland in the days and weeks following. For an entry fee of three pounds, forty-eight lives had been lost in the inferno. It seemed to be the indictment of a country ill at ease with itself, the economic 'basket case' of Europe. The events that terrible night in Dublin were in keeping with the pessimistic mood in the North. In Belfast a rally in support of the hunger strike was cut short as a mark of respect to the dead of the Stardust tragedy. On the morning of Sunday 1 March Bobby Sands refused food and wrote in his diary:

> I am standing on the threshold of another trembling world. May God have mercy on my soul. My heart is very sore because I know that I have broken my poor mother's heart, and my home is struck with unbearable anxiety. But I have considered all the arguments and tried every means to avoid what has become the unavoidable; it has been forced upon me and my comrades by four-and-a-half years of stark inhumanity.
>
> I am a political prisoner. I am a political prisoner because I am a casualty of a perennial war that is being fought between the oppressed Irish people and an alien, oppressive, unwanted regime that refuses to withdraw from our land. I believe and stand by the God-given right of the Irish nation to sovereign independence, and the right of any Irishman or woman to assert this right in armed revolution. That is why I am incarcerated, naked and tortured.

Sands, *Writings from Prison*, p. 219

The 'fast to the death, if necessary' had begun. A statement issued by the Republican prisoners of H Blocks 3, 4, 5 and 6 accused the British government of adopting a racist attitude towards Irish prisoners in refusing to grant political status. At Dunville Park in Belfast a mass rally was addressed by Mrs Rosaleen Sands, mother of Bobby, who was joined on stage by her visibly upset daughter, Marcella. National H-Block Committee Member Jim Gibney appealed to the crowds for mass support and urged people to boycott the government's census, adding that 'We shifted them [British government] during the last hunger strike, and we will shift them again.' In Derry Bishop Edward Daly, however, was warning a congregation of 2,000 teenagers against supporting the hunger strike. The Bishop advised the youngsters that if they were asked to support the fast they should ask the group or individual requesting their support if they 'rejected murder and bombing'. In a wide-ranging speech, the Bishop warned against the 'false freedoms' of sexual behaviour, violent behaviour and consumerism, adding that it would be sinful to be involved with a group that had a policy of murder or destruction. In Belfast Sinn Féin Publicity Director, Danny Morrison, criticised Daly for his willingness to attack the 'so-called immorality' of republicans, compared with his silence on British 'immorality'.

With a waiting game and the inevitable slow build-up in tension in the offing, the whole political situation changed. On the evening of 5 March the death occurred of Frank Maguire, MP for Fermanagh and South Tyrone. Maguire collapsed at his home in Lisnaskea and died at Enniskillen Hospital of heart failure. Known as the 'the silent man' at Westminster, Maguire had been elected as an independent MP in the British general election of October 1974. Opposed to violence, yet republican by instinct, his appearances in the House of Commons were rare; yet, tellingly, he lobbied hard on Irish prisoners' issues. History will recall that his abstention, as well as Gerry Fitt's, during a vote of confidence in March 1979 would lead to the fall of Jim Callaghan's Labour government. Two months later Margaret Thatcher would begin an eleven-year term of office in Downing Street. However, in early March 1981 the prospect of a by-election arose in a seat that had, in 1955, returned Philip Clarke, an IRA member serving ten years in Belfast Prison for his part in a raid on Omagh Barracks in 1954. The constituency retained a slight nationalist majority and, with Bobby Sands now ending his first week on hunger strike, an opportunity to bring his plight to world attention presented itself. But the notion that Bobby Sands could place himself before the electorate was a dangerous high-wire act. Whilst there was a republican tradition within the constituency, the potential existed for political embarrassment in the event of Sands being beaten in the poll. The other alternative for republicanism was to do nothing; and, with Sands fading, that was not an option.

That a Belfast IRA man incarcerated in the Maze Prison might win the hearts, minds and votes of the Fermanagh and South Tyrone nationalist electorate was no foregone conclusion. Crucially, Sinn Féin had won the seat in 1955 when Philip Clarke had defeated Robert George Grosvenor – the fifth Duke of Westminster. Clarke had polled over 30,000 votes but was to be disqualified when the High Court in Belfast ruled that he was ineligible because he was in prison – Grosvenor was duly declared elected. In 1955 the IRA was still preparing for its border campaign and a vote for a prisoner could, in theory, not be construed as tacit support for armed struggle. However, by the late 1950s, with the IRA campaign ongoing, the Sinn Féin vote had collapsed. By 1981 Provisional Sinn Féin had never contested a Westminster election. The last concerted campaign by Sinn Féin before the split between the Provisional and Official wings had been in 1966 when, under the guise of 'Independent Republican', they had garnered a respectable 62,182 votes or 10.5 per cent of the Northern electorate. Tellingly, in Fermanagh and South Tyrone that year, Ruairí Ó Brádaigh had polled 10,370 votes, which placed him third in the poll. What had not been tested throughout the Troubles, though, was the notion that nationalists en masse could vote for somebody who was associated with armed struggle.

While there were major psychological barriers to address for republicans, the physical ones seemed daunting also. The Maguire Clan can trace their ownership of the lands around County Fermanagh back to the year 1302. In 1981 all that remained of the fiefdom of the Maguires was the family's Stag's Head bar in Lisnaskea. Naturally, speculation was rife that the successor to the Westminster seat vacated by Frank Maguire would be his brother Noel: his papers were duly deposited in Dungannon on 25 March. Into the equation also came the name of Bernadette McAliskey, who had been, as Bernadette Devlin, returned in 1969 in Mid-Ulster as the youngest ever female member of the House of Commons. Despite being hit with nine assassins' bullets two months previously, McAliskey declared herself 'interested' in standing on a 'Smash H-Block/Armagh and Anti-Repression' ticket. The bottom line, nevertheless, was that McAliskey was still recovering from her brush with death and the physical strains that a campaign would pose could be a major hindrance. Accordingly, early on in the process she indicated that she would stand aside should a prisoner be nominated. The great unknown in nationalist ranks was the stance of the SDLP. At a convention in Irvinestown the party nominated Austin Currie, who had trailed in behind Frank Maguire by 12,000 votes in 1979, as its candidate for the seat. It was a no-win situation for the SDLP. They would, at best, achieve third place in the poll and the net result of that eventuality would see Bobby Sands defeated and unionism retain the seat.

On 15 March a second hunger striker joined the fast. He was Francis Hughes from Bellaghy in County Derry, who had once been considered 'Northern Ireland's most wanted man'. Born in February 1956, Hughes joined the Provisional IRA after flirting with the Official IRA, and soon made the rugged terrain of south Derry as formidable to the British Army as south Armagh. For three years he lived the life of a rural guerrilla. He had been the absolute bane of the security forces throughout the 1970s, but his luck ran out on St Patrick's Day 1978, near the town of Maghera. Twelve hours before his arrest, Hughes and his unit had been involved in a shoot-out with undercover soldiers, during which David Jones of the Parachute Regiment was killed and Hughes was badly wounded. Hughes, though, managed to escape across fields and hid, but was eventually tracked down and arrested. Ironically, his arrest saved his life and he was to spend ten months in hospital in Belfast where, after operations on his wounds, his thigh bone was shortened by almost two inches. Undeterred by his ordeal, Hughes refused to crack when interrogated in Castlereagh Holding Centre, refusing food and water for fear that he would be drugged. In the end, Hughes was sentenced to life imprisonment in February 1977 for the murder of David Jones and a range of other offences. The RUC in south Derry breathed a sigh of relief. From their point of view, a murdering, hardened and dedicated terrorist had been taken out of circulation. But within republican circles the legend of Francis Hughes had been born and would be embellished with each recollection of his feats. Francis Hughes was, however, as a convicted murderer, putty and propaganda in the hands of unionists and Margaret Thatcher.

On 26 March the ante was raised considerably when the name of Bobby Sands, Anti-H-Block/Armagh Political Prisoner was announced for inclusion on the ballot paper. This move had come about due to prominent Belfast republican Jim Gibney, and the former Chief of Staff of the IRA, Dáithí Ó Conaill, both of whom had sold the idea to the hierarchy within the party. The bottom line was that a split nationalist vote would let a Unionist candidate take the seat. However, only one candidate was in prison on hunger strike, and that would prove decisive. In the Ulster Unionist camp, former party leader Harry West was selected as their candidate at a party convention. West was in the twilight of a colourful political career that had seen him cast into the political wilderness after being trounced by Ian Paisley in the 1979 European Election. He was right-wing in nature – 'a big, bluff farmer from Northern Ireland's rural west' – and was considered a safe and staunch pair of hands to win back the seat for unionism. The historian Eamon Phoenix described Harry

West thus, 'He was suspicious of nationalism, he was suspicious of London and he was opposed to change. He took his cue from his ancestral voices' (*Independent*, 7 February 2004). Who better to stand in the way of Bobby Sands? In essence, West must have thought that his political ship had come in. Nationalism seemed divided, while he had seen off the challenge of Ian Paisley's preferred candidate, Roy Kells. The seat was West's for the winning.

In 1957, in response to a journalist's question on what issue was most likely to blow a government off course, Harold Macmillan responded famously: 'Events dear boy, events'. Accordingly, events in the background began to work against Harry West within the constituency. Firstly, the moral pressure grew on Noel Maguire to stand aside. Since McAliskey was out of the equation, Maguire was visited by Gerry Adams and Jim Gibney who put the case for giving Sands a clear run. With the closure of nominations due to take place on Monday 30 March, the SDLP acted first and its party executive decided to withdraw Currie from the poll leaving the way open for Maguire to face off with Sands for the nationalist vote. Currie was not best pleased at the move and would be left incandescent at the turn of events the following day. In the end, the pressure told on Maguire and, with moments to spare, he withdrew his nomination papers. As Jim Gibney recalled:

> My anxious wait ended well within the time set for withdrawing a nomination. The solitary figure of the white haired Noel Maguire ascended the steps outside the Electoral Office. It was obvious he had decided to pull out of the contest. In keeping with his gentle demeanour he announced in a soft voice to the waiting journalists that he was withdrawing from the by-election because he had been told it would help save Bobby's life. He could not have it on his conscience that any action of his would endanger another person's life.
>
> *Saoirse*, 7 April 2006

The unofficial motto for the Sands campaign was chosen to play on the electorate's emotions: 'his life in your hands'. The philosophy was summed up best by senior Sinn Féin official, Francie Molloy, who recalled, 'Once we stood we had to win. That was pretty much the pitch we made at the doors. We were saying to local nationalists, "look, let's set aside our differences. If we can get him elected that will put it up to Thatcher." Let's get him elected and we can deal with any issues afterwards' (*An Phoblacht*, 13 April 2006).

The 1981 Census for the United Kingdom was scheduled to take place on 5 and 6 April. In republican areas a boycott of the process was urged as a mark of low-level disobedience, and as a valid statement of Irish nationality. Marches in support of the hunger strikers that weekend ended with the lighting of bonfires onto which people were encouraged to throw their forms in a symbolic act of defiance. However, on Tuesday 7 April the issue of the non-completion of the UK Census reverberated throughout the world when Joanne Mathers was killed in Derry while carrying out her work as an enumerator. It was a truly shocking murder that threatened to destroy the relative credibility that had built up around the election campaign for Bobby Sands. She was standing at the door of a house in Anderson Crescent, in the nationalist Gobnascale area of the city, when she was attacked by a masked man. Twenty-nine-year-old Joanne, who was married with one young son, was shot in the head and died instantly. As Bobby Sands, Francis Hughes, Ray McCreesh and Patsy O'Hara lay dying for Ireland, so too was Joanne Mathers. Revulsion spread like wildfire and the gun was later linked to the IRA by the RUC. The campaign of Bobby Sands stared into the abyss as a storm of condemnation awaited. The polls in Fermanagh and South Tyrone opened at 7.00 a.m. on the morning of Thursday 9 April. The turnout was expected to approach 90 per cent. In the House of Commons the voters of the constituency were to be on the receiving end of some advice from Northern Ireland Shadow Spokesman, Don Concannon, whose words, whilst questionable with a by-election ongoing, were forthright and typically blunt:

> Does he recognise that it is our view that a vote for Mr
> Sands is a vote of approval for the perpetrators of the
> La Mon massacre, the murder of Lord Mountbatten at
> Warrenpoint [sic] and all the other senseless murders
> that have taken place in Northern Ireland over the years,
> including the latest brutal and inhuman killing of Mrs
> Mathers, the census enumerator. We sincerely hope that
> those in Fermanagh and South Tyrone who attend the
> election today will take that attitude into the polling booth
> with them.

Hansard HC (series 6) vol. 2, cols 1099–102 (9 Apr. 1981)

The tension on Friday 10 April in Enniskillen's Technical College
was palpable as it was clear that the count was too close to call.
Eventually the Returning Officer Alistair Patterson, who would
in later years become the chief executive of the Ulster Unionist
Party, took to the podium to announce the incredible: 'Sands,
Bobby, Anti H-Block/Armagh Political Prisoner, 30,492, West,
Harry, Unionist, 29,046.' The result was absolutely astounding
and the news spread like wildfire that Sands had been elected
to the British House of Commons. Rather like the death of
President Kennedy, or the events of 9/11, everyone of a certain
age in Northern Ireland can recall where they were when they
heard the result of the April 1981 Fermanagh and South Tyrone
by-election. The situation had changed but soon the British
government announced that the election of Sands would not
change its position with regard to special category status.

In the aftermath of Sands' election, the tension mounted
on the streets. The killing recommenced on 16 April when the
INLA shot dead UDR man Jack Donnelly in his local bar in
The Moy, County Tyrone. The condemnation was swift and
the bitterness at the result in Fermanagh and South Tyrone was
evident among unionist voices. Ian Paisley claimed that Sands'
victory had given republicans a mandate for a 'campaign of
Protestant genocide', while John Taylor of the Ulster Unionist

Party suggested that Mr Donnelly had 'lived amongst 30,000 potential accomplices to murder'. On Easter Sunday 19 April the messages of defiance were sent out from numerous republican gatherings. In Crossmaglen a masked man warned that the struggle would go on and 'if democratic methods were not heeded, then only by armed struggle will they get a hearing'. Later that evening, in the Creggan Estate in Derry, two teenagers, James English and James Brown, died when they were hit by an army jeep during disturbances. Rioting had been ongoing in the city for five nights and the deaths of the two teenagers was accompanied by a war of words between relatives and the army.

As Bobby Sands' life ebbed away, Margaret Thatcher was criticised throughout the world. Having long enjoyed her image as the 'Iron Lady', her indifference and intransigence in the face of the prisoners' demands was noted in many quarters. Whilst criticism of Mrs Thatcher was to be expected from the Tass news agency in the Soviet Union and many left-leaning European daily papers, a lead article of 30 April in *The New York Times* caused consternation within the British government. The article spoke of Thatcher's stance and said that 'by appearing unfeeling and unresponsive, she and her Government are providing Bobby Sands with a death bed wish: the crown of martyrdom'. Into the limelight on 1 May came the British Labour Party who sent Don Concannon to the Maze, at the behest of their leader Michael Foot, to advise Sands that Labour did not support the fast. Concannon, who in his time at the Northern Ireland Office had been one of the architects and staunchest defenders of the prison regime, was, in theory, visiting the hunger strikers to advise them that their fast was futile. However, the six-foot-four-inch former miner soon was embroiled in a political argument with Sands, which, considering that he was faced with a man on his deathbed, says perhaps more about the pugnacious attitude of Concannon than it does about Sands. The criticism of the visit was almost universal within the nationalist community. John Hume described it as a 'cheap and offensive publicity stunt';

Danny Morrison described Concannon as Pontius Pilate; while *Republican News* called the event 'ghoulish'.

When 2 May dawned, it was taken as read that Bobby Sands would die. The hotels of Belfast were full of the world's journalists, while food stockpiling and stories of sending children over the border to escape the backlash were widespread. Rosaries were recited at street corners while Unionist MP Robert Bradford called for the establishment of a ring of steel around 'Republican ghettos'. Others, however, were less circumspect, as is illustrated by the loyalist public relations 'guru' Sammy Duddy, who suggested that 'if Sands dies, there will be blood and guts all over the place. The guns will come out but we are ready for them.' One of the starkest images of those days was that of Rosaleen Sands appearing before the world's media outside the prison on 4 May and saying, 'My son is dying. I want to appeal to the people to remain calm and have no fighting or deaths. My son has offered his life to improve prison conditions and not for death and destruction.'

The death of Bobby Sands occurred at 1.17 a.m. on Tuesday 5 May 1981. The word soon reached the streets of Belfast, Derry and beyond, and crowds were summoned on to the roads by the sound of bin lids and whistles. Within moments of the announcement serious rioting had broken out. Calls for restraint were rendered useless as burning barricades shrouded Belfast in acrid smoke. The genie was out of the bottle and the mobs ran amok. In the nationalist New Lodge district of north Belfast, a crowd attacked a milk float belonging to Eric Guiney, who was doing his rounds along with his fourteen-year-old son Desmond. The milk float was assailed by a hail of missiles and careered into a lamp-post: Eric Guiney would succumb to his injuries the following day, his son died a week later. Mr Guiney's brother, David, spoke of his anger at the attack, comparing the massive publicity generated by Bobby Sand's death to that generated by his brother's and nephew's deaths. The following evening, less than a quarter of a mile from the spot where the Guineys were attacked, RUC officer Charles Ellis died after being hit by a bullet as his patrol attended an incident on the so-called peace line at Duncairn Gardens.

Most editorial comment after the event asked if Bobby Sands' death had made him a martyr. International opinion was certainly not kind to Margaret Thatcher. In Paris thousands of socialists took to the street in a mark of solidarity. Tellingly, *Le Monde* noted that after thousands of meaningless deaths, the hunger strike had served to 'internationalise' the conflict in Northern Ireland. *The New York Times* (6 May 1981) noted that 'by willing his own death, Bobby Sands has earned his own place in Ireland's long roll of martyrs and bested an implacable British Prime Minister'. In another article in the paper entitled 'Britain's Gift to Bobby Sands', it was noted that 'this dying young man made it appear that her stubbornness, rather than his own, is the source of a fearful conflict'. It added that Thatcher's gift to Sands had ultimately been the 'gift of martyrdom'. Outside the British Consulate in New York a crowd of 1,000 protesters burnt the union flag; on the docks, a boycott of British ships was imposed. In India the opposition party stood for a minute's silence as a mark of sympathy, while the *India Express* depicted Mrs Thatcher on its cover as an ostrich with its head in the sand. In the Soviet Union the Tass news agency said that Bobby Sands had been killed in the 'Long Kesh Concentration Camp'. In her memoirs BBC journalist Kate Adie would write a particularly cold recollection of her visit to the Sands' family wake. Ironically, her book was called *The Kindness of Strangers*: 'In his coffin, Mr Sands did not present a pale face of suffered humanity. He looked like a banana. Luminous yellow. I sniffled and coughed and looked hard. This was not the time and place to comment on the effects of hepatitis A and liver failure – nor the fact that the local embalmer had apparently used furniture varnish by the look of it. Thank God no one put a friendly arm round my shoulder at my supposed overcome state. I'd just learnt what actors meant by corpsing' (Adie, p. 179).

In what was obviously a well-prepared editorial, the London *Times* had no sympathy for Bobby Sands. Entitled 'Who Killed

Bobby Sands?', the article congratulated the government for refusing to yield to 'blackmail' and affirmed that it bore 'no responsibility' for his death. 'He committed suicide, in full knowledge of what he was doing . . . He was not hounded into death . . . He was not in prison for his beliefs, but for proved serious criminal offences,' it added. With a pompous *coup de grâce*, the editor ended his tirade by answering the conundrum that he had posed in the heading: 'There is only one killer of Bobby Sands and that is Sands himself' (*The Times*, 6 May 1981). The Speaker of the House of Commons, Sir George Thomas, rose to make the following announcement to parliament: 'I regret to have to inform the House of the death of Robert Sands Esquire, the Member for Fermanagh and South Tyrone.' And then he sat down. Two months previously, as was convention, a similar announcement had been made in the house: 'I regret to have to inform the House of the death of Meredith Francis Maguire Esquire, Member for Fermanagh and South Tyrone, and I desire, on behalf of the House, to express our sense of the loss we have sustained and our sympathy with the relatives of the Hon. Member.' The message was clear: Bobby Sands and his family would not be afforded any sympathy from the House of Commons. It was petty in the extreme; Bobby Sands' death was allocated twenty-two words and approximately seven seconds of the Speaker's time. Prior to the announcement one imagines that there may well have been a prolonged debate in the Speaker's chamber as to whether the word 'regret' was appropriate. The House immediately moved on to note that the British Railways (Victoria) Bill had been read for a second time in the Lords.

The death of Bobby Sands set in motion preparations for, perhaps, the largest funeral ever to be witnessed on the streets of Belfast. Sinn Féin spokesmen confirmed that Sands would be given a 'full military funeral', and that the coffin would be taken from his family home in the Twinbrook Estate to Milltown Cemetery, a journey of three miles through Andersonstown to the Falls Road. The death notices section of *The Irish News* was inundated with hundreds of tributes to Bobby Sands from across the island, and indeed the whole of the Irish diaspora. The funeral Mass would be held in the newly built St Luke's Church in Twinbrook; the wisdom of this was questioned by Cardinal Basil Hume, since he maintained that Sands had committed suicide. It fell to a spokesman for the Catholic Church in Dublin to address the criticism by pointing out that 'only God can judge the intentions of one man and that the sacraments and other comforts of the Church should not be denied'. The Grand Master of the Orange Order, Thomas Passmore, showed his personal concern for the credibility of Catholic doctrine in claiming that 'by blessing dead IRA martyrs, the Roman Catholic Church is acting as a recruiting agent for the IRA and putting the whole Roman Catholic community into the hands of the terrorists'. Across Northern Ireland the upsurge of violence that had greeted the death of Sands waned as the funeral approached. The accepted wisdom was that the trouble had only been put 'on hold' in order to permit a dignified burial. On *Top of the Pops* The Undertones from Derry City sported black armbands as they sang 'It's Gonna Happen', a song aimed specifically at Margaret Thatcher's intransigence. The hotels of Belfast were booked solid as the world's media came to the city; they would not be disappointed by the scenes that they captured on Thursday 7 May.

From early morning along the route of the funeral, buses and cars arrived from across Ireland and the bustle of thousands was drowned by the omnipresent sound of army helicopters. For schoolchildren in nationalist areas school was out of the question, and businesses were seriously affected as people failed to appear for work. The route of the funeral was bedecked in black flags and barricades were moved temporarily to allow the procession to take place. Gerry Adams appealed for restraint from the mourners and said that 'we will bury our dead with the dignity denied to them while living.' In the end most commentators placed the numbers in attendance in the region of 100,000; *The Sun* newspaper, a staunch supporter of Thatcher, typically, suggested that there were a mere 20,000 mourners. After one o'clock Mass the coffin of Sands, accompanied by an IRA colour party, left Twinbrook and travelled towards Andersonstown. It was a massive show of solidarity and strength. At the urging of South Belfast Unionist MP, Robert Bradford, the funeral was diverted away from the loyalist Suffolk Estate and through Lenadoon, where tens of thousands lined the route in silence. As the procession reached Andersonstown, it stopped momentarily as a volley of shots was fired over the coffin; this was the scene that the world's media had wanted. In the falling rain a massive and prolonged roar filled the air as clapping and clenched fists greeted the gunshots. In the midst of the set piece young men scrambled to claim the priceless shells that fell from the weapons to the ground. The police and army could only observe from the skies; unionists were apoplectic. *The New York Times* described the final stages of the funeral:

> At the military-style funeral that the IRA staged for Mr Sands in the 'republican plot' of a rain-swept Belfast cemetery, Gerry Adams, who is thought to be one of the banned organization's leaders, delivered a chilling eulogy that seemed to presage more violence and death. Deploring the death of the hunger strikers as 'British murder', Mr Adams warned, 'Bobby Sands's organisation is quite capable in its own time, not the British Government's time, of making its response.'

> *The New York Times*, 8 May 1981

The funeral continued on its solemn way and by early evening the body of Bobby Sands was interred in the republican plot. Owen Carron gave a defiant and final tribute at the graveside:

> We shall never surrender. We have humiliated the British Government and the British Government has sown the seeds of its own destruction in Ireland. We can only conclude that we must take away what they will not give and there is no way that freedom can be given and then

maintained except by armed men. Final victory to the
soldiers of the Republican Army.

The Irish News, 8 May 1981

In the midst of thousands of mourners, the world's media, by
the graves of republican legends, Carron's speech was dramatic
and fitting. Soon, however, the moment was over. The camera
crews packed up, the crowds dispersed; there was to be no
return to the severity of the rioting of previous nights. The
British government had not moved one iota. Margaret Thatcher
commented at the Scottish Conservative Conference on 8 May:
'One of their members [Bobby Sands] has chosen to kill himself
– a needless and futile waste of his life. I say "futile" Mr President,
because the political status sought by the hunger strikers will not
be granted. The Government's position is clear. Crime is always
crime, whatever the motive. Murder is never anything other than
murder' (Thatcher Archive CCOPR 413/81).

Northern Ireland did not stop functioning with the death of
Bobby Sands, far from it. After his funeral the media moved on
to the next world flashpoint. The fact is that, far from becoming
Armageddon, the situation returned to relative normality quite
quickly. There was to be no abyss, no crossroads, no Rubicon,
no breaking point; it was a return to the usual picture of
controlled anarchy. Bobby Sands' death had not moved Margaret
Thatcher and her government one inch. More importantly,
despite numerous naysayers predicting an all-out civil war on the
streets, the violence was confined to the usual flashpoints. The
conundrum for the IRA and the INLA was that indiscriminate
attacks would act against the prisoners' cause and prove counter-productive. By 1981 the RUC and British Army were, by
and large, able to confine rioting within the republican districts
of Belfast and Derry. There might be ongoing disorder in one
area, but, given Belfast's peculiar demographics, daily life might
trundle along peacefully a mile away. As John Hermon, the then
Chief Constable of the RUC recalled, the violence, though
serious, was contained: 'His [Sands'] death had been anticipated,

so the police and army were on full alert. The ensuing violence throughout that month, when two other hunger strikers died, was at the worst since 1969. Nevertheless, our containment strategy succeeded, even though 100,000 lined the streets for Sands's funeral' (Hermon, *Holding the Line*, pp. 123–4).

The rioting and shootings continued on a daily basis. However, the word 'sporadic' soon replaced 'serious' in the media descriptions of the disturbances. The visit of the English soccer team to Windsor Park to play Northern Ireland late in May was cancelled due to the concerns of the English Football Association. On 11 May the death was announced of reggae legend Bob Marley. In Rathcoole, the area where Bobby Sands grew up, 1,000 mourners followed the coffin of fourteen-year-old Desmond Guiney, who had been injured on his father's milk float on the Antrim Road during rioting. In the Maze Prison the news on the condition of Francis Hughes was reported to be 'grave'. Oliver Hughes, brother of Francis, advised the media that his mother 'had bidden him [Francis] her last farewell. He is now in a coma and has hours to live.' When asked who could save his brother's life, Oliver Hughes responded that only Margaret Thatcher could do that by granting the Five Demands. At 5.45 p.m. on Tuesday 12 May Francis Hughes died on the fifty-ninth day of his fast. Immediately, the streets that had witnessed a temporary lull in strife were alive with crowds and the noise of the banging of bin lids. Rioting soon broke out at the usual flashpoints. At the Lenadoon Estate, fourteen-year-old Julie Livingstone was struck by a baton round fired from a passing army vehicle; she died the following day. An inquest jury was to find that Julie Livingstone was 'an innocent victim' who had not been rioting. At the Divis Flats complex INLA member Emmanuel McLarnon was shot and killed by the army during disturbances. The organisation described McLarnon as having been on 'active service' when he was killed. In Derry over 300 petrol bombs were thrown at the police and army during clashes, while serious disturbances were reported also in Newry, Armagh and Strabane. On the nine o'clock BBC news Oliver Hughes was interviewed and referred, much to the consternation of the Conservative establishment, to the Prime Minister as the 'murderess Thatcher'.

Reaction was swift to Hughes' death. In essence, his violent career in the IRA was putty in the hands of the hardliners opposed to the hunger strike. Armagh Unionist MP Harold McCusker described Hughes as a 'mass murderer' and suggested that 'no one in Northern Ireland should mourn'. Gerry Adams urged Margaret Thatcher to 'accept that her attempts to stare down this hunger strike have failed'. Paddy Joe Hughes said of his son that 'he fought a good fight, soldier to soldier, he fought back to the end with the only weapon he had in a British jail'. Margaret Thatcher was in defiant mood in the House of Commons on 14 May, holding to, and seemingly wallowing in, her hard line: 'What the hunger strikers are asking for – the one who died last was in fact a murderer, let us not mince our words – is political status by easy stages. They cannot have it. They are murderers and people who use force and violence to obtain their ends. They have made perfectly clear what they want. They cannot and will not have it' (Hansard, HC (series 6) vol. 4, col 306W (14 May 1981)).

The deaths, sorrow and mourning continued unabated. In Newtownabbey, Eric Guiney was buried beside his son Desmond. The Church of Ireland Bishop of Down and Connor described the ordeal of Mrs Roberta Guiney, who had buried her son and husband within three days, as 'intolerable' and suggested that 'the full force of evil was at work'. In St Oliver Plunkett Church in Lenadoon the body of Julie Livingstone lay overnight prior to her burial at the City Cemetery. In the lower Falls district a piper and masked men led the procession for Emmanuel McClarnon to Milltown Cemetery. In the Ballymurphy district 23-year-old Constable Samuel Vallely was killed in an IRA rocket attack; he left a pregnant wife and sixteen-month-old daughter behind. The Reverend Ian Paisley called the murder 'vicious' and appealed for the 'shackles' to be taken off the security forces. Amid the anarchy, the world was shocked to hear that Pope John Paul II had been shot in St Peter's Square in Rome. It seemed that the madness was spreading.

The burial of Francis Hughes was a bitter affair. Originally, arrangements had been made to bring his coffin along the full length of the Falls Road; however, the authorities were in no mood to have another IRA show of strength so soon after the funeral of Bobby Sands. The body of Hughes was kept in Forster Green Hospital on the outskirts of Belfast and, on its release, the RUC refused to allow the tricolour-covered coffin to go into west Belfast. Kate Adie encapsulated the attitude of the police when she wrote 'Mr Hughes, they reckoned [the RUC], was being sent on a final lap of honour through national heartland and they weren't having that' (Adie, *The Kindness of Strangers*, p. 179). In effect, there was massive political pressure on the police to prevent the funeral becoming a propaganda coup. Accordingly, the 1954 Flags and Emblems Act was invoked by the RUC and, 'in the interest of public order', a stand-off between the Hughes family and the police began. The National H-Block Committee described the actions of the RUC as 'a callous body-snatching exercise', but, with no resolution in sight, the cortège, accompanied by scores of RUC Land Rovers, eventually left for the Hughes family home in south Derry. The following day saw a massive security operation thrown into place around Bellaghy and the funeral procession was forced to go a circuitous route to get to St Mary's Church in the village. Again, the estimates of the number of mourners ranged from a meagre 10,000 to a more optimistic 40,000. The RUC, however, failed to prevent a further IRA show of strength; suddenly, from within the crowd, a dozen members of the IRA appeared and a volley of shots was fired over Hughes' coffin.

At the requiem Mass for Francis Hughes, Father Michael Flanagan summed up the feeling of pessimism present throughout south Derry and beyond. 'It seems as if the Lord has been very far away from us for the past twelve years,' he said. The procession to the cemetery was along long and winding country roads, led by Gerry Adams and other leading members

of Sinn Féin. It fell to Martin McGuinness to give the message
of defiance at the graveside:

> The enemy feared him so much, there were roads no
> British soldier could travel safely . . . His body lies here
> beside us but he lives in the little streets of Belfast, he
> lives in the Bogside, he lives in East Tyrone, he lives in
> Crossmaglen. He will always live in the hearts and minds
> of unconquerable Irish republicans in all these places. They
> could not break him. They will not break us.

> Associated Press, 16 May 1981

In February 2007 Oliver Hughes would recall bitterly the death
of his brother:

> When my brother died, the coroner's office returned his
> estate to my father. I talked to my sister about this the
> other evening. My brother had nothing when he died I
> said. Eight pence, she said, he had eight pence, a box of
> matches and a miraculous medal. I grieve for that chap, for
> he walked the hills and valleys with no shoes on his feet,
> not much clothes on his back, no food in his stomach and
> no money in his wallet. He was a very active member of
> the IRA, he was on active service for a long number of
> years, and whilst we'll not discuss his involvement in the
> war too deeply, he certainly was a key player.

> *The Times*, 11 February 2007

The killings on the streets continued. On 16 May the UDA
burst into the house of 38-year-old Catholic Patrick Martin and
shot him dead as he lay in his bed. The rumour mill reported
that he had been shot by the IRA after he had 'disobeyed' the
organisation by refusing to close his shop on the day of Francis
Hughes' funeral. The story, regardless of its source, travelled
around the world. Patrick Martin was just another victim of
Belfast's squalid sectarian conflict. On 19 May the IRA in south
Armagh detonated a 1,000-pound bomb as a Saracen army

vehicle was passing. Five members of the Royal Green Jackets travelling in the vehicle were killed in the explosion, two miles from their base in Bessbrook. The debris from the blast littered a wide area of the countryside and closed the Belfast to Dublin railway line, which ran parallel to the scene. It was a devastating attack that had seen the biggest loss of life suffered by the Army since the deaths of eighteen soldiers at Narrow Water in August 1979. Speaking at the scene of the explosion, Secretary of State Humphrey Atkins pointed out that 'it is a sobering thought that those responsible might well claim political status'. The IRA's South Armagh Brigade issued a statement that denied that the plight of Raymond McCreesh (who had joined the hunger strike in March and whose condition was now deteriorating) had been the cause of the attack. The statement released was piercing in its clarity:

> It is interesting to note that those Loyalist hypocrites most vocal in condemning this IRA operation were totally silent when innocent Nationalist civilians were murdered recently by British soldiers and RUC men in Belfast and Derry. British soldiers should recognise that the English public and English politicians do not give a damn about the waste of their lives. How many times have you been told that the IRA has been defeated? You are fighting a war you cannot win.
>
> *The Irish News*, 20 May 1981

Inside the Maze Bik McFarlane sent out a communication that referred to the bomb attack: 'PS Have just heard about that cunning little operation in S. Armagh. Oh, you wonderful people!! Far from home they perish, yet they know not the reason why! Tis truly a great shame. They kill and die and never think to question. Such is the penalty for blind folly. God Bless. Bik' (O'Connor, *In Search of a State*, p. 103).

May 1981 had become a very sad and bitter month. The hunger strike continued.

Chapter 12

Diplomacy and Duplicity

'Where there is doubt, may we bring faith; and where there is despair, may we bring hope.'

Margaret Thatcher, 4 May 1979

As May drew on, the search for a solution to the hunger strikes hit a brick wall. The government, outwardly, remained indifferent to the protest; since the carnival of reaction that had accompanied the death of Sands and Hughes had been localised and controlled, a crisis had been averted. The main nationalist paper *The Irish News*, however, was receiving a stream of letters from residents of the Lower Falls Road complaining that 'hooliganism' and 'thuggery' had been the order of the day for almost a month. In essence, gangs of youths had been allowed carte blanche to riot, hijack and burn virtual no-go areas for police and army, leaving the residents to bear the consequences of the antisocial activity undefended. Regardless, the procession to death inside the prison continued. On Sunday 22 March Raymond McCreesh and Patsy O'Hara had joined the fast and both were deteriorating as the twentieth day of May approached.

Raymond McCreesh was from the village of Camlough in south Armagh and was born on 25 February 1957. South Armagh was, and is, a place apart and throughout the Troubles it was to be the nemesis of the British Army. It was a staunch republican area and Raymond McCreesh soon found himself embroiled in the conflict, having risen through the ranks of Fianna Éireann to the IRA. In June 1976 McCreesh, together with his long-time friends, Danny McGuiness and Patrick Quinn, was captured by an undercover army team as they prepared to ambush paratroopers. In March 1977, despite refusing to recognise the court, McCreesh received a fourteen-year sentence and was immediately sent to the Maze, where he joined the blanket protest. Such was his dedication to the protest that he refused for almost four years to accept his monthly family visit, since in the course of a visit he would have to wear prison garb. He was not, however, totally isolated from his family, as occasionally his brother Brian, who was a priest, travelled to the prison to say Sunday Mass.

Patsy O'Hara was at the time of the fast the Officer Commanding of the approximately thirty INLA prisoners within the Maze. The INLA was an off-shoot of the Official IRA that had been established in December 1974 to offer a radical socialist alternative to the Provisional IRA. It remained small in comparison to the Provisionals, but was to be hindered in its early years by internecine warfare with former comrades that depleted its numbers and called into question any ideological credibility it claimed to possess. The INLA arrived on the international stage in March 1979, when it was responsible for the assassination of Margaret Thatcher's close confidant, Airey Neave, as he left the House of Commons in his car. Patsy O'Hara had truly been a child of the Troubles. Born in Bishop Street in Derry City in 1957, he had witnessed the strife in the city at first hand and had become highly politicised, developing a left-wing critique of the situation that had led him to the INLA. Having spent various periods in prison throughout the 1970s, O'Hara's final prison term in the Maze began in January 1980, when he received eight years for possession of a gun. Immediately, he went on the blanket protest. The image of Patsy O'Hara that adorned the lamp posts of nationalist areas during the hunger strike was eye-catching. The picture captured a young and bearded revolutionary and idealist, in the style of Che Guevera or some other 1960s icon. It was a photograph that portrayed the essence of the man and the revolutionary zeal that he stood and died for. Prior to embarking on the hunger strike, he wrote:

> We stand for the freedom of the Irish nation so that future generations will enjoy the prosperity they rightly deserve, free from foreign interference, oppression and exploitation. The real criminals are the British imperialists who have thrived on the blood and sweat of generations of Irish men . . . They have maintained control of Ireland through force of arms and there is only one way to end it. I would rather die than rot in this concrete tomb for years to come.

> *IRIS*, 1, 2 November 1981

As both men faced death, the propaganda war continued. From within the Northern Ireland Office, a story emanated that McCreesh had asked for food on the fifty-sixth day of his fast. 'Prison sources' reported that on Saturday 16 May the prisoner had asked to end his strike and immediately his family had been called to his bedside. Sinn Féin reacted to what they described as 'black propaganda'. The McCreesh family responded by saying a prison doctor had told them that their son had been in a state of shock after being given the last rites and, when asked did he want some milk, he had become confused and had said, 'I don't know.' On their arrival, the McCreesh family found their son in a state of hallucination, believing that he was in Scotland. They added that when asked if he knew what Long Kesh was, he responded 'a concentration camp'. The family reaffirmed that they would respect their son's wish that no intervention would be allowed if he lapsed into a coma.

Despite the war of words, both Raymond McCreesh and Patsy O'Hara edged closer to death as they reached the sixtieth day of their fast. Father Brian McCreesh, the brother of Raymond, received a 'no surrender' response from Mrs Thatcher (through her personal secretary Clive Whitmore) when he wrote to her asking that she intervene to save his brother's life. Her reply to the priest was cold, blunt and heavy on indifference: 'The aim which your brother and his fellow strikers declared, or which was declared on their behalf, is simply not in any responsible Government's gift,' she advised the priest. The letter continued that it was the Prime Minister's 'profound hope' that 'those to whom your brother listens, and whom he trusts, will explain this to him so that, even now, a chance can be taken to save one life at least' (*The Irish News*, 20 May 1981).

On 20 May Northern Ireland went to the polls for its local government elections. At stake was the governance of the twenty-six local councils – yet in reality, as ever, it was the very constitution that was at stake as far as the politicians were concerned. Sinn Féin would, as in previous years, not field candidates in the elections. The anti-H-Block ticket, on which Bobby Sands had been elected to the House of Commons the previous month, was not an option on the ballot papers; it may seem as if this was a missed opportunity for Sinn Féin and the anti-H-Block campaign to add political clout to the hunger strike. However, in strictly practical terms, the shock value of the Fermanagh and South Tyrone victory had come too late to assist in mounting an organised campaign at local government level. Moreover, for most, if not all, of the wider republican movement, the minutiae of local government within Northern Ireland (which had effectively been stripped of its powers in 1972) did not merit consideration. In the Republic, however, Charles Haughey announced that he was going to the country on 11 June. It was an election that had been postponed in the wake of the Stardust tragedy in February, and the date was now set for June due to the ongoing hunger strike crisis. The Taoiseach said he would be seeking a 'clear mandate because of the grave situation in Northern Ireland'. On 19 May, in Bobby Sands' home estate of Twinbrook, an eleven-year-old girl, Carol Ann Kelly, had been struck by a plastic bullet fired by the British Army as she returned home with a carton of milk from a local shop. Carol Ann Kelly died from her injuries two days later. As usual a war of words between the army and locals erupted over the circumstances; it was, however, open season for the use of plastic bullets. The Belfast H-Block Information Centre issued a bulletin about the condition of Patsy O'Hara who had, it was reported, suffered a minor heart attack. The bulletin continued: 'so fragile is Patsy's body that the blankets covering him are supported by a cage. His eyes have completely sunk into his head, his tongue has swollen to twice its normal size and he is coughing up clots of blood.' Brendan McLaughlin, who had replaced Francis Hughes on the fast, was experiencing extreme discomfort and was moved to the prison hospital, while Raymond McCreesh had not 'moved in days'.

In the hours prior to Raymond's death Brian McCreesh celebrated Mass at his brother's bedside; he died at 2.11 a.m. on the morning of Thursday 21 May. The H-Block Committee said the death was a direct result of Margaret Thatcher's 'Death Wish' policy. Cardinal Ó Fiaich made no apologies as he appealed again to Mrs Thatcher to act or be 'faced by the wrath of the whole Nationalist people'. Patsy O'Hara's death was announced just after midday on the same day; both men had survived for sixty-one days on the fast; the city of Derry prepared to bury its first hunger striker. Rioting and sniper fire returned to the streets of Belfast and Derry as the INLA issued a statement threatening 'fierce retaliation' for the death of O'Hara. Inside the Maze Kieran Doherty from Andersonstown joined the hunger strike.

Again the procession of funerals drew the world's media to Northern Ireland. In Camlough a massive crowd gathered to witness the final journey of Raymond McCreesh. Pipers, guards of honour and masked men and women accompanied the tricolour-draped coffin to St Malachy's Church, where loudspeakers relayed the proceedings to the mourners. The service was led by Brian McCreesh and concelebrated by five other clerics. Afterwards, the procession made its way from the church to the nearby cemetery where, at the graveside, a volley of shots rang out to cheers and applause. Sinn Féin President Ruairí Ó Brádaigh (who had been banned from Northern Ireland, but was present nevertheless) paid tribute to McCreesh and his dedication to the same cause for which Terence MacSwiney had died. Of the British government, he said, 'Where now is their Ulsterisation? Where now is their normalisation? Where now is their criminalisation? These hungry and starving men in their beds of pain, by superior moral strength, have pushed the British government to the wall and have shamed them in the eyes of the world.' Patsy O'Hara's funeral provided the INLA with the opportunity to demonstrate that it was just as capable as the IRA of mounting a show of strength. In all, thirty-five masked and armed men flanked the coffin as it made its way through the Brandywell and Bogside to the city cemetery; tens of thousands followed or lined the streets. O'Hara's coffin was draped with the tricolour and the Starry Plough and led by a lone girl piper who played a lament. At the graveside IRSP spokesman Jim Daly, whose wife had been murdered by loyalists less than a year earlier, paid tribute to O'Hara. Daly turned his ire on the Prime Minister, accusing her of being a hypocrite. 'Mrs Thatcher, who stood on the steps of 10 Downing Street and read aloud the prayer of St Francis of Assisi. That prayer belonged not to her, but to Patsy O'Hara,' said Daly.

On 26 May Brendan McLaughlin, who had been suffering excruciating pain and internal bleeding due to a stomach ulcer, ended his fast. On 29 May he was replaced by Martin Hurson. The H-Block Information Centre commented on McLaughlin that 'to have continued in his critical condition would have meant immediate death, before the effects of a long hunger strike would have built up the necessary pressure to break the British Government's intransigence'. In the aftermath of the deaths of four hunger strikers, the statement was somewhat optimistic. In the background, however, the National H-Blocks/Armagh Campaign was busy finalising its candidates for the Republic's elections due to take place on 11 June. In the end nine candidates were forwarded for election. The four men on the fast at the time were nominated: Martin Hurson for Longford–Westmeath, Kieran Doherty for Cavan–Monaghan, Joe McDonnell for Sligo–Leitrim and Kevin Lynch for Waterford. The other five candidates were Sean McKenna – who had almost died during the first fast – together with Tony O'Hara, brother of Patsy, Paddy Agnew, Tom McAllister and Mairéad Farrell, who had partaken in the first fast at Armagh Prison. Twenty-four years earlier, in the emotional aftermath of the deaths of Seán South and Feargal O'Hanlon during the IRA border campaign, Sinn Féin had returned four members to the Dáil. In 1981 such a performance was again entirely feasible.

Belfast was to receive a surprise visitor on Thursday 28 May. In the midst of the human tragedy that was unfolding, Margaret Thatcher arrived in the city to renew her attack on the IRA and the hunger strikers. It was a carefully stage-managed publicity stunt to demonstrate that her position was unchanged, and the decision to come had been entirely down to Mrs Thatcher herself. On the previous Sunday she was being given a security briefing at Chequers by the Chief Constable of the RUC, Jack Hermon, who records that she suddenly called her Diary Secretary, announcing 'I must go to Ireland.' She arrived at Stormont Castle and described the hunger strike as a 'futile cause' and turned the tables on the IRA by accusing *them* of being 'inflexible' and 'intransigent'. She did, however, offer her sympathy to the relatives of the dead hunger strikers and added that it was a tragedy that young men should be 'persuaded, coerced or ordered to starve themselves to death'. With words that were obviously well choreographed, the Prime Minister claimed that 'they [the IRA] have turned their violence against themselves', but her next line was one that would haunt her in future years. 'The men of violence, faced with the failure of their discredited cause, have chosen to play what may well be their last card.' Since she was a woman whose every word was scripted, it was obvious that her visit was one for bravado as well as propaganda. In the wake of the IRA's killing of five Royal Green Jackets the previous week, as well as its statement that the

British were fighting a war they could not win, Thatcher's trip was an act of defiance. There may well have been an element of semi-elation within government circles arising from the fact that the hunger strike had not brought Northern Ireland to its knees. However, it was a poorly judged remark by Mrs Thatcher to say that the IRA's last card was being played.

On 8 June Thomas McElwee from south Derry joined the fast. Two days later republican prisoners again stole world headlines as eight inmates on remand in Belfast's Crumlin Road Jail escaped in what was a very daring IRA action. The escape was well received in republican districts and, two days later on 12 June, the H-Block campaign was to receive a further boost as election results rolled in across the Republic. From the outset, it was evident that Fianna Fáil had been wounded. However, the performance of the anti-H-Block candidates bordered on the stunning, as both Kieran Doherty and Paddy Agnew were elected to the Dáil. It was Doherty's performance in Cavan–Monaghan that was the most impressive, since he secured 9,121 first preference votes, almost 15 per cent of those cast. In Louth, Paddy Agnew polled 8,368 first preference votes, while Joe McDonnell secured 5,634 in Sligo–Leitrim. Martin Hurson polled well and gained 4,573 of the poll in Longford–Westmeath, while in Kerry North, Sean McKenna received 3,860 of the first count. In Waterford, Kevin Lynch received 3,337 of the first preferences and in Dublin West Tony O'Hara gained 3,034 votes, almost 1,000 more than future President of Ireland Mary Robinson. Mairéad Farrell received a creditable 2,751 votes in Cork North Central and in Clare Tom McAllister secured 2,120 votes. Given that Section 31 of the Broadcasting Act had effectively barred anybody – including the prisoners themselves – from campaigning for the prisoners on television or radio, the results shook the political establishment. In the end, Haughey's Fianna Fáil was to be damaged severely by the performance of the prisoners, who took 3.1 per cent of the total first preference votes. With Haughey's position weakened, Garret FitzGerald, in coalition with the Labour Party, secured the votes of a majority of the independents in the Dáil to be elected Taoiseach by 81 votes to 78 on 30 June.

Confirmation that the election of Bobby Sands had shaken the British establishment to its core came on 12 June, when the Conservative government began the process of amending the Representation of the People Act. On its introduction to the House, the Home Secretary outlined the aim of the amendment, in the words of the bill, 'to disqualify for standing for election to this House and for membership of this House those convicted persons detained in prison in the United Kingdom in pursuance of a sentence of more than twelve months'. During the debate the IRA was mentioned a total of 117 times, Bobby Sands a total of 62, while 'Fermanagh and South Tyrone' received 57 references; it was evident that the election of Bobby Sands had caused deep anguish within Thatcher's government. The following day *The Times* published an editorial, which was headed 'Let Them Stand, But Not Sit'. The thrust of the article being that, in the interests of democracy, all felons should be allowed to stand for election, yet not sit in the Commons. The editorial went on to suggest that the barring of prisoners from nomination – never mind election – was logical, but that it might just have been a step too far by the government. This argument was because British democracy had a tradition of allowing the electorate to vote for candidates who could not sit in parliament, such as Tony Benn, then Viscount Stansgate, in 1961. The piece finished with an assertion that 'the election of Bobby Sands was indeed embarrassing, but it was not disastrous ... such an embarrassment may not be repeated, but is in any case worth the risk'. However, the fact was that the argument was deeply flawed and that the law was amended for one reason and one reason only: the result of the Fermanagh and South Tyrone election of 9 April. The violence continued as June drew to a close. In the space of a month the IRA would claim the lives of three members of the RUC, two soldiers, and two Catholic civilians (one killed in crossfire and one labelled an 'informer'). In the background, the issue of the hunger strike had divided the communities in

Northern Ireland to unprecedented levels. It was within this context that East Derry Unionist MP Willie Ross suggested that 'the Roman Catholic population of Northern Ireland should be paid to leave the country and settle elsewhere'.

The morale of the prisoners, it seemed, was undaunted. In late June Paddy Quinn, Mickey Devine and Lawrence McKeown all joined the fast in the Maze. Margaret Thatcher, as ever, was the main target of republican ire at a mass march and rally scheduled for Dunville Park on the Falls Road at the end of June. The advertisements for the event sent out the message that supporters must 'Break Maggie Thatcher'. The tone of the anti-H-Block Campaign was still upbeat as it issued a statement that the British had 'murdered four prisoners on Hunger Strike', adding that 'They are set to murder more.' It also claimed, somewhat bombastically, that the election of both Kieran Doherty and Paddy Agnew to the Dáil had 'rendered the Free State ungovernable for the first time in its history', and that the message remained the same: 'nothing less than the five demands'. On the day of the march itself, 28 June, approximately 30,000 gathered at the rally. Goretti McDonnell, wife of Joe, who had entered the fifty-second day of his fast, gave a stark assessment of her husband's condition. 'He [Joe McDonnell] is no longer the man with the big frame that you see on the posters. His teeth are protruding and his cheeks have sunk into his face. He has a skeleton-like figure.'

In early July speculation began to grow that the British were about to 'move' to offer a solution to the crisis. After the deaths of the first four hunger strikers it may have seemed to some that a breathing space had been created before the fifth hunger striker, Joe McDonnell, entered his 'crisis' phase. However, a statement released by Secretary of State Humphrey Atkins on 29 June seemed to cast doubt on this notion. Saying that the prisoners had nothing more to prove, Atkins then criticised the leadership of the IRA: 'it suits them better to have the strike go on, manipulating and intimidating those who do not agree with them, and exploiting the human emotions that the strikes inevitably give rise to.' In response, the prisoners labelled Atkins 'arrogant and callous', while Ian Paisley suggested, again, that the British government was preparing to grant political status to the prisoners as a precursor to a United Ireland. The key to progress at that time seemed to lie with the newly installed Dublin government under Garret FitzGerald. He had met in late June with Goretti McDonnell and pledged that he would contact the British government in relation to the hunger strike, should he be elected Taoiseach.

On 1 July FitzGerald, accordingly, made contact with the British about the feasibility of permitting the Irish Commission for Justice and Peace (ICJP) to intervene in the dispute. This body was an offshoot of the Irish Catholic Bishops' Conference, which had been established in 1970. Its *raison d'être* was to consider issues regarding peace, justice and human rights. On 3 June the Commission had issued a statement on the hunger strikes suggesting that, whilst full political status was in its view out of the question, it would support moves to enable male inmates to wear their own clothing – as was permissible for female inmates in Armagh Jail. In addition, the Commission proposed that greater association should be granted and that 'prison work' could be redefined within the context of educational or cultural activities. It was a measured statement that outwardly seemed to offer some form of limited compromise. Led by Dublin Bishop Dermot O'Mahony, the Commission's intervention over the weekend of 4–6 July perhaps presented the most important attempt to broker a deal throughout the fast. One of its members was Father Michael Crilly, who was a cousin of Thomas McElwee, and it was this link that had initially brought the work of the Commission into the equation. At stake was the life of Joe McDonnell; time was running out as he had been afforded the last rites on 3 July. That day the Commission held an eight-hour meeting with the Northern Ireland Office Prisons' Minister, Michael Alison.

On 4 July the republican prisoners, under the leadership of Brendan (Bik) McFarlane and Public Relations Officer, Richard

O'Rawe, issued a statement that reiterated their determination to win their Five Demands. The tone was considered remarkably conciliatory, as it suggested that the British government could resolve the hunger strike without losing face by extending prison reforms to the entire prison population. But Atkins was adamant that there would be no beginning to prison reform until the fast had ended. As the Commission spoke at length to the hunger strikers, Atkins refused permission for McFarlane to join in the discussions on the Saturday.

At the same time as talks were ongoing within the prison, the British government, through its intermediary 'Mountain Climber' made contact with the republican leadership outside the prison. The IRA assigned Gerry Adams as its intermediary for these contacts and, insisting on the utmost secrecy, Mountain Climber outlined proposals that would grant concessions beyond those that the ICJP understood were on offer. It was believed that one of these additional concessions would include enhanced educational facilities, such as access for prisoners to Open University courses. On Sunday 6 July the Sinn Féin Director of Publicity, Danny Morrison, was permitted to meet with the other prisoners and outlined briefly to them the proposals that Mountain Climber had offered, should the fast be terminated. It was suggested that, initially, the government would make 'gestures' on three of the Five Demands as a compromise. This was a breakthrough of sorts, but it was also recognition that there could not be an absolute victory for either side. Morrison was advised that the prisoners felt there was still existed an issue of trust and substance; in essence, the prisoners needed guarantees. Morrison then went to an office and phoned Gerry Adams to describe the mood of the prisoners and suggest that he should try to secure viable concessions and more evidence of the government's good faith. As the matter progressed towards some sort of agreement, Bik McFarlane was briefed on the situation and permitted to see the hunger strikers. As Danny Morrison recalled, with such a delicate process ongoing, certain individuals within the prison were unhappy that they had not been consulted.

Indeed the turn of events, according to Morrison, were a sign
that hidden hands were trying to undermine the negotiations:

> The prison officers were very unhappy that day and
> considered my presence in the jail on a Sunday, having
> been brought in through the prison officers' gate, as a
> 'sell out'. But as I waited to go back in to see the hunger
> strikers (Bik and I were not allowed in together) a deputy
> governor called John Pepper stormed into the room and
> told me to get out of his jail! I explained to him that I was
> there with the authority of the government and was trying
> to resolve the hunger strike. He didn't care – I was thrown
> out and some of the prison officers that were angry when
> they saw me coming in were now laughing that I was
> getting kicked out. This, not inconsequential incident, was
> one of the grounds for suspecting that the British were
> either toying with the hunger strikers in their weakened
> condition [raising their expectations, only to crash them]
> or that the British were divided between the Northern
> Ireland Office or Home Office and the Foreign Office
> (who, it seems, were the ones who had got me in).

> Correspondence from Danny Morrison to the author, 14
> February 2011

With Morrison now outside the prison, the situation stalled.
In short, there were proposals on the table but no deal. Bik
McFarlane, who was unaware that Morrison had been put out
of the prison, returned to his cell in the belief that nothing had
been agreed. As the minutes passed, the good faith and hope,
if any, that had been established between the sides began to
dissipate.

Adams, in confidence, advised the ICJP that further
concessions had been proposed in the course of this secondary
negotiation. At this point Bishop O'Mahony confronted
Michael Alison and insisted that an envoy be sent to the prison
to verify exactly what was on offer. Accordingly, after discussion,
the prisoners were told that they would receive a visit from a

government envoy at nine o'clock the following morning, 7 July.

As midday approached on 7 July the prisoners had not received the anticipated visit. By now Bishop O'Mahony had become distressed that the British government appeared to have acted in bad faith and organised a press conference to outline the British concessions. This move prompted Alison to contact O'Mahony to assure him that a government official would enter the prison that afternoon. By six o'clock the situation remained unchanged. At ten o'clock that evening Alison phoned O'Mahony to tell him that the envoy would be sent early the next morning. Joe McDonnell died at 4.50 a.m. on 8 July; the prisoners were visited hours later by the official and told that the government's position remained unchanged. The Commission described the statement read to the prisoners as nothing like 'a serious attempt to seek a resolution in the light of the discussions we have had and of the position clarified to us by the minister' (*The Irish News*, 9 July 1981).

In 2005 the publication of *Blanketmen* by Richard O'Rawe opened up a debate, perhaps chasm, within the wider republican family over the extent of the negotiation and offer at this time – and how acceptable this offer might have been to the prisoners, Sinn Féin and the IRA. The crux of O'Rawe's argument is that IRA prisoners and their leader within the Maze, Brendan McFarlane, had accepted the proposals as a basis for ending the strike, only for Sinn Féin and the IRA leadership to reject it on their behalf. The net result of this action, O'Rawe suggests, is that the lives of Joe McDonnell, Martin Hurson, Kevin Lynch, Kieran Doherty, Thomas McElwee and Michael Devine were lost. Moreover, O'Rawe suggests that the IRA leadership made this decision because it calculated that Owen Carron would be in a better position to reclaim the Fermanagh and South Tyrone seat left vacant by the death of Bobby Sands if the hunger strike was still ongoing. Given the gravity of this allegation, it is not surprising that there has been much flak exchanged between former comrades. Indeed, leading republicans, including the

IRA commander in the prison at the time, Bik McFarlane, Jim Gibney and Danny Morrison, have contradicted vehemently O'Rawe's claims. Gerry Adams has diplomatically and characteristically remained silent.

But O'Rawe is emphatic that, even as Joe McDonell's life was ebbing away, McFarlane had indicated to him from his cell that the proposals offered formed the basis for a settlement. McFarlane allegedly accepted O'Rawe's suggestion that a deal could be struck and said (O'Rawe claims), '*Aontaim leat, scriobhfaidh me chun taoibh amuigh agus cuirfidh me fhois orthu.*' ('I agree with you, I will write to the outside and let them know.') But when the message was sent out to the IRA leadership by McFarlane it was (allegedly) rejected and, accordingly, the prisoners were left with no option but to continue their fast. In his book, O'Rawe says, 'Bik and I were shattered.' Bik McFarlane rejects this as nonsense. And indeed, O'Rawe's cellmate, Colm Scullion, is adamant that there was no deal on the table:

> What is being said is untrue. There was no deal. I agree with Richard that there was certainly an offer which Richard was made aware of by Brendan McFarlane who was a few cells away. I didn't hear anything like what Richard is saying. We all desperately hoped that there would be a deal. Unfortunately, the British government refused to stand over or verify what it was offering. It refused to send any of its representatives in to meet the hunger strikers and tragically Joe McDonnell died and his death was followed by five more of our comrades.

> *Derry Journal*, 8 April 2008

Unfortunately, from the historian's point of view, there is no independent witness to the exchange between O'Rawe and McFarlane. The net result is that the IRA and Sinn Féin leaderships of the time have been portrayed with the deaths of six hunger strikers on their hands. Richard O'Rawe states in his book's prologue that when, in 1991, he began questioning the role of the IRA leadership (and by inference that of Gerry

Adams) over the weekend of 4 to 6 July, he was advised that he 'could be shot' for opening his mouth. On the final page of his book O'Rawe makes a heart-felt appeal to the families of the hunger strikers to believe his story:

> I ask the families of the dead hunger strikers to understand why I have written this book. Not only does it cast some light on a critical part of our lives, but I believe that you have the right to know the facts as I knew them . . . Your loved ones [the deceased hunger strikers] are more than faces on a gable wall to me; they are dear friends and valued comrades. Furthermore, my children, your children and future generations of Irish have a right to the truth; history will judge us very harshly if we skim over such a momentous event, as we have up to now.

> O'Rawe, *Blanketmen*, p. 261

The foregoing passage would seem to contradict a communication that O'Rawe sent out from the Maze in the wake of the failure of the negotiations. Hindsight is always 20:20, but this statement in July 1981 does seem curiously at odds with his subsequent recollection:

> The British government's hypocrisy and their refusal to act in a responsible manner are completely to blame for the death of Joe McDonnell . . . The only definite response forthcoming from the British government [to the prisoners' 4 July statement] is the death of Joe McDonnell . . . This morning [Secretary of State] Mr Atkins has issued us with yet another ambiguous and self-gratifying statement . . . That statement, even given its most optimistic reading, is far removed from our July 4th statement. At face value it amounts to nothing.

> *Derry Journal*, 18 April 2008

The 'whatabouteries' of the affair raged on and were further compounded in November 2010 when O'Rawe published his second book, *Afterlives: The Hunger Strike and the Secret Offer That Changed Irish History*. In this book, O'Rawe elaborates on his argument, suggesting that Gerry Adams was personally behind the decision to reject the offer, thus overriding the prisoners' own wishes and causing the needless deaths of six hunger strikers. O'Rawe's logic is that Adams believed Sinn Féin needed to oversee the victory of Owen Carron (Bobby Sands' election agent who would be nominated as a 'proxy prisoner' candidate in the Fermanagh and South Tyrone August by-election) in order to establish a Sinn Féin electoral strategy. For the followers of this argument, the timeline is convenient. The last hunger striker to die, Michael Devine, passed away on 21 August, the day that Carron retained Sands' seat. In the 5 September 1981 edition of *An Phoblacht*, an 'authorised' spokesman for the IRA endorsed the idea that Sinn Féin should contest the West Belfast seat at the next British general election. The hunger strike ended on 3 October 1981. Within a month the Sinn Féin electoral policy was approved at its Ard Fheis in a motion calling for Sinn Féin to 'contest all local government elections both north and south'. That very day Danny Morrison delivered his famous speech, namely, 'Who here really believes that we can win the war through the ballot box? But will anyone here object if, with a ballot paper in one hand and the Armalite in the other, we take power in Ireland?' That speech was the foundation of what became known as the 'Armalite and ballot box strategy' of Sinn Féin.

For those who feel that O'Rawe's argument is poppycock, the case is clear-cut. To argue that six hunger strikers died, at the behest of the Sinn Féin leader, for the sake of the party's vaulting political ambition stretches reality to the extreme. For O'Rawe to make an assertion without primary evidence, and to personalise his argument against Adams to the obvious relish of many anti-Sinn Féin commentators, detracts from his case. In short, O'Rawe's attack is unmerited. To infer that, over the particular weekend of 4 to 6 July 1981, Gerry Adams could have formulated a plot that foresaw Sinn Féin's thirty-year electoral rise based on the unlikely victory of Owen Carron is far-fetched in the extreme. The argument brings new meaning to the term Machiavellian. The bottom line was that nobody at that time was sure when the by-election for Fermanagh and South Tyrone would take place. Adams, therefore, would have been gambling with the lives of the hunger strikers on a future date that neither he, nor the British government, could identify. The writ for holding the election was fast-tracked through the Commons and was heard on 28 July – three weeks after the alleged offer had been made. In protest at the government's apparent haste, Gerry Fitt asked the Speaker of the House of Commons, George Thomas, to postpone the move, since 'the emaciated dead or dying body of an IRA hunger striker is a more lethal weapon than an Armalite rifle in the arms of the men of violence'. Whether Fitt's outburst was aimed at the IRA or an attempt to persuade his former comrades in the SDLP to stand is unclear. By that stage, very few people in Irish nationalist politics were taking Fitt seriously.

The date for the poll was set for 20 August. The biggest impediment to a Carron victory in early July, aside from a Unionist–Unity candidate, lay in the intentions of the SDLP. For Adams to gamble, at that time, that the SDLP would give a Sinn Féin-supported candidate a clear run would have been a serious error. The party had been crucified for its decision to withdraw three months earlier from the first by-election and had made it clear that it would stand in the August poll. The party executive of the SDLP then voted by 11 votes to 7 to recommend that a candidate be put forward, only for this to be rejected on 5 August by the local party on a 48 to 44 vote. On 6 August, the SDLP announced, reluctantly, that it would not field a candidate: a month after Adams, allegedly, had made his calculation on fielding Carron in Fermanagh and South Tyrone.

A number of other contradictions plague O'Rawe's assertion. There was no need for Gerry Adams to prove that there was mileage in electoral politics; the argument had been put to bed by Sands' triumph in Fermanagh and South Tyrone in April that

year. In truth, the republican movement had already accepted
that it had missed a prime opportunity to make electoral gains
and to highlight the prisoners' cause in the local government
elections of May. That 'oversight' was rectified at the Sinn Féin
Ard Fheis later in the year, when the decision was taken to
stand in future local government elections. If anything, Owen
Carron's subsequent victory was an unexpected bonus for the
republican movement that, in early July, not many commentators
would have predicted. All evidence, indeed, would support the
fact that in the summer of 1981 there was a debate ongoing
within Sinn Féin on the viability of entering electoral politics.
However, it is absurd to suggest that this internal debate hinged
on the participation of Owen Carron in the Fermanagh and
South Tyrone by-election. It is even more incredible to say, after
long and silent consideration of the events of that time, that
dying men were sacrificed on the altar of political convenience
to prove a point.

Chapter 13

Intervention and Disintegration

'I told him that I would intervene if he lapsed into a coma.'
Mrs Philomena McCloskey

Joe McDonnell died on 8 July on the sixty-first day of his fast.
Again rioting broke out in the early morning as news of the
fifth death broke. Just like the proverbial stable door that was
locked after the horse had bolted, an official from the British
government arrived to advise the prisoners that its position was
unchanged. Pat McGeown joined the fast the following day. A
statement issued by the republican prisoners in the Maze stated
quite simply that 'Joe McDonnell need not have died.' The press
release on behalf of the 420 prisoners continued:

> The British Government's hypocrisy and their refusal to
> act in a responsible manner are completely to blame for
> the death of Joe McDonnell . . . For a considerable period
> of time they stood on ceremony, asserting again and again
> that they would not talk to the prisoners in order to find a
> solution. Yet after Joe's death they decide to send an official
> into Long Kesh to talk to us – or rather talk at us.

> *Daily Ireland*, 11 June 2006

H–Block organiser, Jim Gibney, called on Mrs Thatcher to accept the five deaths as sufficient sacrifice for each of the demands, describing the latest statement of denial issued by Humphrey Atkins as 'rubbish'. John Hume described the death of Joe McDonnell as a 'tragedy', adding that 'Mrs Thatcher has once again shown a disastrous failure to understand the situation.' In the Republic, Charles Haughey, who found himself in opposition and seemingly free of the diplomatic shackles of power, commented that there 'was a serious obligation on the British to resolve the dispute', adding that the hunger strike had the 'most serious and far-reaching implications for the political life of this country' (*The Irish Times*, 9 July 1981). For many observers though, Haughey's newfound articulacy was, perhaps, a tad too late.

The hunger strike was proving to be a propaganda coup for the republican movement. The series of mass funerals, together with their defiant displays of paramilitary strength, were a thorn in the side of the British government. It seemed to most foreign observers as if the IRA and the INLA were, literally, calling the shots, and the situation was causing the British acute embarrassment. Pressure on the Thatcher government, the RUC and the British Army to act decisively came from Unionist politicians. Just prior to McDonnell's death, in the midst of the rumour and counter-rumour over a 'deal' with the prisoners, one Robert Bradford MP had placed his views on the record.

Speaking in the Commons on 2 July in a debate concerning the renewal of the Northern Ireland (Emergency Provisions) Act (1978), Bradford pleaded, rather characteristically, that the 1351 Treason Act should be included in the schedule of the Emergency Provisions Act to deal with the IRA. This, he argued, would 'increase the powers of the court and . . . safeguard us from needless IRA propaganda', allowing for capital punishment. In words that were clearly measured as a criticism of the government's inability to match the republicans in the propaganda battle, Bradford continued:

There is a need to deny terrorists the possibility of

ventilating their views in newspapers, magazines, on the radio and on television, either directly or through a non-proscribed sister organisation. The Ulster people have been insulted again and again by spokesmen for Sinn Féin appearing on television and the radio spewing out venom, poison and hatred on behalf of IRA convicts. We must do something by statute to curb the ventilation of IRA propaganda, either directly or indirectly . . . I warn the Rt. Hon. Gentleman [The Secretary of State] that the IRA is a past master at taking an inch, then a foot, and then a mile. If, as he said, he is prepared to fight the IRA within the law, let him apply the law that no uniforms or guns should be produced in public places – whether during a funeral or otherwise. If he allows that law to go unapplied in the Province the IRA will soon find other laws to flout in the face of the Government and the much-beleaguered people of the Province. We need a new policy on security forces' involvement when uniforms, guns and all the trappings of the paramilitary demonstrations emerge in the Province.

Hansard, HC (series 6) vol. 7, cols 1053–106 (2 Jul. 1981)

It was evident that there was a political expectation among leading unionists that the authorities would intervene at the next IRA funeral. The burial of Joe McDonnell, on Friday 10 July, was to provide the opportunity for the police and army to act. The procession from McDonnell's home in Lenadoon was attended by upwards of 15,000 people and as usual the coffin was accompanied by masked men in combat fatigues. On the Andersonstown Road a volley of shots was fired over the coffin, but the colour party was being monitored from a helicopter and the British Army moved in to a nearby street to try and arrest the IRA men. As news of the arrest operation spread, rioting broke out in the vicinity and soon hundreds were crouching in terror as troops and rioters engaged. In all, the police arrested four men, who they believed had been part of the colour party, seized three Garand rifles, military fatigues and arrested a woman into whose house the men had fled. The IRA was not slow in its criticism of the operation, claiming that the 'cream of the British military and RUC paramilitary force are reduced to mounting an attack on mourners to capture a small number of weapons' (*The Irish News*, 11 July 1981). In the House of Commons East Belfast MP, Peter Robinson, told the Secretary of State that he could 'take it from me that many people in Northern Ireland have been greatly encouraged . . . by the actions of the security forces at the funeral of Joseph McDonnell . . . given the success of that operation, will the Secretary of State now recommend that such operations be stepped up?' (Hansard, HC (series 6) vol. 8, cols 1370–2 (16 Jul. 1981)).

With the Orange parades due to take place across Northern Ireland on Monday 13 July, the tension on the streets was ratcheted up further when news broke of the death of Martin Hurson. The 27-year-old bachelor from Cappagh, County Tyrone, died on the forty-fifth day of his fast. He had been sentenced to twenty years imprisonment in September 1979 for possession of explosives and had replaced Brendan McLaughlin on the fast in May. Late on the evening of Sunday 12 July the father of Martin Hurson had been called to the Maze because his son's condition had deteriorated. According to a bulletin released by the H-Block Information Centre, complications had been caused by Hurson's inability to take any fluids and his condition had worsened significantly. His sudden death came as a shock and was announced by the Northern Ireland Office in brutally simplistic terms: 'Edward Martin Hurson died today at 4:30 a.m. He took his own life by refusing food and medical attention for 45 days.' The coffin of Martin Hurson was given a police escort from the Maze to the heartland of County Tyrone, but was unaccompanied as it made its way to the Hurson home in the republican stronghold of Cappagh. With the scenes at the funeral of Joe McDonnell still reverberating around the world, Sinn Féin vowed that Hurson would be given full military honours. In the end wise counsel prevailed, and the police and army made no attempt to interfere with the funeral. Accordingly, eight masked men appeared at the graveside at St John's Church in Galbally and fired a volley of shots over Hurson's coffin, while two Army helicopters filmed proceedings. In the Maze the conveyor belt of hunger strikers continued: Matt Devlin from Ardboe, County Tyrone, replaced Hurson on 15 July.

On Saturday 18 July Dublin hosted a mass rally on behalf of the hunger strikers. With the pressure now shifting to the Republic to shore up support for the fast, a crowd of almost 20,000 descended on the capital to deliver a letter of protest to the British Embassy in Merrion Road. But the Irish government was in no mood to contemplate a repeat of the scenes in February 1972, when the previous British Embassy had been stormed and razed to the ground during a demonstration in the aftermath of Bloody Sunday. Over 2,000 Gardaí were on duty to protect the embassy – the police were ready for trouble and so, too, were a significant number of the protesters. Consequently, when the march made its way through Dublin and reached the leafy vicinity of the embassy it was greeted by a wall of Gardaí. After a stand-off, Bernadette McAliskey led a small deputation into the embassy where a wreath was handed over. Then the inevitable happened. A section of the crowd attacked the Gardaí. The Gardaí, in no mood to take prisoners, were immediately on the offensive. The news that evening was dominated by scenes of battered protesters: it had been an abject lesson in baton-wielding and riot control.

In Belfast the unionist-leaning *News Letter*'s editorial the following Monday applauded the actions of the Gardaí: 'What was memorable about the Dublin riot on Saturday was the sight of the vast crowd turning tail and fleeing in abject panic, when a far smaller number of the Civic Guard, fed up with being passive targets, charged the rioters and put them into ignominious flight.'

Whilst the rioting in Dublin stole the headlines, another initiative occurred that week in the form of an International Red Cross visit to the prison to investigate, at the behest of the British government, the conditions under which the inmates were held. The group, led by Frank Schmidt, arrived at the prison from

Geneva on 18 July and held talks with the hunger strikers and other Maze prisoners. The omens, however, were poor and the IRA issued a statement indicating that the intervention would do nothing to break the deadlock, as a settlement of the dispute was in the gift of the British government. A week later, perhaps in exasperation, the group left with Schmidt noting sadly that 'the two sides would not meet and we found we had no role to play' (*Keesing's Record of World Events*, November 1981).

In the H-Blocks Kevin Lynch and Kieran Doherty edged closer to death. In the United States Mrs Thatcher met with President Ronald Reagan but, despite speculation that the matter of the hunger strike would be discussed, protocol on the American side forbade it because it was 'an internal United Kingdom' issue. On 21 July Humphrey Atkins claimed on BBC Radio that both Kieran Doherty and Kevin Lynch had requested a meeting with Northern Ireland Office officials to clarify the government's position. In his clipped tones Atkins gave his own sanitised version of events, saying that the hunger strikers thought they were going to 'negotiate' with the officials, with Bik McFarlane in attendance. Atkins continued, 'we were not prepared to negotiate with convicted prisoners', and the officials promptly left. Atkins' version of events angered many within the republican family, and Kieran Doherty's father, Alfie, called on Garret FitzGerald to visit the prisoners. Among the sightseers to the prison at that time was Major-General Miles Francis Stapleton Fitzalan-Howard, better known as the Duke of Norfolk. As the only member of the House of Lords to take up the offer of a 'general interest' visit, the Duke was given a tour of the prison and commented that the conditions were the 'best he'd ever seen'. In an editorial, the *News Letter* took a keen interest in this story since not only had the prison been visited by a duke, but this particular duke was also a 'leading Roman Catholic peer' to boot. It was all mere megaphone rhetoric, as both Lynch and Doherty received the last rites; death was now a sad and predictable reality.

In London on 29 July the marriage of Prince Charles to Lady

Diana Spencer took place amid scenes of pageantry seldom seen. The world stopped for a day but the fast continued regardless. The gravity of the situation led to an eight-hour meeting in the prison, during which Gerry Adams, Owen Carron and Seamus Ruddy, together with a number of clerics and the family members, assessed the situation for the hunger strikers. The meeting seemed to mark a watershed, in that Gerry Adams was given permission for the first time to see the hunger strikers. Afterwards Adams told the waiting press that he had advised the prisoners that they would 'all soon be dead'. In a tone that was markedly conciliatory, Adams added that he had pointed out to the hunger strikers that there 'was no problem with anyone on the outside if they wished to end their fast', a clear indication that the onus to surmount the impasse was now with the prisoners, rather than the government. The unity that had been evident prior to this point had also recently been threatened when the INLA expressed its own concerns at the direction of the fast. However, the hunger strikers themselves remained steadfast and, individually and collectively, they avowed their determination to see the fast through. Then came the news that this solidarity had been broken: Mrs Catherine Quinn, the mother of Paddy Quinn who had been fasting for forty-seven days, signed forms ordering medical intervention.

The pressure on the hunger strikers' families from the higher echelons of the Catholic clergy had been growing steadily, most notably from Bishop Edward Daly and Father Denis Faul. Quinn had lapsed into a coma and the thought of letting their son die was proving too agonising for his family. Quinn had already told his mother that she was not to take him off the hunger strike if he lapsed into coma, saying, 'You either back me or you back Maggie Thatcher.' Paddy Quinn maintains that his mother was brought to the hospital deliberately in order to influence her decision. 'She heard me roaring. [They] thought I had a couple of hours to live' (*Guardian*, 4 March 2006). He met with his mother in the prison hospital a few days later and described himself as 'blind and angry'. He would not rejoin the fast and the matter was never discussed by Quinn and his mother again. Nevertheless, the government officials were hopeful that the momentum of the fast had been broken and, with hindsight, they were to be proved right. The prisoners released a defiant statement on 31 July, stating 'Our position has not and will not alter until the British Government decide to honourably settle this issue.' Within two days both Kevin Lynch and Kieran Doherty were dead.

The funeral of Kevin Lynch was to be shrouded in controversy as six gunmen, against the wishes of the Lynch family, entered the grounds of St Patrick's Church in Dungiven and fired a volley of shots over the Starry Plough-draped coffin. The family had given express orders that the funeral was not to have paramilitary trappings and the actions of the INLA on the day caused them acute embarrassment. The tension between the Lynch family (who would not have considered themselves 'political') and the republican movement in general had worsened as their son's fast continued. At one stage Kevin Lynch's father had called upon Gerry Adams to replace his son on the fast, such was the family's despair. At the funeral mass Father John Quinn called for an end to the hunger strike and the 'agonising pain' that it was bringing to the families. He added that the mother and father of Kevin Lynch had been 'day and night at Kevin's bedside, but despite the pressures put on them from every quarter and despite raised and dashed hopes so many times, they bore their crosses with Christian resignation' (*News Letter*, 4 August 1981). Although there had been scenes of violence in Andersonstown at the funeral of Joe McDonnell three weeks previously, Kieran Doherty's funeral was afforded full paramilitary honours on 5 August. From early morning black taxis blocked the roads close to St Teresa's Church to prevent any incursion by the police or army. Under normal circumstances the death of a TD would have prompted the government of the Republic to send an official representative: none appeared.

On 9 August the death of Thomas McElwee occurred. The 23-year-old from Bellaghy, County Derry, had survived sixty-two days on the fast and his passing ignited rioting in Belfast and Derry, since it a;so coincided with the ninth anniversary of the reintroduction of internment without trial. In October 1976 he had lost an eye after a premature explosion, which also injured his brother Benedict. In April 1977 he received a twenty-year prison sentence and immediately joined the no-wash protest. At his funeral Father Michael Flanagan made a pointed attack on those 'who had called for the hunger strike and who had refused to call it off following the election successes of Republicans on both sides of the border'. He added that the strike should end and this was greeted by the stamping of feet within the church in protest. The remarks were described by Bernadette McAliskey as 'insulting', and some mourners left the church in anger. A full paramilitary funeral was afforded for McElwee and he was buried in the same graveyard as his cousin Francis Hughes.

Pat Sheehan, who was chosen as Kieran Doherty's replacement, refused food on 10 August. At twenty-three years of age, Sheehan thus became the seventeenth prisoner to embark on the 1981 hunger strike. His name had been chosen from among the volunteers who had indicated that they were prepared to join the fast. When he joined the fast he experienced a tough inner struggle, which came with the realisation that he might soon be facing death:

> The hardest part of going on the hunger strike is the difficulty in getting focussed on what lies ahead. There was no doubt that we, as prisoners at that time, remained absolutely determined to carry through the fast and there was palpable anger as so many had been allowed to die. In reality, the fact is that you would in all probability be dead in two months and this was something that had to be faced up to. Self-doubt is something that becomes a constant factor, but it soon became apparent to me that I would need to overcome that doubt and remain focussed on what lay ahead for me. There was without question a severe emotional impact on myself and my family as death was always a possibility. However, my mindset had to be

100 per cent certain that what I was doing was the right thing and that was critical. Nothing else mattered at that time and winning the psychological battle was crucial. For me, preparing for the fast was made even more emotional and draining to my psychological well-being when my father visited me and broke the new that my sister Louise had been diagnosed with leukaemia. In the circumstances, I could have opted out of the fast but I was determined and was prepared to die. The actual process of starvation is frightening. You soon become aware that you are making yourself very seriously ill and the body, as is natural, will rebel against you. As the fast progressed I remained very lucid and very, very calm within myself. I recall that everything became blurred and distant and that all I could see were shadows.

Author interview with Pat Sheehan, 11 November 2010

A week after Sheehan embarked on his fast, Belfast man Jackie McMullan, aged 25, joined the hunger strike. He was the replacement for Thomas McElwee. The third of a family of seven, McMullan had studied in Athlone as a boarder and had been sentenced to life imprisonment in 1976 for the attempted murder of an RUC officer. From his arrival in the H-Blocks until Christmas 1979 McMullan saw his mother only twice, since he refused to wear a prison uniform. The last visit from his mother was at Christmas 1979 and her next scheduled had been due in March 1980. As McMullan recalled, 'I was in my cell waiting to take a visit. The door opened. The priest walked in' (*An Phoblacht*, 21 August 2006). She was dead and McMullan was refused compassionate parole to attend her funeral.

On Thursday 20 August the voters of Fermanagh and South Tyrone went to the polls to elect the successor to Bobby Sands In the constituency the voters had a stark choice between Owen Carron, the articulate election agent to Bobby Sands, or Ken Maginnis, a well-liked and capable local headmaster and former UDR member, who represented the Ulster Unionist Party and was fancied to take the seat. Many observers suggested that the 'Bobby Sands' factor may have prompted many local nationalists to 'lend' their vote to the fasting anti-H-Block candidate in April, and, accordingly, a Carron victory was considered far less likely.

The SDLP had decided to opt out of the poll, something which was manna from heaven to their unionist critics. In early August Austin Currie, who had originally been nominated to stand against Sands, told his constituency party that he would not stand in the latest poll for 'personal reasons'. In a parting shot, however, he added that it was 'absolutely essential' that the party stand a candidate against Owen Carron. The pressure was therefore on John Hume's party to stand, but the decision fell to the local constituency who decided to opt out. Hume defended the choice, claiming that it had been taken democratically in light of the 'different circumstances' that existed within the constituency. South Belfast MP Robert Bradford described the SDLP as an 'extremist republican party', while the DUP said that the SDLP had 'capitulated and surrendered to the republican extremists'. The other candidate of note was the Lisburn-based Seamus Close of the Alliance Party, who was seeking to attract the 'moderate' vote. From the political wilderness the Workers' Party Republican Clubs candidate Tom Moore – who, for some reason, had become a darling of the unionist media – argued that economic considerations should be at the forefront of voters' minds. However, such arguments, while creditable in any other constituency, were naive in the circumstances and his nomination was seen as an attempt to undermine the voting base of Carron.

As counting began, news broke that Michael Devine had become the tenth hunger striker to die. His death cast a shadow over the count and pundits predicted that the 86.9 per cent turnout recorded in April had been exceeded. The poll attracted a turnout of 88.6 per cent, which was marginally up on the turnout recorded for the April poll. In what was an even more spectacular result than Sands', Carron was elected with a personal vote of 31,278 – almost 800 votes more than Sands had accrued in April. Ken Maginnis received 29,048 votes, two more than

Harry West's tally in April. What made Carron's victory even more notable was that the three other candidates had attracted over three thousand votes, yet Carron's mandate had surpassed all expectations. Accusations of widespread vote stealing were made against Carron's supporters, and Maginnis noted that 'the wind that blew here today will turn into a whirlwind when the murderers that Owen Carron represents come shooting innocent people' (*News Letter*, 22 August 1981).

In his acceptance speech Carron said that his election had provided a basis for a resolution to the H-Block crisis. *The Irish Times* suggested that 'there was a vehemence and vituperation about the post declaration speech of Mr Carron which may hearten some of his supporters, but promises no great future for the politics of Northern Ireland'. Carron's first action was to call for a face-to-face meeting with Margaret Thatcher; she refused and suggested that he could meet with a junior minister in the Northern Ireland Office. In Dublin Garret FitzGerald also turned down a request to meet with the newly elected MP without providing a reason. Now that the roads to Downing Street and Leinster House were blocked, Carron went to seek support from Charles Haughey, leader of Fianna Fáil. The meeting, which took place on 1 September at Haughey's palatial mansion in Kinsealy outside Dublin, was not, however, marked by a meeting of minds. The Fianna Fáil leader was described as 'blunt' and he rejected Carron's requests that he support a move to expel the British Ambassador to Ireland, Sir Leonard Figg, and give his backing to demands that Irish troops be removed from security duty at the border. With hindsight, it would have been politically insensitive for Haughey to endorse such proposals, given that five years earlier the IRA had assassinated the then British Ambassador, Christopher Ewart-Biggs.

On 24 August 30-year-old Bernard Fox, who was serving a twelve-year sentence for possessing explosives and bombing a hotel, replaced Patrick Quinn. A week later he was joined by 25-year-old Hugh Carville, a well-known Gaelic footballer from County Down who was serving a fourteen-year sentence for

arson and possession of weapons. Within a week the fast began
to unravel. Lawrence McKeown entered the sixty-seventh day
of his fast and was described as 'extremely weak'. Despite this,
his family were being denied daily visits since, according to the
prison doctor, his condition did not 'warrant' them. At this stage
McKeown weighed just over seven stone and his family were
sent home believing that they might not see him alive again.
For the family of Matt Devlin, who had endured fifty-two
days on the hunger strike, the situation became unbearable on
4 September and they ordered medical intervention when he
suffered a violent epileptic fit and kidney failure. The decision of
the Devlin family was duly noted and, on Sunday 6 September,
Laurence McKeown's mother signed the necessary forms to
save his life through medical intervention. It was a decision he
respected:

> I didn't feel any way different about her because I just
> knew that she had stood by me all that time anyway. I
> could understand her point of view. A number of people
> had made interventions. She wasn't politically committed
> to my ideas but she was committed to me as a son. I
> certainly didn't ever say anything to her that would have
> been hurtful. I think much was left unspoken.

> http://www.iisresource.org/Documents/HS30 Laurence
> McKeown–Ireland in Schools (accessed 5 January 2011)

With the hunger strike apparently on the verge of collapse,
the protest was dealt a further blow when the INLA prisoners
issued a statement declaring that they would not be replacing
Michael Devine on the fast. Liam McCloskey, then entering
his thirty-sixth day on hunger strike, was to be the last representative of the republican socialist prisoners. In a demoralising
statement the INLA pointed out that 'The British government
has been much more intransigent than we expected and at this
current rate all of our prisoners would be dead in six months'
(*The Irish News*, 7 September 1981). The families of the IRA
hunger strikers remained defiant and issued their own statement.

Nevertheless, their request for a response from the British government hints that they, too, were feeling the pressure:

> We, the families of the present Hunger Strikers in the H-Blocks of Long Kesh, wish to state our public support for the political prisoners' struggle for their 5 demands and for our loved-ones on hunger strike. We call upon the British Government to ensure a permanent ending to all the prison protests by implementing the conditions outlined by the prisoners. We request a public response from the British Government to this appeal.

The Irish News, 7 September 1981

As far as the British were concerned, the hunger strike was collapsing from within. Looked at objectively, there is no doubt that the fast had been weakened and was facing a crisis of confidence. However, at this critical stage 25-year-old John Pickering from Andersonstown became the twenty-first prisoner to join the strike. In London Margaret Thatcher shuffled her team at the Northern Ireland Office and into the equation was sent the 'wet' Jim Prior, who had apparently called into question some of the Iron Lady's economic policies. For Prior the job as Secretary of State for Northern Ireland was a demotion that was widely perceived, within the context of the hunger strikes, as a poisoned chalice. Humphrey Atkins' reward for holding the line in Northern Ireland was promotion to Deputy Foreign Secretary.

On 14 September, the day after Prior's appointment, 21-year-old Gerard Hodgkins from Turf Lodge in Belfast joined the hunger strike. Later that day, either through curiosity or in a serious attempt to begin to draw a line under the fast, Prior visited the Maze. He observed the condition of Liam McCloskey, who had entered the forty-fifth day of his fast, and spoke briefly to a number of other prisoners. His only diplomatic comment on the subject of the visit was that he 'wanted to take a look around. It is very important for me to go' (*News Letter*, 15 September 1981). Yet the fact that he had visited the prison at all indicated that resolution was now at the top of his agenda. Slowly the prisoners were coming to terms with the reality that concessions, if any, would not be forthcoming while the fast continued. The government had been placed in a stronger position by the intervention of the families of the hunger strikers, and it seemed clear that the families, if not the prisoners themselves, were divided over the viability of the fast. At this point the Catholic Church again entered the arena, adding its weight to the pressure for the fast to be called off. In early September the Bishop of Down and Connor, Dr William Philbin, had called for an end to the strike, but the main advocate for its termination was Father Denis Faul. Now that the condition of Bernard Fox and Liam McCloskey was reported as very grave, Faul appealed to their families to 'step in at the earliest opportunity to save their lives . . . fathers and mothers have a responsibility for the physical and spiritual welfare of their sons, and they should take courage knowing that they have the support and prayers of all the people of Ireland' (*The Irish News*, 24 September 1981).

On 25 September the condition of Bernard Fox, who had been on the fast for thirty-two days, deteriorated when his kidney became blocked and he was unable to hold down water. Brendan McFarlane was called to the prison hospital and it was decided that Fox would receive medical assistance. He became the sixth hunger striker to come off the protest. The pressure, accordingly, was growing on the mother of Liam McCloskey to act. McCloskey was almost blind and unless he received vitamin injections he would lose his sight. Faul described Mrs Philomena McCloskey as a 'very private person' who had been thrust into the public spotlight and indicated that he believed that she was 'a very loving mother who will do what is right for her son'. There were seven men remaining on the fast and that number was reduced to six on 26 September when Liam McCloskey 'voluntarily' ended his fast. McCloskey had spent the day in discussions with his family and his mother had told him that she was not prepared to let him die. Mrs McCloskey, who had spoken to James Prior during his visit to the Maze, issued a statement clarifying her position:

> My son reluctantly ended his hunger strike after I
> convinced him that I would not let him die. I told him
> that I would intervene if he lapsed into a coma and it was
> better if he came off the hunger strike now rather than run
> the risk of permanent damage . . . I urge Mr Jim Prior to
> bring the hunger strike to an end by sending officials into
> the prison to negotiate.

Saoirse, 31 July 2006

It seemed that Father Faul was winning the psychological battle
with the families and that the end of the fast was now just a
question of time. From within the prison the IRA issued a
statement describing Father Faul as a 'conniving treacherous man,
not in the least shy about twisting the truth to his own ends'.
The statement continued, 'He has insinuated that those mothers
who stood by their sons [and refused medical intervention]
were somewhat less than loving mothers and we utterly deplore
such devious manipulation of emotional words to maximise
the pressure on the families.' Faul responded that the statement
was 'nonsense' and 'balderdash', that the hunger strike was in a
'different phase', and that no more prisoners should die. The
tail end of the fast had now degenerated into a war of words
between a chaplain and the prisoners; the British sat back and
waited for the inevitable (*The Irish News*, 28 September 1981).

On Friday 2 October the Prisons Minister, Lord Gowrie,
met with relatives of five of the six remaining hunger strikers
at Stormont Castle. It was a meeting that three months earlier
would have been considered unthinkable. Gowrie outlined to
the families what might be on offer if the strike were called off,
but he also emphasised that conceding to the Five Demands was
out of the question. The dynamic had moved on and it soon
became apparent that the relatives had made a collective decision
not to allow their sons to die. Father Faul was advised of their
stance – the fast was effectively over. In Belfast senior Sinn Féin
spokesman Richard McAuley summed up the situation, noting
that 'unless the prisoners can find a means of overcoming the

intervention of their families, they must reassess the hunger strike' (*The Irish News*, 3 October 1981). He attributed the blame for the collapse of the hunger strike to the government of the Republic, the Catholic hierarchy, and the SDLP, all of which had 'actively' subverted the prison fast campaign for the Five Demands by 'putting pressure on the relatives'. In a somewhat crass statement of fact, he further asserted that 'in order for pressure to be maintained on the British Government, cold though it may seem, prisoners have to die' (*The Irish News*, 3 October 1981). Cold comment indeed, and also, given that the British had not been brought to the negotiating table after ten deaths, perhaps too simplistic an observation.

On Saturday 3 October the fast ended. The statement issued from within the Maze was defiant, detailed and bitter. It began, 'We, the protesting republican prisoners in the H-Blocks, being faced with the reality of sustained family intervention, are forced by this circumstance, over which we have little control at the moment, to end the hunger-strike.' The statement then went on to highlight the achievements, the highs and lows of the strike, and named and shamed those who had undermined the fast in the wider political community. It noted angrily and gloomily that:

> Despite the electoral successes, despite the hundreds of thousands at hunger-strikers' funerals, despite massive and unprecedented displays of community support and solidarity, the British government adhered rigidly to the precept that 'might is right' and set about hammering home the point that nothing has really changed since the fall of Stormont or from inception of this state. That is, that nationalist Ireland must always be subjected to the British and loyalist veto.

> *The Irish News*, 5 October 1981

The statement concluded that the prisoners would 'reaffirm their commitment to the achievement of the Five Demands by whatever means we believe necessary and expedient. We rule nothing out.' Accordingly, the lives of Pat Sheehan (fifty-five days), Jackie McMullan (forty-eight days), John Pickering (twenty-seven days), Gerard Hodgkins (twenty days), Hugh Carville (thirty-four days) and Jim Devine (thirteen days) were saved. The following day Father Faul re-entered the Maze to celebrate Mass. Commenting outside the prison on the wave of criticism he had received from the prisoners for 'manipulating' the families of the hunger strikers, he replied, 'I can take it, I don't mind, if they want a scapegoat I don't mind.' The MP for East Derry, William Ross, who had called during the strike for the repatriation of Catholics to the Republic, said that the end of the fast was a 'massive and humiliating defeat for the IRA'. South Belfast Unionist MP, Robert Bradford, told the press that he 'smelled a rat' and predicted that 160 IRA men would soon be free as part of a deal (quotations from *News Letter* and *The Irish News*, 5 October 1981).

To some, the end of the dispute came as a surprise. To most observers, it seemed to have staggered to an inconclusive halt. Both sides maintained that they remained unbroken. What is certain is that within days there began serious evaluation of the status of both republican and loyalist prisoners. Without the pressure cooker of an ongoing hunger strike, the British demonstrated that they could be flexible. In the face of the trauma that had gripped Northern Ireland throughout 1981, it was evident that the republican prisoners would not be faced down. Out of the glare of the world's press, the Five Demands were to be granted eventually. All would soon change, and change utterly, both inside and outside the Maze. Five weeks after the ending of the hunger strike the IRA assassinated Robert Bradford while he was holding a constituency surgery on 14 November. In the midst of a renewed bout of sectarian murders, the IRA had chosen to kill Bradford as punishment for his outspoken comments throughout the hunger strike. It was a symbolic but nakedly sectarian and gratuitous murder of the man who had described the hunger strikers as 'sub-human vermin'. He was the one hundred and seventh person to die as a result of the Troubles during 1981

(McKittrick, Kelters, Feeney & Thornton, *Lost Lives*, p. 886). In the summer of 1981 ten Republican prisoners died inside the Maze Prison. On the outside sixty-two others died in the violence surrounding the protest. The republican movement had begun its slow but certain shift to the political sphere and the value of propaganda and international sympathy had been understood. The growth of Sinn Féin was thus assured.

Father Denis Faul referred later to one rather ironic consequence of Margaret Thatcher's inflexibility during the hunger strike: 'She built up the Sinn Féin Party to an enormous degree and it's still a very big power in Northern Ireland. And she left the hunger strikers up on the walls of every Catholic home in Northern Ireland, like the men of 1916' (BBC *Frontline*, 'Behind the Mask: The IRA and Sinn Féin', 21 October 1997). As later political events in Ireland, both north and south, have demonstrated, the 1981 hunger strike was a pivotal moment. Just as the death of Thomas Ashe in 1917 altered somewhat the course of Irish history, the deaths in the Maze Prison in 1981 showed that history can turn on unexpected events that have far-reaching consequences. The bitterness of the hunger strike era is, thankfully, far behind us. Today Belfast's Falls Road is a Mecca for tourists where the mural of Bobby Sands looks out from the side of the headquarters of Sinn Féin in Sevastopol Street. The image is stark and colourful and beside the familiar face of Sands is written a quote attributed to him:

> Everyone, Republican or otherwise, has their own particular role to play. Our revenge will be the laughter of our children.

It is a statement that has underpinned the growth of Sinn Féin as a political party. That growth began with the election of Sands to the House of Commons in April 1981 – and it still continues.

Appendix I

'For Micheal Gaughan and Frank Stagg' by Gerry Kelly

It was not the hunger
Though it gnawed its way
Through slim pickings of fat
To muscle tissue

And into every dream
So that in the most
Outlandish of images
Central to its theme was...food

After nineteen foodless days
The pain of hunger
This usurper of senses
Was itself usurped by fear

For some hours since
The dapper doctor announced
That he would return
To force-feed the prisoner

(He later changed this to
'Artificially feed the patient')
Fear had feasted
On his self doubt

From the ballad of his schooldays
From the archives of his mind
The spectre of Tom Ashe's
Force-fed death appeared

The dramatisation
Of the brutal process
By cynical warders
Ate at his imagination

The clinical recitation
Of dangerous possibilities
The tube entering the lung
'By mistake of course'

But most acute
The fear of failing
Once the gauntlet
Was thrown down

So when the trolley
Rattled to the cell
The young man
Lotus-like on the bed
Faced them, bone naked
To the blanket round his waist
Talisman of rosary-beads
About his neck

The key turned
With a clack
An intrusive unknown
Churning in his gut

Twelve-handed they entered
In angry flood
Frothing hospital white
On incriminating blue

While the doctor
From deep-seated elitism
Affected detachment
In civilian hue

The initial struggle
Was painfully brief
Boney resistance
Was cruelly subdued

Prison stripped
To helplessness
Then stretched
To hopelessness

Under doctor's orders
Trailed up the bed
With jack-knifed body
To the high end

Hair-pulled head forced back
For a throat to stomach line
That would be straight and true
Steel cold to his neck

Fear fought dedication
In the rebel heart
As his breath battled
Through gated teeth

'Now' ordered the doctor
'Open your mouth'
And so it began
In clenched mute refusal

Naivety left the naked
To join the clothed
And both discovered the power
Of a spirited 'No'

Forearm anchored forehead
Knuckles boring jaw joints
Forceps scraping gums
Ryles-tube searing nostrils

The soft membrane
Hot with pain and blood
Surgeon turned jailor
In prison's privacy

Jaw muscles are strong
But not strong enough
Gasping with pain
A clamp kills the cry

No time for self pity
As the clamp is adjusted
To steer a tube
Down famine throat

Motionless dread
Fills the pinioned body
Movement is rebellion
And clinically suppressed

No speech is possible
Nor motion of limbs
Protest undiluted
In dilated eyes

This is the surreal
Experience of nightmares
Where great danger
Invokes paralysis

The doctor knocks clumsily
At the swing door in the throat
One way to the stomach
The other to lung filled death

Tom Ashe, Tom Ashe
Comfort and fear
A pounding drum
A temple beat
All of which, the doctor
Hypocratically explained
Was for his own good
To save his life

Then the flap swings right
The tube rams through
A choking of liquid
Crowds his shrunken belly

As the pain ebbs
And relief tingles
In sweat beads
His drowning stomach heaves

Heaves a thick white eruption
With involuntary spasms
On chin and chest
And uniforms

Until some clever warder
Wielding a kidney-dish
Collects the dripping remains
Of this expensive fare

Which the doctor described
Without hint of irony
As equivalent to
'A meal at The Savoy'

For his final trick
With nausea on the wane
The chef returned the contents
To the prisoner's stomach

And so it ends for one day
With a hasty exit
Of the tube from the throat
And the squad from the cell

Leaving the Irishman
To clean up the mess
To recover his dignity
And fret about the many next times

The doctor in charge
Known by the official title of
'Principal Medical Officer'
Was clearly affected by the scene
For the remainder of the hunger strike
He entered the cell
Only after the prisoner
Had been subdued

A man of intellect and eloquence
Who spoke of Arthur Koestler,
Oliver St John Gogarty
And his own flag-waving youth

While he went about his task

Selected Bibliography

Adams, Gerry, *A Farther Shore – Ireland's Long Road to Peace*, (London, Random House 2003)

Adie, Kate, *The Kindness of Strangers – The Autobiography*, (London, Headline Book Publishing, 2002)

Anderson, Brendan, *Joe Cahill – A Life in the IRA*, (Dublin, O'Brien Press, 2003)

Barry, Denis, *The Unknown Commandant – The Life and Times of Denis Barry, 1883–1923*, (Cork, The Collins Press, 2010)

Behan, Brendan, *Confessions of an Irish Rebel*, (London, Arrow Books, 1967)

Bennett, Richard, *The Black and Tans*, (Ontario, Spellbound Publishers Limited, 2001)

Beresford, David, *Ten Men Dead*, (London, HarperCollins, 1987)

Bishop, Patrick & Mallie, Eamonn, *The Provisional IRA*, (London, Corgi Press, 1989)

Bowyer Bell, John, *The Secret Army – A History of the IRA 1916–1970*, (London, Sphere Books, 1970)

Berresford Ellis, Peter, *A History of the Irish Working Class*, (London, Pluto Press, 1996)

Campbell, John, *Margaret Thatcher – Volume Two: The Iron Lady*, (London, Vintage, 2007)

Carroll, Joseph T., *Ireland in the War Years 1939–1945*, (New York, David & Charles, 1975)

Coogan, Tim Pat, *The I.R.A.*, (New York, Fontana Books, 1970)

—*De Valera – Long Fellow, Long Shadow*, (London, Arrow Books Limited, 1995)

—*The Troubles – Ireland's Ordeal, 1969-96, and the Search for Peace*, (New York, Palgrave, 1995)

—*Michael Collins – A Biography*, (London, Arrow Press, 1991)

Cullen Owens, Rosemary, *Smashing Times – History of the Irish Suffragette Movement 1899–1922*, (Cork, Attic Press, 1984)

Devlin, Paddy, *Straight Left – An Autobiography*, (Belfast, Blackstaff Press, 1994)

English, Richard, *Armed Struggle – The History of the IRA*, (London, Macmillan, 1993)

Farrell, Michael, *Northern Ireland – The Orange State*, (London, Pluto Press, 1976)

Feeney, Brian, *Sinn Féin – A Hundred Turbulent Years*, (Dublin, O'Brien Press, 2002)

FitzGerald, Garret, *All in a Life*, (Dublin, Gill & Macmillan Ltd, 1991)

Kiberd, Declan, *1916 Rebellion Handbook*, (Dublin, Mourne River Press, 1998)

Gallagher, Frank, *Days of Fear – The Diary of a 1920s Hunger Striker*, (Cork, Mercier Press, 2008)

Hermon, John, *Holding the Line – An Autobiography*, (Dublin, Gill & Macmillan, 1997)

MacBride, Seán, *That Day's Struggle – A Memoir, 1904–1951*, (Dublin, Currach Press, 2005)

MacEoin, Uiseann, *The IRA in the Twilight Years 1923–1948*, (Dublin, Argenta Publications, 1997)

—*Survivors – The story of Ireland's struggle as told through some of her outstanding people*, (Dublin, Argenta Publications, 1980)

MacSwiney, Muriel, *Letters to Angela Clifford*, (Cork, Athol, 1996)

McKittrick, David, Kelters, Seamus, Feeny, Brian & Thornton, Chris, *Lost Lives – The Stories of the Men, Women and Children Who Died as a Result of the Northern Ireland Troubles*, (Edinburgh, Mainstream Publishing, 1999)

McGuffin, John, *Internment*, (Belfast, Anvil Books Ltd, 1973)

Mulcahy, Risteárd, *My Father, the General – Richard Mulcahy and the Military History of the Revolution*, (Dublin, Liberties Press, 2009)

O'Callaghan, Sean, *The Easter Lily – The Story of the I.R.A.*, (Dublin, Wingate, 1956)

O'Connor, Fionnuala, *In Search of a State – Catholics in Northern Ireland*, (Belfast, Blackstaff Press, 2003)

O'Malley, Ernie & Dolan, Ernie, *No Surrender Here! – The Civil War Papers of Ernie O'Malley 1922–1924*, (Dublin, Lilliput Press, 2007)

O'Rawe, Richard, *Blanketmen – An Untold Story of the H-block Hunger Strike*, (Dublin, New Island Books, 2005)

O'Hegarty, Patrick Sarsfield, *A Short Memoir of Terence MacSwiney*, (Dublin, P. J. Kenedy and Sons, 1922)

Price, Dolours, & Price, Marion, *Venceremos Sisters*, (Belfast, Cathal Brugha Cumann (Sinn Féin), 1975)

Priestly, J. B., *The Edwardians*, (London, Penguin Books Ltd, 2003)

Ryder, Chris, *The RUC – A Force Under Fire*, (London, Mandarin Paperbacks, 1992)

—*Inside the Maze – The Untold Story of the Northern Ireland Prison Service*, (London, Meuthen Publishing, 2000)

Sands, Bobby, *Writings from Prison*, (Cork, Mercier Press, 1998)

Taylor, Peter, *Provos – The IRA and Sinn Féin*, (London, Bloomsbury Publishing, 1998)

White, Robert W., *Ruairí Ó Brádaigh – The Life and Politics of an Irish Revolutionary*, (Indiana, USA, Indiana Press, 2006)

Yeates, Padraig, *Lockout – Dublin 1913*, (New York, Palgrave, 2001)

Index

Aberdeen, Lord 10–11
Adams, Gerry 137, 138, 139, 150,
      188, 195, 199, 209, 216, 217,
      220, 221, 235, 236, 238–9,
      240–41, 249, 250
Adie, Kate 214, 221
Agnew, Paddy 230, 231, 233
Aiken, Frank 67–8, 69–70, 72–3, 74
Albany Prison 163
Aldershot 145
Alison, Michael 192, 194, 234,
      236–7
Amnesty International 183
An Phoblacht 20, 42, 75, 210, 240, 252
Anglo-Celt 97–8
Anglo-Irish Treaty 61–2, 64
Arbour Hill Prison 90, 92, 106, 115
Armagh 194, 219, 222–3, 224–5
Armagh Prison 133, 157, 160, 179,
      182, 190, 194, 230, 234
Armstrong, Billy 146
Ashbourne 25
Ashe, John 27–8
Ashe, Thomas 18–19, 24–38, 45, 47,
      149, 261
Asquith, Herbert 3, 8–9, 15, 16
Associated Press 51, 53, 58, 64, 69,
      71, 222
Atkins, Humphrey 186, 192–3, 194,
      195, 197–9, 223, 233–4, 235,
      239, 244, 248, 256

Bagnel, Patrick 67
Baker, Albert 'Ginger' 166
Bala internment camp 76
Ballina 156, 167, 169–71, 172–3
Ballinalea 25
Ballinrobe 71
Balymurphy 195
Ballyseedy Wood 67
Bandon 41
Barrett, Richard 66

Barry, Bartholomew 77–8
Barry, Denis 'Dinny' 60, 76–81
Barry, Kevin 59
Baxter, Patrick 75
Beál na mBláth 63
Behan, Brendan 119
Behan, Tom 67
Belfast 41, 51, 113, 118, 129–30,
      134–5, 136, 140, 142, 151, 165,
      166–7, 178–9, 183, 188, 193,
      194, 199, 202, 203–5, 213–14,
      216–18, 219, 221–3, 224, 227–8,
      230, 233, 250, 261
Belfast Prison 43, 113, 124–5, 206
Belfast Telegraph 187
Bell, Ivor 139
Belleeks 165
Benedict XV 54
Benn, Tony 232
Birmingham 89, 159
Black and Tans 40, 45, 55, 58, 59, 97
Bloody Sunday 127, 128, 131, 145
Blueshirt movement 75
Blythe, Ernest 73, 75
Boland, Clerk 32–3, 34
Boland, Gerald 86, 91–2, 93, 95–6,
      98–9, 100–101, 110, 111–12,
      114–15, 120, 122–4
Bonar Law, Andrew 23
Boston Globe, The 73
Bourne, Francis 54
Bowers, Thomas 25
Boyle, Martin 132, 135
Bradford, Robert 160, 213, 217,
      244–5, 253, 260
Brady, Ian 152–3
Brady, Martin 146
Breen, Dan 71
Brennan, Lily 68
Brixton Prison 39, 41, 44, 49, 52–6,
      150
Brockway, Fenner 157

Brown, James 212
Browne, Robert 83
Bunting, Ronnie 200
Burke, Liam 109
Burke, Seamus 92
Byrne, Alfie 37
Byrne, James 11–12
Byrne, James 94–5

Cahill, Joe 129, 130, 170
Callaghan, James 178, 205
Campbell, James 33
Campbell, Robert 132, 134–5
Carron, Owen 217–18, 237, 240,
    241–2, 249, 252–4
Carville, Hugh 254, 260
Casement, Roger 51
Casey, Patrick 83
Cassidy, Peter 63
Ceannt, Éamonn 14
Ceannt, Tomás 14
Chance, Sir Arthur 30–31
Channon, Paul 140
Charles, Prince of Wales 248–9
Childers, Erskine 64
Childers, Molly 76
Churchill, Winston 12, 62
Civil War 60–68, 77
Clare 21
Clarke, Kathleen 95
Clarke, Philip 206
Clarke, Thomas 14, 67
Close, Seamus 253
Cobh 57, 58
Coholan, Daniel 80–81, 83
Colbert, Con 14
Colby, Bainbridge 57
Coleman, Charles 135
Collins, Gerry 172
Collins, Michael 17, 20, 27, 41, 61–3,
    64, 65, 76–7
Collins Barracks 94
Concannon, Don 179, 210–11,
    212–13
Connacht Sentinel 169

Connery, Margaret 10
Connolly, James 10–11, 14
Connolly, Fr Michael 155–6
Connolly, Nora 68
Coogan, Tim Pat 115
Cooley peninsula 107
Cooney, Patrick 155, 170
Cooper, Brian 155
Cork 39–43, 55, 56–7, 58–9, 76–7,
    80–81
Cork Examiner 80–81
Cork Prison 51, 52–5, 56–7, 73, 77
Cosgrave, Liam 173
Cosgrave, William T. 73, 75, 76, 77,
    78
Cousins, Margaret 10
Coventry 89, 123, 144–5, 163, 165
Cowan, John 133
Crean, Cornelius 41
Crilly, Fr Michael 234
Crooks, John 201
Crossmaglen 212
Crumlin Road Prison 51, 128, 129,
    132–5, 138, 143, 231
Culhane, Sean 41
Cullen, Malachy 133
Cumann na mBan 68–9, 84
Cumann na nGaedheal 70–71
Curragh Camp 67, 70, 73, 76, 77,
    79, 116
Currie, Austin 207, 209, 253

Daily Chronicle 16, 21, 66
Daily Ireland 243
Daily Mail 5, 9
Daily Mirror, The 146
Daily Telegraph, The 6, 21, 26
Daly, Edward 14
Daly, Edward, Bishop of Derry 179,
186, 205, 249
Daly, Jeremiah 90, 91
Daly, Jim 229
Daly, Miriam 200
Darcy, Louis 97
Darcy, Tony 94, 95, 96–8, 100–101, 104

Davern, Paddy 106
Davison, Emily 6–7
de Lacy, Larry 107
de Valera, Éamon 14, 17, 21–2, 27, 62, 70–71, 78, 85–6, 88–93, 96, 98, 100, 102, 110, 111, 115, 121, 124
de Valera, Síle 188
Deansgrange Cemetery 12
Democratic Unionist Party (DUP) 177, 253
Derry 128, 136, 166, 193, 205, 210, 212, 213, 218, 219, 221–2, 225, 228–9, 250
Derry Journal 238, 239
Derry Prison 150
Devereux, Michael 105–6
Devine, Jim 260
Devine, Michael 1, 233, 237, 240, 253
Devine, T. J. 20
Devlin, Bernadette *see* McAliskey, Bernadette (neé Devlin)
Devlin, Matt 247, 255
Devlin, Paddy 138, 157
Diamond, Harry 118
Dillon, John 14, 22
Doherty, Alfie 248
Doherty, Kieran 228, 230, 231, 233, 237, 248, 250
Doherty, Nicholas 94
Donnellan, Michael 122
Donnelly, Jack 211–12
Donovan, Thomas 52
Dougherty, Joe 106
Doyle, Mary 190
Drumm, Máire 135, 165, 167, 179
Dublin 47–8, 55, 64, 73, 107, 108–9, 118, 153, 156, 167, 190, 204, 247
Dublin Lockout 10–12
Duddy, Sammy 213
Duffy, George Gavan 92
Duke, Henry 16, 28–9, 35, 37
Dundalk Prison 43
Duval, Victor 1
Dwyer, George 156

Dwyer, John 94
Dynan, John 113

Easter Rising 13–16, 24–5, 42–3, 76
Éire 73
Elizabeth II 190
Ellis, Charles 213–14
Emery, Fred 198
English, James 212
English, Richard 144
Evans, Gladys 8, 9
Evans, Gwynfor 184–5
Everett, James 111–12
Ewart-Biggs, Christopher 254

Farrell, Mairéad 190, 230, 231
Farrell, Tom 107
Faul, Fr Denis 199, 249, 257–8, 260, 261
Faulkner, Brian 127–8, 130, 153
Feeney, Hugh 145, 146, 147, 154, 157, 160
Fell, Fr Patrick 163
Fermanagh 205–11, 237, 240–42, 252–4
Fermoy 54–5
Fianna Fáil 85, 86, 100, 115, 121, 172, 188, 231
Figg, Leonard 254
First World War 12–14, 21, 22
Fisher, James 63
Fitt, Gerry 152, 178, 189–90, 205, 241
FitzGerald, Garret 168–9, 231–2, 234, 248, 254
Fitzgerald, Michael 54–5
Fitzgerald-Kenny, James 87
Flanagan, Fr Michael 221, 251
Flanagan, Oliver 112, 113–14
Fleming, David 113, 124–5
Foot, Michael 212
Ford, Robert E. 15
Fortnight 137
Fox, Bernard 254, 257
French, Lord 40, 46, 49
Frongoch internment camp 16–17, 20

Gaffney, John 63
Gallagher, Frank 46–7, 48–9
Galway 97
Gardiner, Lord 175–6
Gaughan, John 154–5
Gaughan, Michael 152–3, 154–6,
    160–61, 162, 163–4, 167,
    170–71, 172–3
George V 65
Gibney, Jim 205, 208, 209, 238, 244
Ginnell, Laurence 28
Gladstone, Herbert 2
Gladstone, William 13
Glasgow 50
Glasgow Herald 94, 154
Glasnevin Cemetery 26–7
Glencree 107
Golden, Frank 152
Gormanstown Camp 73
Goulding, Cathal 129, 166
Gowrie, Lord 258
Graham, John 113
Green, Leo 186
Green, Max Sullivan 28–9, 33, 34
Green, Thomas 92
Greenwood, Hamar 48, 58
Griffith, Arthur 17, 22–3, 52, 59, 62
Grogan, Larry 89
Grosvenor, Robert George 206
Guiney, Desmond 213, 219, 220
Guiney, Eric 213, 220

Hales, Sean 65
Hales, Tom 65
Halifax, Viscount 88–9
Hanna, Henry 27, 31–3
Hannaway, Liam 137
Hardie, Keir 4
Harte, Pat 65
Harte, Tommy 105
Hartnett, Noel 115, 117, 120–21
Harty, John 58
Haughey, Charles 188, 193, 195, 198,
    227, 231, 244, 254
Hayes, Stephen 99, 103–5, 106–9, 123

Healy, Timothy 15–16, 26, 27–8,
    30–31, 33–4, 35, 65
Heath, Edward 130, 152
Heath, Mark 187
Heenan, John 166
Hennessey, Sean 52
Henry, Denis 46
Henry, Kevin 132, 133
Hermon, John 186, 218–19, 230
Heuston, Sean 14
Hewitt, James 189
Highstead, Derek 167
Hilditch, Stanley 201
Hillock, Bobby 204
Hodgkins, Gerard 256, 260
Hogan, Martin 171–2
Holloway Prison 1, 2
Hollymount 162–3, 167
Holmes, Paul 146, 152
Home Rule movement 9, 12–13,
    19–24
Hopkinson, Michael 73
Hoskins, Barbara 10
Hughes, Brendan 'The Dark' 186,
    195–7
Hughes, Francis 207–8, 210, 219–22,
    251
Hughes, Oliver 219–20, 222
Hughes, Paddy Joe 220
Hume, Basil 216
Hume, John 136–7, 192–3, 203, 212,
    244, 253
Hunt, Tom 105
Hunter, Thomas 46
Hurson, Martin 229, 230, 231, 237,
    246–7
Hyland, Richard 92, 105

Independent, The 128, 187, 208–9
India 214
International Red Cross 247–8
Irish Commission of Justice and
Peace (ICJP) 234, 235, 236–7
Irish Constitutional Convention 22–4
Irish Independent 48, 56, 63, 77, 78,

83, 84, 87–8, 90, 132, 133, 135, 137, 156

Irish National Liberation Army (INLA) 181, 186, 189, 193, 211, 218, 225, 228, 229, 244, 249, 250, 255

Irish News, The 27, 119, 179, 188, 190, 191, 192, 194, 197, 198, 199, 203, 215–16, 217–18, 223, 224, 226, 237, 246, 255, 256, 258, 259, 260

Irish Parliamentary Party (IPP) 8, 19, 20, 22, 28

Irish Republican Army (IRA) 40–41, 43, 61–2, 65–6, 69, 76, 85–95, 97, 99–100, 102–15, 121–5; *see also* Provisional IRA

Irish Republican Brotherhood (IRB) 25, 26

Irish Republican Socialist Party (IRSP) 191–2, 229

Irish Times, The 21, 27, 74, 95–6, 97, 101, 116, 119, 120, 121, 184, 188, 190, 199, 244, 254

Irish Volunteers 24–5, 26, 42–3, 54, 56, 57, 76

Irish World, The 15

Irwin, Sir John 29

Jameson, John 50

Jenkins, Roy 155, 156–7, 158–60, 164, 166, 168

John Paul II 187, 191, 220–21

Johnson, Thomas 66, 78

Johnston, Joe 67

Jones, David 208

Jones, Edward 181

Jones, Herbert 7

Keane, Fr Michael 156

Kells, Roy 209

Kelly, Carol Ann 227–8

Kelly, Gerry 145, 146, 147, 148–50, 154, 157, 160

Kelly, Pearse 107

Kent, David 81

Kerry 24, 26, 67, 121

Kilfedder, James 138–9

Kilkenny 76

Kilkenny Prison 73

Kilmainham Jail 14, 63, 68, 76

Kilroy, Michael 69–70, 72, 100

Labour Party (Britain) 212

Labour Party (Ireland) 231

Larkin, Jim 10

Le Monde 214

Lehane, Con 90, 110, 115

Leigh, Mary 3, 4, 8–9

Leigue cemetery 156, 169–71, 172–3

Leixlip 67

Lennon, John 193

Leonard, Malachy 132, 135

Lewes Prison 21, 23, 25, 37

Lincoln Prison 43

Lisburn 41

Little, Patrick 120–21

Liverpool 50, 89

Livingstone, Julie 219, 220

Lloyd George, David 7, 16, 19, 22, 23, 40, 45, 52, 55

Logue, Michael 13

London 50, 51–2, 89, 140, 144–6, 155–6, 167

Long Kesh Prison 1, 137, 138, 150, 177, 178, 179–84, 185–6, 191–201, 202–5, 207–8, 219, 223, 224–9, 232–42, 243–61

Long Lartin Prison 164

Longford 20–21

Loughran, Seamus 166–7

Loyalist News 132

Lynch, Finian 33, 35

Lynch, Jack 167–8

Lynch, John 90, 91, 92

Lynch, Kevin 230, 237, 248, 250

Lynch, Liam 43, 65, 76, 82

Lynch, Patrick 21

Lynch, Tony 163

Lyons, Joe 94
Lyttle, Noel 200
Lytton, Lady Constance 4–5

MacAirt, Proinsias 133
McAliskey, Bernadette (neé Devlin) 131, 135–6, 190, 194, 200, 207, 247, 251
McAllister, Tom 230, 231
McArdle, Dorothy 68
McAteer, Hugh 113
McAuley, Richard 258–9
MacBride, John 14
MacBride, Seán 92, 98, 100–101, 103, 105, 110, 115–18, 124
McCarthy, Charlie 107
McCarthy, Matthew 41
McCarthy, Richard 90, 91, 92
McCartney, Raymond 186, 191–2, 196–7
McCaughey, Seán 102–4, 106–25
McCloskey, Liam 255, 256, 257
McCloskey, Philomena 257–8
McCorley, Roger 41
McCorkell, Michael 139
McCormack, T.J. 115, 117
McCreesh, Fr Brian 226, 228
McCreesh, Ray 210, 223, 224–5, 226, 228–9
McCurrie, James 130
MacCurtain, Tomás 39–41, 52–3, 76
MacCurtain, Tomás (Jr) 93, 94
McCusker, Harold 220
MacDiarmada, Seán 14
MacDonagh, James 29
MacDonagh, Joe 33
MacDonagh, Thomas 14
McDonnell, Goretti 233, 234
McDonnell, Joe 230, 231, 233, 234, 237, 238, 239, 243–4, 245–6
McElduff, Jack 152
McElwee, Thomas 231, 234, 237, 250–51
McFarlane, Bik 223, 234–6, 237–8, 248, 257

McFeeley, Tom 186
McGarry, Sean 67
McGeown, Pat 180, 243
McGlade, Charlie 106
McGoldrick, Patrick 41
McGowen, Emily 6
McGrath, Joseph 49
McGrath, Patrick 90, 91, 92, 105
McGuigan, Billy 133
McGuinness, Danny 225
McGuinness, Joe 20–21
McGuinness, Martin 139, 222
McGuinness, Seán 86–8
McIlhone, Henry 130
McKearney, Maura 186–7
McKearney, Tommy 186, 195
McKee, Billy 129–30, 131, 132, 134–6
McKelvey, Joe 66
McKenna, Patrick 21
McKenna, Reginald 5
McKenna, Sean 186, 194–5, 196, 199, 230, 231
McKeown, Lawrence 233, 255
McKeown, Patrick 92, 105
McLarnon, Billy 146, 147
McLarnon, Emmanuel 219, 220
McLaughlin, Brendan 228, 229, 246
MacLogan, Paddy 115
McMahon, Philip 33
McManus, Frank 138
Macmillan, Harold 209
McMillen, Liam 129
McMullan, Jackie 252, 260
McNearney, Roisin 146–7
McNeela, Seán 94–5, 96–7, 98, 100–101, 104
MacPherson, Ian 48
McQuade, Johnny 152
McQuade, Owen 189
Macready, Sir Nevil 49
Mac Stíofáin, Seán 136–7, 139–41
MacSwiney, Annie 64, 68–9
MacSwiney, Mary 52, 53, 58, 64–5, 68–9, 73, 80–81

MacSwiney, Muriel 43, 51, 57
MacSwiney, Seán 55–6, 57–8
MacSwiney, Terence 17, 39, 41–5,
    51–9, 80, 81, 155
Maginnis, Ken 252, 253–4
Maguire, Frank 154, 205, 207
Maguire, Noel 207, 209
HMS *Maidstone* 128
Mallin, Michael 14
Mallow 82, 83–4
Manchester 89
Manchester Guardian 15
Mangan, Patrick 67
Mannix, Daniel 54
Manns, Rowley 145
Markievicz, Constance 11, 14
Marley, Bob 219
Marsh, Charlotte 3
Martin, Patrick 222
Mason, Roy 178, 179, 182
Mater Hospital, Belfast 135, 165, 200
Mater Hospital, Dublin 24, 26, 27,
    30, 32, 64
Mather, David 143
Mathers, Joanne 210–11
Maudling, Reginald 128, 131
Maxwell, John 13–16
Mayo 156, 162–3, 167, 169–71,
    172–3
Maze Prison *see* Long Kesh Prison
Meagher, Fr Brendan 195–6
Meehan, Martin 135, 182–3
Meelin 77
Mellows, Liam 66
Millar, Jim 204
Millar, Ronnie 183
Milltown cemetery 118, 215, 220
Milton, Frederick 146
Molloy, Francie 210
Molyneux, James 192
Monaghan 153
Monaghan, Paddy 133
Mongan, Seamus 94–5
Monro, Charles 32
Mooney, George 86–8

Mooney, James 70
Moore, Brian 67
Moore, James 152
Moore, Tom 253
Moore's Bridge 67
Morrison, Danny 198, 205, 213,
    235–6, 238, 240
Moss, Frank 12
'Mountain Climber' *see* Oatley,
Michael
Mountbatten, Lord 185, 211
Mountjoy Prison 9, 10, 11, 25, 27,
    28, 30, 31–3, 36, 44, 46–9, 59,
    64, 66, 69–70, 72–4, 82, 86–7,
    94–5, 97–9, 100, 101
Moverley, Fr Gerald 166
Moynihan, Maurice 115
Mulcahy, Richard 63–4, 66, 69, 74,
    78, 79
Mullan, Seamus 189
Mullingar 21
Mullins, Thomas 87
Murphy, Joseph 56–7
Murphy, Paddy 110
Murphy, Sean 151
Murphy, Timothy 79
Murphy, William Martin 10
Murtagh, Joseph 40
Musgrave Park Hospital 183
Myles, Albert 181
Myles, Sir Thomas 30

National H-Blocks Committee 193,
    200, 202, 205, 221, 228
Neave, Airey 185, 225
Neill, Robert 130
New York 214
New York Times, The 4–5, 7, 16, 23,
    52, 55, 73, 93–4, 212, 214, 217
Newbridge 79
Newbridge Barracks 73, 75
Newport 100
Newry 166, 219
News Letter 247, 248, 250, 254, 256,
    260

Niedermayer, Thomas 151
Nixon, John 186, 195
Nolan, Patrick 67
Norfolk, Duke of 248
Northern Ireland 126–41, 142–4, 145, 151–2, 153, 160, 166–7, 174–201, 202–23, 224–42, 243–61
Norton, Patrick 87
Noyes, Alfred 7
Nugent, Kieran 179
Nugent, Mairéad 190

Oatley, Michael 195, 235
Ó Brádaigh, Ruairí 154, 170, 173, 177, 188, 206, 229
O'Brien, Conor Cruise 121
O'Brien, William 10, 49
O'Byrne, John 83
O'Callaghan, Donal 56, 58
Ó Conaill, Dáithí 136–7, 139, 156, 208
O'Connell, J. J. 62
O'Connor, Fionnuala 190
O'Connor, James 67
O'Connor, Rory 62, 66
O'Connor, T. P. 47
Ó Deirg, Tomás 108
O'Donnell, Peadar 72
O'Donoghue, Paddy 121
Ó Fiaich, Tomás 180, 183, 186, 194, 198, 203, 228
O'Hanlon, Feargal 230
O'Hanrahan, Michael 14
O'Hara, Cathal 118
O'Hara, Patsy 193, 210, 224, 225–6, 228, 229
O'Hara, Tony 230, 231
O'Hare, Fergus 202
O'Hegarty, Sean 81
O'Higgins, Thomas 67
O'Kane, Tony 133
O'Kelly, James Joseph 19

O'Kelly, Seán T. 113
O'Mahony, Dermot 234, 236–7
O Máille, Pádraic 65
O'Malley, Ernie 71, 76
O'Neill, Annie 68
O'Neill, Laurence 28–9, 78
Orange Order 216, 246
Oranmore 97
O'Rawe, Richard 234–5, 237–42
O'Shannon, Cathal 66
O'Sullivan, Andrew 60, 82–4
O'Sullivan, Michael 82
O'Toole, 'Black Dan' 109
Oxford Prison 20

Paisley, Ian 177, 178, 186, 191, 208–9, 211, 220, 234
Palin, Michael 167
Parkhurst Prison 152–3, 157, 164
Pankhurst, Christabel 7, 9
Pankhurst, Emmeline 7
Passmore, Thomas 216
Patterson, Alistair 211
Pearse, Padraig 14, 15, 41–2
Pentonville Prison 21
Philbin, Wiliam 257
Phillips, Veronica 165, 170
Phoenix, Eamon 208–9
Phoenix Park 93, 113
Pickering, John 256, 260
Pius XI 68
Plaid Cymru 184
Plant, George 106
Plunkett, George Noble 19–20, 27
Plunkett, Horace 23
Plunkett, Joseph 94–5
Plunkett, Joseph M. 14, 20
Plunkett, Josephine 84
Pollitt, Geoffrey 164
Portlaoise Prison 106, 110–13, 121–2
Portobello Barracks 64
Powell, Enoch 186, 198

Price, Albert 150, 152
Price, Dolours 145, 146, 147,
  150–51, 153–4, 157–8, 160
Price, Marion 145, 146, 147, 150–51,
  153–4, 157–8, 160
Prior, Jim 256, 257–8
Protestant Telegraph 190
Provisional IRA 126–41, 142,
  144–7, 151–3, 155–7, 163,
  167–73, 174–84, 186, 189–93,
  200, 203, 206, 207, 210, 217,
  218, 220, 221, 222–3, 225, 229,
  230–31, 232, 235, 237–8, 240,
  241, 244–6, 248, 255–6, 258,
  260; *see also* Irish Republican
  Army (IRA)
Purser, Mabel 10

Quinn, Catherine 249–50
Quinn, Fr John 250
Quinn, Patrick 225, 233, 249–50

Reading Jail 43
Reagan, Ronald 188, 248
Redmond, John 8, 19, 21–2, 28
Redmond, William 21
Rees, Merlyn 152, 153, 160, 165,
  174–6, 177
Republican News 213
Rice, Liam 106, 109
Roberts, Ernie 186
Robinson, Lennox 119
Robinson, Mary 231
Robinson, Peter 246
Robinson, Seamus 124, 160–61
Roche, John 93
Roscommon 19–20
Ross, William 165, 233, 260
Royal Irish Constabulary (RIC) 25,
  40, 41, 43, 45, 46
Royal Ulster Constabulary (RUC)
  118, 177, 194, 208, 213, 218,
  221, 230, 232, 246

Royal Victoria Hospital 136, 196
Ruddy, Seamus 249
Rush, Thomas 163
Russell, Seán 88, 97, 100
Ryan, James 108
Ryan, Nellie 68
Ryan, Willie 49

Sachs, Michael 167
St Bricin's Hospital 82–3, 95, 97,
  99–100
St Finbarr's Cemetery 59
San Quentin Prison 122
Sands, Bobby 160, 186, 196, 198,
  199, 201, 203–4, 206, 208–18,
  232, 261
Sands, Marcella 205
Sands, Rosaleen 205, 213
Saoirse 99, 209, 258
Schmidt, Frank 247–8
Scullion, Colm 238
Second World War 85, 86, 88, 89,
  102–3
Shaw, George Bernard 9, 60
Sheehan, Pat 185, 251–2, 260
Sheehy-Skeffington, Hanna 71
Sherlock, Lorcan 8
Short, Renee 158
Sinn Féin 19–24, 40, 42, 45, 47,
  61–2, 70–71, 73, 85, 163, 165,
  174, 185, 188, 190, 191, 198,
  206, 215, 222, 226, 227, 229–30,
  237–8, 240–42, 245, 246, 258–9,
  261
Sinn Féin 71, 72–3, 74, 77
Social Democratic and Labour Party
  (SDLP) 136, 143, 157, 177,
  207, 209, 241, 253, 259
South, Seán 230
Soviet Union 212, 214
Special Branch 94, 97, 104–6
Spencer, Lady Diana 248–9
Stack, Austin 33, 34–5, 71, 72

Stagg, Bridget 168–70, 171
Stagg, Frank 152–3, 154, 157, 160,
    162–73
Stagg, Joseph 164
Stagg, Mary 171
Stallard, Jock 157
Stardust nightclub 204, 227
Strabane 219
Stronge, James 200–201
Stronge, Norman 200–201
suffragette movement 1–10, 26
Sullivan, Jobie 109
Sun, The 216–17
Sunday Independent 171
Sunday News 132
Sunday Times 157
Swanzy, Oswald Ross 40, 41

Taylor, John 211–12
Thatcher, Margaret 182, 183, 184–5,
    187, 188, 191–2, 194–5, 199,
    205–6, 212, 214, 218, 220,
    226–7, 228, 229, 230–31, 233,
    244, 248, 254, 256, 261
Theatre Royal, Dublin 8–9
Thomas, Sir George 215, 241
Time 151
Times, The 53, 198, 214–15, 222, 232
Toombs, Ivan 200
Tralee 121
Traynor, Michael 94, 95, 96, 99
Troup, Sir Edward 49
Tullamore Prison 10
Turnly, John 200
Twohig, Richard 63
Twomey, Maurice 86, 87–8
Twomey, Seamus 139
Tynan Abbey 200
Tyrone, 205–11, 237, 240–42, 252–4

Ulster Defence Association (UDA)
    190, 222
Ulster Defence Regiment (UDR)
    177, 200, 211, 252

Ulster Unionist Party (UUP) 177,
    208, 211–12, 252–3
Ulster Volunteer Force (UVF) 132,
    153, 190
Undertones 216

Valente, Peter 200
Vallely, Samuel 220

Wakefield Prison 43, 164–5, 166
Wales 184–5
Wallace-Dunlop, Marion 1–3
Walsh, Michael 106
Walsh, Robert 146
Walsh, William 47
War of Independence 39–40, 43,
    45–6, 59, 61, 65, 82
Warnock, Edmond 124
Warrenpoint 185, 200
West, Harry 208–9, 211
Wexford 70
Wexford Prison 70
White, Stephen 67
Whitelaw, William 131, 132, 134,
    136–9, 140, 152, 185
Whitmore, Clive 227
Whitty, Joseph 60, 70
Williams, Tom 113
Wilson, Harold 152, 153
Wilton Jail 4–5
Wimbourne, Lord 15
The Wind that Shakes the Barley 61,
    65
Windlesham, Lord 138
Winston Green Prison 3–4
Woodfield, P. J. 139
World in Action (TV programme)
    191–2
Wormwood Scrubs Prison 44,
    49–51, 148–9